OST AND FOUND IN JOHANNESBURG

ARK GEVISSER is one of South Africa's pre-eminent authors and urnalists. His last book, *A Legacy of Liberation: Thabo Mbeki and the ture of the South African Dream*, won the Sunday Times 2008 Alan ton Prize. His journalism has appeared in publications and journals cluding *Granta*, the *New York Times*, the *Guardian*, *Newsweek*, *Vogue*, e *Wall Street Journal* and the *Los Angeles Times*. He lives in Cape own.

evisser brilliantly maps out multiple worlds fractured by race, class, d history, in a story as complex and beautiful as any memoir I've er read' Dinaw Mengestu, author of *How to Read the Air*

Gevisser] is unflinching in his account of the complex contradictions at still haunt his country' *New Yorker*

epicts a profound sense of place' *Sunday Times*

yrical and achingly touching ... a riveting and enchantingly nuanced e of a young white writer-to-be's growing understanding of the cially charged land he was born into, as well as a more personal urney: his coming out as a gay man' *LA Times*

LOST AND FOUND IN JOHANNESBURG

A MEMOIR

MARK GEVISSER

GRANTA

Granta Publications, 12 Addison Avenue, London W11 4QR

First published in Great Britain as *Dispatcher: Lost and Found in Johannesburg*
by Granta Books, 2014
This paperback edition published by Granta Books, 2015

A CIP catalogue record for this book
is available from the British Library.

1 3 5 7 9 10 8 6 4 2

ISBN 978 1 78378 099 0
eISBN 978 1 84708 859 8

Typeset by M Rules

Printed and bound by CPI Group (UK) Ltd, Croydon, CRO 4YY

www.grantabooks.com

To my mother
and to Maggie Davey and Bridget Impey

Here is your map. Unfold it, follow it, and then throw it away, if you will. It is only paper. It is only paper and ink, but if you think a little, if you pause a moment, you will see that these two things have seldom joined to make a document so modest and yet so full with histories of hope or sagas of conquest.

Beryl Markham, *West with the Night*

The Nation is an administrative term, consequently artificial.
The Native Land is a sentimental term, consequently natural.
The Nation has fixed frontiers (conventions established by wars, treaties, victories and defeats). A material fact.
The Native Land converges on one centre, one heart.
There are no frontiers to the Native Land.
It is an act of faith, a spiritual conception.

Le Corbusier, *Aircraft*

CONTENTS

AUTHOR'S NOTE

Several names in this book have been changed, at the request of the people whose stories I have told. The reasons for this will become evident when reading the stories of Phil and Edgar, of Hopey Molefe, of Adam, and of Bea and Katie.

PROLOGUE

Wildsview

On the night of 11 January 2012, I went to visit my friends Katie and Bea in their flat at Wildsview, high up on Killarney Ridge. Our plan was to continue watching the Australian TV mini-series, *The Slap*, based on Christos Tsolkas's celebrated novel of the same name. I was living in France at the time, but was back in Johannesburg for a couple of months to finish working on this book. I parked the old BMW convertible I had borrowed from my mother, said hello to Jonah, the doorman-cum-security guard, and bounded through the grand lavender-painted lobby into the lift and up to the fourth floor.

I know the place well: my partner C and I had lived in this generous and somewhat shabby flat ourselves, with its scuffed parquet floors and high ceilings and little touches of stucco, before we passed the lease on to Katie and Bea. Wildsview was built in the mid-twentieth century for the comfortable elderly Jews who came to be associated with Killarney and who are still to be seen, perhaps less comfortable, amid the gay people, students, and large multi-generational Muslim families who now call the suburb home.

When we moved here in the early post-apartheid years from the decaying inner-city suburb of Troyeville, it was at a time when many white South Africans were emigrating and were being replaced by upwardly mobile people, younger and darker. One of our friends quipped that the suburb was known as the 'departure lounge': everyone was en route to somewhere else – off this mortal coil, or following children to San Diego or Perth, or to the ultimate middle-class goal of a house in the northern suburbs. When we went looking for a place to rent, there was the smell of chicken soup and incontinence in some of the long, glass-enclosed corridors of these old blocks that took me right back to the frequent visits I used to make, in my childhood, to Killarney aunts and uncles.

We loved the flat we finally found at Wildsview, which we rented from the retired Jewish gynaecologist and his wife who lived in the penthouse and owned the whole block. Wildsview seemed to perch on a threshold, at the edge of a ridge that housed the mansions belonging to the city's wealthiest mining magnates: you could look north over the green canopy of Johannesburg's lush northern suburbs, or east and south over The Wilds towards the wall of Hillbrow's highrises announcing the inner city beyond.

Living at the lip of The Wilds was a disconnecting experience. It is a magnificent, forty-acre, indigenous wooded botanical garden along two rocky ridges of the Witwatersrand, and it was landscaped somewhat incongruously in the form of English parkland, with stone paths winding down into a kloof between the ridges carved by the Sandspruit stream. The river's headwaters are buried beneath the concrete of Hillbrow, and its bed now carries cavalcades of motor vehicles – largely minibus taxis – between the inner city and the M1 highway to Alexandra township. When we lived there, the din of invisible traffic along Houghton Drive often brought to my mind a perpetually thunderous herd of elephants, particularly before or after a big soccer match, when the trumpeting of *vuvuzelas* provided an antic bass line to the incessant hooting.

There were other sounds: the burglar alarm sirens that were as much a part of our aural landscape as the birdsong of the loeries who canoodled in the stately blue gum outside our bedroom window; the pre-dawn Tracker helicopters searching out stolen cars; the skid and crash of an accident across the Houghton Drive intersection; the shattering of glass from yet another smash-and-grab by petty assailants using The Wilds' vegetation as cover; a woman's screams of terror and pain rising up out of the dark.

The gardens of The Wilds were separated from our apartment block by a palisade fence, and I looked out over them every day for five years. In my childhood, the park's rocky pathways had provided routes for adventure; in my teenage years, refuges for romance or solitude. But now that I looked out over the Wilds every day, I never entered the park. Almost no one did, because of its reputation for crime, until a pioneering resident from Yeoville on the other side set up a dog-walking club on Sunday mornings: there would be strength in numbers. Despite the fact that The Wilds was immaculately maintained by a team of City Parks gardeners, the park had come to inhabit its name in an entirely new and unwelcome way: it became a lung as dark as it was green in the middle of the city.

On the night of the 11th of January 2012, at about 9.30 p.m., three men were exhaled out of this lung across the palisade fence into Wildsview while I was watching *The Slap* with my friends. The men crossed the terrace of the ground floor flat, scrambled over the service gate, and climbed the service steps until they could go no further. They opened the locked kitchen door of Katie and Bea's flat without any force.

Something seemingly irrevocable changed, that night, in my relationship to Johannesburg, my home town, the place I have lived for four decades, the place of this book.

PART ONE

DISPATCHER

OUTWARD BOUND

Closed City

When I was a boy, in the 1970s, I used to play a game I have retro-actively called Dispatcher, for hours on end, using my parents' street guide, *Holmden's Register of Johannesburg*. Ring-bound with a blue cloth cover, its whimsical title and archaic typography conjured a nostalgia for less turbulent times – although I knew none of that, of course, aged seven or eight, when I found a whole world between its covers.

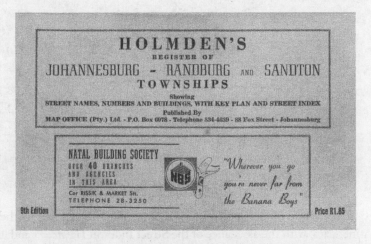

Somehow, perhaps with the help of a parent, I found our road in Sandton, the bucolic new dormitory town north of Johannesburg, on page 77 of the *Holmden's*, and then plotted it on the key plan in the front. On Sunday afternoons, accompanying one or the other of my parents as they drove my Granny Gertie home, I would sit in the back of the car and look at the street signs, finding them in the index of the

Holmden's and piecing together our route, all the way along Oxford Road and then across Killarney into Houghton Drive on page 19, through The Wilds and up onto Louis Botha Avenue to Paul Nel Street in Hillbrow, where she lived in a residential hotel called The Lloyd. These forays into the lower numbers of the *Holmden's* took me tantalisingly close to a place called the 'Fort' on page 3, which was barely my finger's length away from Granny Gertie's hotel and yet thoroughly beyond my reach. I remember my distress when, sitting in the back of the car with the street guide, I realised that the Queen Elizabeth Bridge crossed railway lines rather than a river as in the London Bridge of nursery rhymes; I expected the same kind of romance from the Fort and was suitably gratified when told that it was Johannesburg's jail, and that the only time I would be visiting it would be in the back of a police van.

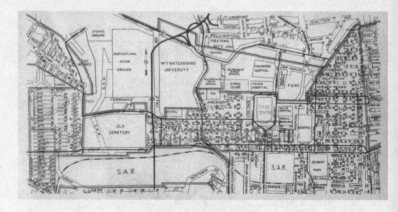

Once I tired of plotting Granny Gertie's route home, I found other itineraries, with the assistance of the Street Index in *Holmden's* and its inescapable companion, the *Johannesburg Telephone Directory*. Here is how the game went: I would open the phonebook at random and settle on a name; say, 'PUPKEWITZ, P., 14 BERYL STREET, CYRILDENE.' I would then look for Beryl Street in the *Holmden's* street index, find it on page 29 of the maps, refer back to the key plan, plot a route there from our home, and then dispatch an imaginary courier to Mr

Pupkewitz, or Mr Papenfus on Pafuri Road in Emmarentia, or Mrs Papadopoulous on Panther Street in Kensington.

Other map-making activities derived from Dispatcher, such as the plotting of new suburbs in the white spaces of the *Holmden's*, or the designing of floor-plans for houses at the addresses I had found. All of these activities conspired to create an obsessive attachment, within me, to the *Holmden's*, which I would spirit out of the car after having been

collected from school and into a quiet corner of our rambunctious house: by the time I was seven I had three younger brothers. I would inevitably forget to return the book to its cubbyhole, an oversight that would only be discovered once it was actually needed on a real journey. Thus did a strict rule come to be made, and vigorously enforced: the *Holmden's* was not, under any circumstances, to leave the car. This meant that I would spend much of

my childhood sitting in my father's Mercedes in the garage, making out my routes and plotting out my suburbs. One of my strongest memories of childhood is asking to be excused from the lunch table and rushing off to the garage with a telephone directory to spend a happy afternoon of Dispatcher and associated activities. In the memory it is always grey and rainy – although it seldom was in Johannesburg – and I am safe and warm, up against the creamy perforated leather until my nanny, Bettinah, comes to coax me out for my bath, or tea.

*

Inevitably, Dispatcher took me places I was not meant to go. I stumbled across one of the few African names in the Johannesburg telephone directory – let's call him 'Mphahlele, M.' – with an address in Alexandra – and discovered how intent the *Holmden's* was on actually losing me. I had, of course, heard of Alexandra: it was that thing

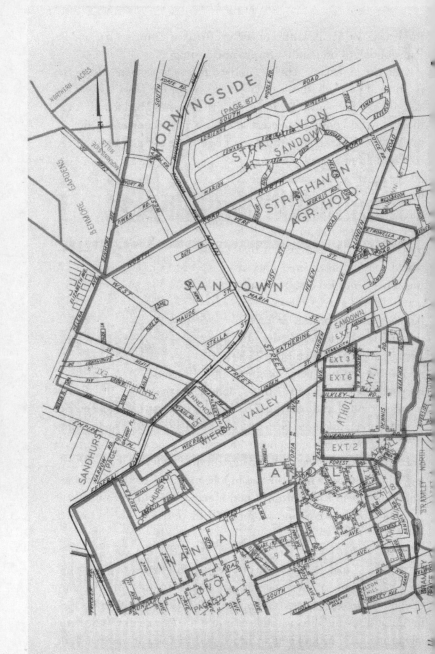

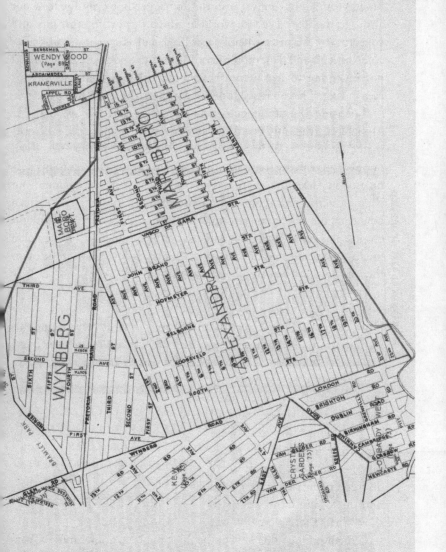

called a 'township', that place where the black people who worked for us would go to church or to visit family on their days off. It would function in adults' conversations as a trigger not only for fear, but also – in the liberal Jewish world in which I grew up – for pity and concern. It was a place where blacks lived, and as such it was unknowable, difficult and dangerous – not least for the poor people who had no choice but to live there. It was on another planet, and for this reason I must have missed it on my journeys through the *Holmden's*.

But using the street guide's index I discovered, now, that Mr Mphahlele lived only two pages away from us, on page 77, far closer than Granny Gertie's hotel or even my school in Victory Park. Even now, I can recall my frustration at trying to get my courier to his destination in Alexandra: there was no possible way of steering him from page 77 across into page 75. Sandton simply ended at its eastern boundary, the Sandspruit stream, with no indication of how one might cross it, or even that page 75 was just on the other side. The key plan might have connected the two pages, but on the evidence of the maps themselves there was simply no way through.

*

How extraordinary it seems to me now that anyone found his way anywhere using the *Holmden's*. There was no logic to the pagination, no standard scale, and no consistent north: some pages had the compass arrow facing left, or right, or, even in a few instances, down. Sets of neighbouring suburbs were grouped – in admittedly pleasing designs – as if they were discrete countries, often with nothing around the edges to show that there actually was  settlement on the other side of the thick red line. Sometimes the cartographers would leave you a turn-page marker as a clue, but just as often the streets would melt away at the page's edges, or – in some instances, such as Riverlea on page 105 – would be surrounded by nothingness, as if islands in a sea of white paper.

I only realised the madness of all this at the age of twelve when, in the aftermath of the 1976 Soweto Uprising, my parents took us to London for six weeks. South Africans of all races and classes were flee-ing the country. Just a couple of pages away from us, children were being funnelled through the hidden alleyways of 'Dark City', as Alexandra was universally known among black people (there was nei-ther electricity nor law), across the border to join the liberation army. Meanwhile, on our side of the Sandspruit, white families were – as the contemptuous cliché had it – 'packing for Perth'. Many in our world were emigrating, to Australia or America, to Britain or Israel, and although my parents did not want to follow, they packed us off to Pimlico for a 'trial run' masquerading as an extended holiday.

What I remember most about the trip was, not surprisingly, the *London A–Z* street atlas; 'over 30,000 streets in your pocket'. In those days, it was available only in black and white, but no matter: the maps were *continuous*, which meant I could dispatch my courier from our rented house in St George's Square all the way to Harrow or to Hackney, to Richmond or to Rotherhithe, just by flipping the pages. Released from the suburbs and a life of being driven around, I could even use it myself, to plot my way down the King's Road or past Buckingham Palace and across Green Park to an exhibition at the Royal Academy. As it began to dawn on me how bizarre the *Holmden's* was, I began to ponder the reasons for its eccentricity. Thus began, cartographically, the dawning of my political consciousness.

*

Alexandra might have been on another planet before my *Holmden's* revelation, but its name was nonetheless familiar as a concept. Soweto, on the other side of the city, was almost entirely beyond my ken. Prior to that terrifying Wednesday in June 1976 when we were sent home from school, most of what I knew about it would have come from the Coca-Cola bottle tops we traded, which had black footballers printed on their foamy undersides. Whites and blacks had different leagues, of course, and my friends all were fanatical supporters of one or other of the white Johannesburg clubs, Highlands and Rangers. But the bottle tops alerted us to the fact that there was a parallel world out there, with fabled heroes named Kaizer Motaung and Jomo Sono, who played for clubs called Kaizer Chiefs and Orlando Pirates. On the playground of King David Primary School, this is what 'Soweto' meant.

I had, in fact, been to the township once – on a field trip in Standard Two (fourth grade) arranged by my Jewish school, to visit the Rabbi of Soweto. Who knows how he acquired his position? Perhaps he had worked for Jews and converted; perhaps he was a member of the Lemba tribe from the north of the country, who, like the Ethiopian Jews, claim direct descendancy from the Israelites and who have practiced Jewish rituals for generations. Whichever: we were piled into a bus, and when we got to his nice enough house in what must have been Soweto's middle-class enclave of Dube, we were met by a jolly little man in a prayer shawl and yarmulke who led us through some incantations and told us that he was happy to have been able to show us that Soweto really wasn't so bad after all.

That trip would be the sum total of my exposure to townships before I left home and went to university at the age of eighteen; certainly it – together with what I heard on the playground about the Pirates and the Chiefs – was all I knew about Soweto in June 1976, when the name found itself, suddenly, on everyone's lips. If the uprising unsettled my parents, it upset me too: black schoolchildren my age were being killed, as were good white people who had gone to the township to *help* blacks. The name of Melville Edelstein, a Jewish doctor who worked at Baragwanath Hospital in Soweto and was murdered by a group of angry rioters, was on every adult's lips.

I sought out the *Holmden's* to find out more.

But I was thwarted. *Soweto wasn't there!* The huge, sprawling agglomeration of townships was a phantom in that bottom-left-hand corner, in that white space below Riverlea and to the left of Robertsham, where I had insouciantly plotted so many of my own fantasy suburbs; unmarked, unheeded, home to hundreds of thousands of people who commuted to the rest of the city to make it to work each day.

Later, looking through older maps of Johannesburg, I came to see that there was a long tradition of Soweto-denial in Johannesburg cartography. Although the township was actually only proclaimed as Soweto in 1963, given its name (an acronym for SOuth WEst TOwnships) by the white winner of a competition run by the City Council's Department of Non-European Affairs, Johannesburg's black people had been settled there, behind the mine-dumps and along the Klip River, since the early twentieth century, as part of a supposed slum-clearance policy. But even though the area constituted a huge part of Johannesburg, both in population and physical size, it did not feature at all on any road maps to the city. From the 1930s, a cunning convention had been established: the enlarged inset of the 'Central City Area' would be placed in the bottom-left-hand corner of a map, filling the space where Soweto should have been. In most instances, there would be no indication at all that this inset was covering a human settlement. But in some brazen examples, such as the *Holmdens'* own hanging street map, the cartographers actually had the audacity to

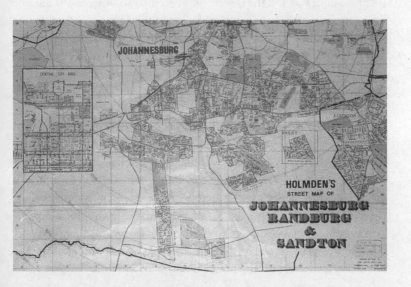

mark out Soweto, albeit in a solid bluish block without any roads or features, before obscuring it with the inset of the downtown area. Thus does it appear, a leering dark underside to the city, its evening shadow.

*

I was not, it turns out, the only one to begin thinking about Soweto in 1976. This was the year that the Map Studio company published its first street guide to the black city. By the end of the decade, Map Studio would bring out its *Street Guide to the Witwatersrand*, which joined all of the region's cities, black and white, together in a series of continuous maps. The *Holmden's* was quickly rendered obsolete: compared to the Map Studio's *Street Guide to Witwatersrand* it was silent films to talkies; black and white to colour; analogue to digital. This explosion into colour and continuity seemed to mirror other awakenings within me, sexual and political. Suddenly, there were whole fields of data across double pages that ran into each other, with roads in yellow and parks in green and industrial areas in grey, with schools in ochre and rivers in blue, and police stations marked with blue dots and hospitals with red crosses; fields of symbols as expansive as the terrain they now populated. Central Johannesburg was still the centre, but it seemed so tiny now, as did our little corner of suburban Sandton. Soweto was mapped. *Soweto*! It was a city. It took up almost as many pages as Sandton. This was a revelation.

The previously undifferentiated notion of the township came into focus as a complex sequence of suburbs, some with familiar names – like 'Orlando' and 'Meadowlands' – and others new to my ears: 'Zola', 'Emdeni', 'Kliptown', and the delightfully paradoxical 'White City Jabavu'. And yet they were mapped with exactly the same precision, exactly the same symbols, as the white suburbs, even if in different patterns. They were not unknowable, not unimaginable: they had streets and parklands; red crosses for clinics, ochre blocks for schools, green ones for parks; traffic lights and main roads and secondary roads, just like anywhere else. This became the cartographical expression of something I had come to believe with early adolescent fervour: even if we were forced to live in different places under different conditions, we were all the same.

But as I grew older and learned more, the *Street Guide to Witwatersrand* became evidence, too, for exactly the opposite: 'they' wanted us to believe that Soweto was 'separate but equal' to Johannesburg, a fully serviced city; when anyone could see, looking at the maps, that it was not. As I studied the *Street Guide* more closely, I came to be struck more by the townships' difference from the suburbs of my childhood than by their similarity. The blocks of land were such tiny slivers that one could hardly imagine houses on them, and the streets were set out in dense, oppressive grids, often identified by bureaucratic strings of letters and numbers rather than the alluring names to be found in white suburbs, if identified at all. There were schools and churches all over the place, but few of all the other symbols which dotted the white parts of town, and I grew sceptical: I knew there were parks in Parktown and oaks in Oaklands, but could there possibly be meadows in Meadowlands?

The *Holmden's* had not been entirely wrong: townships were indeed islands, like Riverlea (which I was later to discover was a coloured township), surrounded by the white space of empty veld, and often with only one access road. This, coupled with the lack of street names in wide swathes of township, made a dispatcher's job more frustrating, and more interesting; thus, through the Map Studio *Street Guide*, did I begin to appreciate, too, how the primary logic in the planning of townships was control.

As I came to understand apartheid, it was fascinating to me that the residential areas for different racial groups were not colour-coded, and I now set about doing this. I used whatever clues I could find – 'Coloured Cemetery'; 'Mosque'; 'Jabulani Street'; 'Shivananda Drive' – and supplemented these with interrogations of those adults to hand: my parents, domestic staff, those very rare teachers who seemed to have an interest in such things. And so I discovered why suburbs like Riverlea were islands: they were established as buffers between the white city and Soweto, to which mixed-race residents of inner-city neighbourhoods had been forcibly removed.

As I learned more about the city, I came to track other journeys: the route down Fuel and Commando Roads the government lorries would have taken as they transported evicted black residents from Sophiatown to their new homes in Meadowlands in 1955; the route black workers took down Louis Botha Avenue during the Alexandra bus boycott of 1957; and yes, finally, the route the Soweto protesters took from the Morris Isaacson School (marked on the map) through Dube, down to Orlando West, where Hector Pieterson was shot at the top of Vilakazi Street, on 16 June 1976.

*

A while ago, while browsing through the Collector's Treasury on Commissioner Street in downtown Johannesburg, I came across an edition of the *Holmden's*, amid the old porcelain, the tattered photoalbums, the ziggurats of books that the owners have salvaged from estates of the deceased or cleared garages. The shop, up a flight of steps off the concrete gulch of Commissioner Street, with its purveyors of cheap sex and cheap Chinese goods on one of the rougher fringes of Johannesburg's now-black inner city, felt like a walk-through *Holmden's* itself, a museum of cast-asides and left-behinds that ossified the first century of white Johannesburg experience into several storeys of musty rooms.

The blue cover of the *Holmden's* was like a river, here, through the dusty shop and the allergenic grit of a hot, dry, highveld afternoon. I bought it immediately. Rediscovering it now, in middle age, and revisiting the memories it has evoked, I have had the eerie but illuminating experience of viewing my childhood from above, as if it were a map itself. Where did the *Holmden's* take me, as I lost myself between its covers during my hours of Dispatcher? And why, as an adult, have I yearned for it so?

In the years since I sat in my father's Mercedes playing Dispatcher, I have lived a life in Johannesburg. I have left the suburbs. I have put my body in those places I dreamed of. And yet I have found, to my perpetual surprise, that my home town eludes me, however assiduously I court it. There is always a suburban wall, there is always a palisade fence, an infra-red beam, a burglar bar, a thick red line, between the city I think I know and the city that is. And then, at 9.30 p.m. on

11 January 2012, there was suddenly not enough of a boundary, as three men with guns slid effortlessly through a locked door on the fifth floor of a block of flats and ruptured that perimeter of denial that all Joburgers have to erect if they are to sleep comfortably at night.

In his unforgettable novel about New York, the Nigerian–American author Teju Cole records his protagonist's wanderings around the city in the way Baudelaire was a *flâneur* in Paris or James Joyce set Leopold Bloom around Dublin in *Ulysses*. Cole's novel is called *Open City*, and it leads me to think about Johannesburg as anything but that: it draws its energy precisely from its atomisation and its edge, its stacking of boundaries against each other. It is no place to wander; no place, either, to throw your windows open and let the world blow in.

On one level, Johannesburg's elusiveness is a condition specific to the city itself; its apartheid history, its risky streets. The people who walk Johannesburg daily are not *flâneurs* at all, but migrants, or workers, to whom the city still denies the right to public transport. Each time they walk it is not only a weight on their feet but a slight on their dignity: the stories their feet tell, unlike those of the idealised *flâneurs* imagined by Baudelaire or Walter Benjamin, are often ones of pain and dislocation. The rest of us drive.

And so, certainly, there are specific historical, social and cultural reasons why Johannesburg remains such an elusive home town. But there is also a personal dimension to this elusiveness, an existential one and perhaps a moral one too, that I have come to understand through my nostalgic attachment to the *Holmden's*. Maps would have no purchase on us, no currency at all, if we were not in danger of running aground, of getting lost, of dislocation and even death without them. All maps awaken in me a desire to be lost and to be found – to find myself – at the same time, and this desire is particularly intense with the *Holmden's*.

Psychiatrists define pathological nostalgia as a condition in which one loses oneself in the past, looking for a route home – a route to oblivion, to death, really – through one's childhood; in which one becomes so preoccupied with this search that one loses sight of the present. But I know that that is not the reason I go back to the *Holmden's*. I find myself going back to it, rather, because it forces me to remember something I must never allow myself to forget: Johannesburg, my home town, is not the city I think I know.

This is why I have to keep on playing Dispatcher.

Treasure Valley

When I was in my early teens, I began 'developing' multiracial suburbs in the white spaces of the *Street Guide*, where we could all live
together. One of these, I remember, was called Treasure Valley. I don't
remember exactly where I put it, but for argument's sake let's say I
plotted it in the white space to the east of Alexandra, between the
Jukskei River and the white suburb of Linbro Park, one of my
favourite *terrae incognitae*. My inspiration came from Robert Louis
Stevenson's *Treasure Island*, which rather predictably entranced me.
The main artery through Treasure Valley was, I think, Long John
Silver Drive; there would also have been Black Dog Boulevard,
Captain Flint Crescent and, of course, Spyglass Hill.

Although my property-developing fantasy life was a pale shadow of
young Jim Hawkins' imagination, I had come to identify deeply with
Treasure Island's hero, who discovers the map leading to buried treasure in the sea-chest of an old mariner and sits brooding over it for
hours: 'I approached that island in my fancy from every possible direction; I explored every acre of its surface; I climbed a thousand times
to that tall hill they call the Spy-glass, and from the top enjoyed
the most wonderful and changing prospects. Sometimes the isle was
thick with savages, with whom we fought, sometimes full of dangerous animals that hunted us, but in all my fancies nothing occurred to
me so strange and tragic as our actual adventures.'

Young Jim's fancies echo those of his creator, who wrote later in his
life that the idea for *Treasure Island* came to him during a wet Scottish
summer when he used his son's watercolours to paint the map of an
imaginary island: 'As I pored upon my map of Treasure Island, the
future characters in the book began to appear there visible among

imaginary woods; and their brown faces and bright weapons peeped out upon me from unexpected quarters as they passed to and fro, fighting and hunting treasure, on these few flat square inches of a flat projection. The next thing I knew, I had some paper before me and was writing out a list of chapters.'

For Stevenson, imagination and creativity sprang out of 'those few flat square inches of a flat projection'. So too did the adventure of his own life, which mirrored young Jim's, albeit in somewhat distorted ways. His own wanderlust severely curtailed by ill health, Stevenson managed nonetheless to fulfill his dream of travel to the South Seas five years after writing *Treasure Island*, and eventually settled in Samoa. Here he bought land, took on the name Tusitala ('teller of tales') and became something of an elder until his death at the age of forty-four, in 1894. Unlike his young protagonist, Stevenson did not come home with booty. But he too found a way to plot a life's journey and the literary treasure of his novel too – off cartographic imagination.

'In all my fancies nothing occurred to me so strange and tragic as our actual adventures'. When I read these words, aged thirteen, at the beginning of *Treasure Island*, I must have asked myself whether I would ever be able to – whether I would ever want to – say the same about my own such fancies.

*

There is indeed a valley separating Sandton and Alexandra, formed by the Sandspruit stream, that uncrossable boundary at the edge of page 77 in the *Holmden's*. When I was growing up, Alexandra and Sandton, neighbours across the stream, were invisible to each other. The vast majority of middle-class white South Africans who lived in Sandton had never set foot in Alexandra, although Alexandra's citizens, of course, crossed daily out of the bounds of page 75 to work in the white city. Today, most white residents of Sandton will still not have gone anywhere near Alexandra, but at least the neighbours are more visible to one another. The towers of Sandton City rise high enough off the landscape to overlook the black township just to the east.

And Alexandra itself has expanded up the steep far bank of the

Jukskei River into the white space wherein I once plotted my utopian suburbs. Today, if you stand amid the developments of the Far East Bank, as my Treasure Valley is now known, you are afforded the startling vista of a city that has managed for so much of its lifetime to conceal its squalor in yards or behind mine dumps. Beneath you, down in the riverbed, are a herd of goats and the squatter-camp of Setswetla. Lift your gaze slightly higher, directly ahead, and you will be looking into 'Old Alex', a dirty mess of zinc sheeting and coalfire-smog punctuated by the handsome gables and red-painted roofs of the original homesteads. Look higher still and you are confronted by the brutalist atrocity of the Zulu migrant-labour hostel perched at the top of the valley, slatted with narrow apertures as if a prison. Look beyond the hostel, up into the flat blue highveld sky, and you will see, rising above the green canopy of the Northern Suburbs – the trees under which my childhood bloomed – Sandton's ostentatious and disorderly cluster of skyscrapers, each one an unfortunate suitor to the caprice of its times, from the concrete mass of Sandton City to the neo-classical pastiche of the Michelangelo Hotel to the asymmetrical contemporaneity of the Norton Rose Towers; all held together by the continent's largest shopping mall, where middle-class black South Africans now outnumber their white compatriots in their conspicuous consumption.

When I want to show visitors how South Africa has changed since the end of apartheid, I take them to Sandton. Alexandra is unchanged, except for the new housing on the Far East Bank, but since my youth the colour of Sandton has been transformed, along with its skyline. The area I grew up in, one of its new developers once told me, was the country's first 'truly aspirational area' – 'aspirational' being a favourite new South African euphemism; adspeak for 'black person spending money'. It has even become a noun, a self-descriptor. The other day I heard a caller to a radio show describe herself, pride tinged with wry irony : 'I'm an aspirational!'

The original Johannesburg was held to a tight, European-style urban grid, but the new Sandton has no such constraints, no master plan, aesthetic or urban, to hold these spires together in the landscape;

there is no interest among its developers, either, in communicating with one another. Johannesburg's gilded new city-on-the-hill, established to provide sanctuary to capital as it fled the decaying inner city, is a product of the grab-what-you-can frontier mentality that has driven the mining settlement from the beginning.

And so the vista presented to you from Alexandra's Far East Bank is startling, particularly if you were raised in a walled, white world: you see before you, over time and space, a vertical cross-section of the city of your birth.

Tompkins's Folly

Once I had rescued the *Holmden's* from the Collector's Treasury and dispatched myself into the cartography of my childhood, I found myself back in a street-map obsession I had not experienced since my youth.

Johannesburg's first commercial street guide, I discovered, was published in 1890, just four years after gold was discovered in the creases of the Witwatersrand to the south of Paul Kruger's Boer republic, in 1886. The map folds out from a rather unassuming leatherbound folio with *Plan of Johannesburg* embossed in gold lettering on its front cover, into a meticulous and magnificent record of the imagination and confidence that drove the early settlement. It is signed by one W. Tompkins, and drawn with the kind of cartographic love that had long deserted commercial map-making by the time the *Holmden's* of my childhood came along. Streets and railway lines and parks are plotted onto a landscape dominated by elegant conical structures, representing the ridges and koppies beneath which the new town was settled. Limpid pools of blue ring the city like sparkling stones in a necklace.

The artist William Kentridge, who has been cutting up street guides of Johannesburg for years and incorporating them into his artworks, owns a copy of this first Johannesburg street map, and he

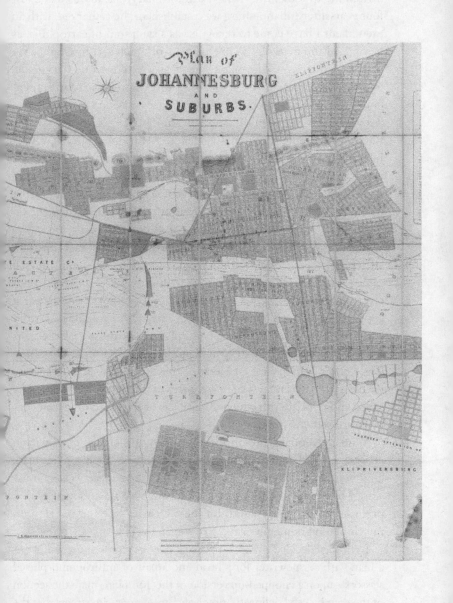

Plan of JOHANNESBURG AND SUBURBS.

invited me to look at it. 'Isn't it extraordinary that it was made just four years after Johannesburg was established?' he remarked, with an excitement I have come to recognise as a symptom of cartophilia, as he opened the map out on one of the work tables in his studio. He drew my attention to the map's legend: six churches, one synagogue, four banks, four theatres, four clubs, three hotels, six government buildings (including post office, police station, hospital and 'Government Entrepot') and around forty 'Other Notable Buildings'. 'On the basis of this evidence,' Kentridge said, 'you'd think Johannesburg was a rather grand colonial town, instead of the chaotic rough-and-ready mining camp we know it was.' He loved the notion that the map must have been an act of will, a determination of what would be, rather than an objective reflection of what was actually on the ground, and he marvelled at the accuracy of its augury.

Johannesburg had none of the allegiances to the past that constrain ancient cities. Everybody came from somewhere else, and they all came for one reason – to make money. The city was a singularly modernist venture: it imposed itself so quickly on the landscape that it appears almost as an optical illusion in early photographs. Its history has been one of 'ceaseless metamorphosis', as the social theorists Achille Mbembe and Sarah Nuttall put it in their book, *Johannesburg: The Elusive Metropolis*: 'A trajectory that in the West took ages to unfold and to mature was here compressed into under a century. The speed and velocity with which the city has experienced modernity has been in itself dizzying.'

William Kentridge attempted to capture this kinetic energy in an artwork he made out of chopped-up segments of the Tompkins map, a monumental tapestry entitled *Office Love*. The piece was commissioned by the Johannesburg Stock Exchange for the lobby of its new premises in the new 'Central Business District' of Sandton, close to my childhood home on page 77 of the *Holmden's*.

Kentridge decided to superimpose characters representing industry – a man with a typewriter for a head and a pair of anthropomorphised scissors – upon a chopped-up version of the Tompkins map; the section of the map he used delineates precisely those inner-city streets that the

Stock Exchange had just abandoned now that the old 'Manhattan of Africa' was beginning to fall in on itself under the weight of the new economic refugees flooding in from other parts of the continent. In this way, *Office Love* uses Johannesburg's first map to call attention to the atomisation of the post-apartheid city: downtown Johannesburg's abandonment by big business at the moment when it finally became accessible to all.

As we looked at the source-map of *Office Love*, Kentridge and I chuckled at how differently we responded to it. He was struck not just by its aesthetic beauty, but by how precise a blueprint it was for the city that would come: the handsome inner-city grid arranged around civic squares between the goldmines to the south and the railway yards to the north; the residential suburbs to the east like shards of glass following the acute angles of pre-existing farms, Braamfontein spilling out along a valley down below the western ramparts of the Fort.

I was moved, on the other hand, by the map's fantasy, or perhaps more accurately, by its drama: that which was plotted but which did not come to pass. These included a network of squares in the inner city, and its extension southward into fantastical residential suburbs (fantastical in so far as they never existed) called Schweizer and Ingramsburg, Mewettville and Casey's. Why 'Schweizer', I wanted to know. And then, why not 'Schweizer'? Who were Ingram and Casey, and why, in the end, did the city's elite choose to settle on the ridges north of the city, leaving the Klipriviersberg in the south to become Johannesburg's own Sherwood Forest, home to the members of the Ninevites gang founded by Nongoloza, the mining town's black Robin Hood?

Some part of the answer lies in the fact that Johannesburg was a speculative venture from the outset, a project of acquisitive capitalism that paid scant attention to the natural qualities that typically define urban settlement: river, port, citadel. Now a conurbation of eleven million people, Johannesburg came into being on an expanse of uninhabited rolling grassland nearly 6000 feet above sea level after an English prospector named George Harrison stumbled upon some gold-bearing rock on the Langlaagte farm, just west of the present-day city. As one of the world's greatest gold rushes ensued, the wily Boer president Paul Kruger famously made a small triangular patch of land available for the establishment of Johannesburg. This unused and unattractive piece of veld was what was known in the Boer republic as '*uitvalgrond*', literally 'left-over-land', but more colloquially 'wasteland': it fell between the demarcated farms of the Boers. Speculators rushed to buy portions of neighbouring farms to prospect: if gold was found, they would lay mine-claims; if not, residential suburbs would be laid out. Often, these speculators would 'sell' land to foreign investors, and only then negotiate with landowners to part with their property; if they were unsuccessful, the deals would fall through. The suburbs plotted by Tompkins that did not come to pass – his Casey's and his Mewettville, his Schweizer and his Ingramsburg – were speculation, then, rather than fact.

Is Johannesburg's first street guide a sales pitch rather than an empirical municipal guide? Not quite: such was the confusion of the commercial and the civic, of randlords and republicans, in this ramshackle boom town scrabbling for lucre, that the map did actually function as the city's blueprint. Tompkins was a city functionary, its surveyor.

Perhaps it was this confusion of roles that led Tompkins and his fellow planners to make their most egregious error in the fiction that is Johannesburg's first street plan. Just beneath the railway station, surrounded by the requisite cordon of open veld, are to be found two tiny portions of six blocks each, allocated for the Coolie Location and Kaffir Location respectively – 'coolies' being workers of Asian descent and 'kaffirs' being black labourers.

When you look at these 'locations' on the Tompkins map, you are struck by two things. The first is that apartheid was embedded in the

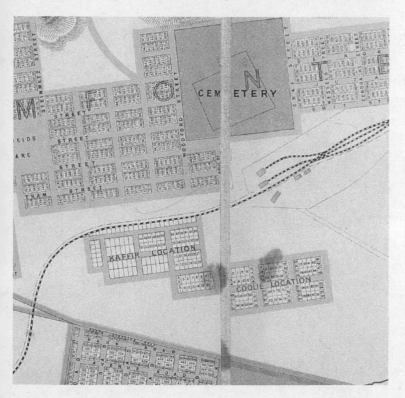

development of Johannesburg from the very start. And the second is that the city's planners actually believed they could contain the labour force they would need to build their metropolis on the highveld into twelve little blocks beside the railway line. Here, represented by the Tompkins map, is the folly of apartheid capitalism and the reason why it was destined to fail, even if it took a century to do so.

In Search of the South African 'Hüzün'

Recently, I was given a set of Super-8 films that my Uncle Leslie had shot on North Beach in Durban, that bustling east coast port where my father, David, was born in 1926 into a large middle-class Jewish family. The films were taken during the Christmas holidays throughout the 1950s, when the cousins from the interior would come down for their annual fortnight by the seaside. Over the course of a decade, Uncle Leslie recorded these get-togethers dominated by garrulous women playing cards, knitting, entertaining the kids and hamming endlessly for the camera, cigarettes always firmly attached to reddened lips. I was struck, watching the footage, by how the older people could well have been in Odessa or Coney Island in the way they slumped, contented and clothed, in their deckchairs: they had staked a mittel-European

anywhere-land at the fringe of this perplexing but bountiful continent so far away from their roots.

Indeed, the only way you knew they were *not* in Odessa or Coney Island was by the army of white-suited, red-fezzed Indian men who buzzed about the peripheries delivering tea trays and ice-cream cones and fizzy drinks. Beaches, of course, were strictly segregated in apartheid South Africa – the Indians were allocated the far more dangerous Battery Beach to the north, and the Africans beyond, at Blue Lagoon. But because these men were servants, they were permitted on the white sands of North Beach, fully clad spectres amid white South Africa undressed and at leisure.

In one sequence, my beloved Aunty Ruby is seen in profile. Someone just outside the frame is lighting a ciggy for her and she engages this person in her usual spirited manner. The shot is disorienting and intriguing: why would the cinematographer show his sister in such animated conversation and yet exclude her interlocutor? It took me a few viewings to figure it out, as I watched a headless white-suited man stomp off into the busy distance, decapitated by the frame, while my aunt mugged for the camera: Uncle Leslie's frame simply did not include the Indian waiter, who lived on the other side of the frontier even as he lit my aunty's cigarettes and served my uncle tea.

There are many photographs of my childhood in the garden, featuring the series of black men and women who looked after us. Much has been written, particularly from the United States, about how black slaves and servants have been posed in white family portraits, and there is a rich archive that documents the uneasy and sometimes transgressive nature of these compositions in apartheid South Africa too. In the photographs of my own childhood, from the 1960s and 1970s, I am struck by the contradictory position often occupied by servants: even though they are incidental – really just there to hold a child to the camera or deliver the tea tray – they are often an image's focal point. Perhaps less used to the dynamics of the snapshot as opposed to the formal studio picture, they look directly and dispassionately at the camera while everyone else gets on with their business.

Sometimes, the servants would come back to our home after their days off bearing formally posed studio portraits of themselves to show us – the men with trousers creased so sharp they could cut you; the women's contours liberated from pastel pinafores and their features brought alive between exotic hats and corsages. If you had asked me, aged six or seven, where they had gone to have these images made, I would probably have said, 'to the olden days', given the way their studied sepia-tinted poses and extravagant costumes resembled those of my ancestors on the study walls – and given, too, how little

I knew about what black people did and where they went when they were not looking after me.

*

Uncle Leslie's home movies remind me that every time a camera is pointed, a decision is made and a frontier is established. This might seem like a statement of the obvious, but it has profound implications, for there is a world beyond each image, a world that might be hinted at by what is in the frame, but that is also often ignored or even rejected. The suburban garden wall is a frontier, much as any frame; how much more so in apartheid South Africa, where – like the laagers of the Voortrekkers of old – one's security within was defined, precisely, by the dangers lurking without. My world, atomised by apartheid, was defined by what it had been walled against, dammed against. I was safe in direct relation to the insecurity of those outside – who were in turn corralled by Bantustan or township borders, borders specifically defined to dispossess them.

Ever since Jan van Riebeeck planted his famous almond-and-thorn-bush barrier in the mid-seventeenth century against the savage 'Hottentots' beyond, being South African has meant the negotiation of such frontiers. It has meant the marking of territories, the separating out of us from them, of the known from the unknown, of the safe from the fearful.

I could have used the words 'being human' rather than 'being South African' above and they would have been equally true. There is no deep mystery to this: from earliest childhood we form our identities by testing ourselves against (or submitting to) the boundaries erected for us by our parents, our schools, our communities and nations. And yet one reason why the South African situation became so acute a marker of iniquity in the twentieth century was because it was an extreme example of the way people could be bounded beyond their own volition; into neighbourhoods, into families, into destinies, into lives, and into jails if they resisted. This strand of self-consciousness about borders and boundaries – a negotiation of frontiers and a fear of what lies beyond – is particularly (even if not uniquely) South African.

If you have ever heard the story of Sandra Laing, you will never forget it for this very reason. Born in 1955, Laing was an Afrikaner child ostracised by her rural small-town community because of her negroid features, the product of a recessive gene carried by both her parents who, like so many Afrikaners, had black antecedents. Sandra's school attempted to expel her by getting her reclassified as black, and even though her father was ultimately successful in waging an epic battle to get her classified back to 'European', she came to understand things as they were. She was black, no matter what the Race Classification Board and her father said, and she would only be able to live her life in apartheid South Africa among other people who looked like her. And so she found love with a black man who worked for her parents; when her parents discovered this, they banished her and set her off on a lifetime of nomadic insecurity.

Recently, my partner C and I were dining with some friends. I am white, C is of Indian origin, and our friends were both from the 'coloured' community. We were bantering about race and ethnicity, as South Africans will do, and Zohra's family history tumbled out. When her mother was a little girl, Zohra's grandfather's family – fair-complexioned folk – decided to get themselves classified 'European'. Zohra's grandmother, who was also fair and with straight hair, was invited to join them in their new life of possibility and privilege. But she could not bear the thought of losing her own family in the process, and so she and the little girl remained behind in the coloured community, abandoned by husband and father. Once or twice, Zohra's grandfather would appear as a spectre through the kitchen door; a few years ago, some children came knocking, to call Zohra's mother to his funeral. His own life appears to have been nomadic; for reasons Zohra and her family do not understand, he was buried in the coloured township of Mitchell's Plain, outside Cape Town.

In South Africa, and particularly in the Western Cape – the heart of the country's coloured community – such stories are almost banal in their frequency, even if rarely told. There is nothing in my personal narrative that even approaches such trauma, the dimensions of the border-crossings that Sandra Laing was forced into or that Zohra's grandfather felt compelled to make. And yet – while making no claim whatsoever to suffering – I find in the relationship of within and without and the negotiation of a boundary between them, a strand of South-Africanness that links my identity, if not my experience, to theirs.

*

In his memoir *Istanbul: Memories and the City*, Orhan Pamuk describes the way that the drawing rooms of his family's apartments were museums of melancholy, reflecting the '*hüzün*', the fundamental melancholy, at the heart of his crumbling city hankering after the glory of its Byzantine and Ottoman pasts. Pamuk uses black and white photographs – from his family's personal collection, as well as of the city and its history – to explore a particular relationship between the collective identity of the city and the individual identity of a child, a poetic soul: 'What I am trying to describe now is not the melancholy of Istanbul,' he writes, 'but the *hüzün* in which we see ourselves reflected, the *hüzün* we absorb with pride and share as a community.' The *hüzün* is Pamuk's own, of course, or perhaps his family's or that of his patrician class: it is not something objective, but rather an internal, subjective emotion that he uses to explore the city of his birth. Or perhaps, conversely, it is a plumb line he takes from the mapping of the city of his birth, and which he uses to plot a journey into the self.

Pamuk writes that to understand Istanbul's essential *hüzün*, you need to visit the city in winter, and watch Istanbullus shuffle across the Golden Horn's Galata Bridge in a blizzard, draped in their coal-black shawls and illuminated by lamplight. The true Istanbul, he suggests, is best represented by the chiaroscuro images of the city's most illustrious photographer, Ara Güler, rather than by the vibrant tourist brochures of imperial splendour, its gold-topped domes glinting against the Bosphorus.

I am similarly tempted to represent Johannesburg through the Kodachrome prints in the family photo albums, although I came to see, as I grew older, that the overabundance of light could be savagely flattening as it burned townships through the thin dry highveld air. If there is a Johannesburg *hüzün* – if *I* have a Johannesburg *hüzün* – it must be found, somehow, in the relationship between the bucolic gardens of my Kodachrome childhood, wooded and green and irrigated, a world of swimming-pools and sprinklers – and the harsh bleached landscapes just beyond its suburban walls. Pamuk's work has provoked me into thinking about how the visual archive I have been collecting for the past two decades – photographs and maps – offers some route into an emotional truth: about what it means, to me, to be a South African, and about how my particular South African identity has been formed within the shadow of how I was defined – by family, by society, by the state.

'South Africanness' is a construct of the twentieth century, much as 'Turkishness' was: there was a nationalist project dedicated to defining some people into the laager, such as my Jewish immigrant antecedents, while defining the black majority out. The liberation struggle was in no small part an attempt to extend that definition to all inhabitants of the geopolitical entity called South Africa; little wonder, then, that post-apartheid South Africa has found itself obsessed with questions of identity and with how a new society might be built around a certain set of common values and identity markers.

I do not possess Pamuk's confidence: I cannot distil my national identity down into an essence such as *hüzün* and name it, the way he does. Still, I would like to adapt the Turkish writer's formulation to set the objective for this book: What I am trying to describe is not the boundaries that define South Africa (or, more specifically, Johannesburg), but the way that we South Africans define ourselves within, and across, and against, these boundaries.

Maybe I feel more comfortable with the personal singular pronoun: The way I define myself within, and across, these boundaries ...

Zita's Map of Želva

Imagination is 'always spatial', wrote the Polish poet Czesław Miłosz in his essay 'Notes on Exile': it 'points north, south, east, and west of some central privileged space, which is probably a village from one's childhood or native region'.

In July 2010 I took a trip with my friends Carol and Jessica, also South African Jews, to Lithuania, Miłosz's native region, which happens to be exactly the part of the world our grandparents came from. Miłosz was from a Polish landed family in Lithuania; our grandparents were Orthodox Jews from the *shtetl*. Still, I kept the poet close as we drove through the Baltic's lush woodlands and gorgeous baroque cities that seemingly carried little trace of my obliterated ancestry. I tried to imagine what it must have been like to come from a place so constantly shifting: now Lithuania, now Poland, now Tsarist Russia, now Nazi Germany, now the Soviet Union. Such instability, Miłosz writes in his memoir *Native Realm*, rendered him a typically formless Eastern European whose good qualities – 'intellectual avidity, fervor in discussion, a sense of irony, freshness of feeling, spatial (or geographic) fantasy' – derived from the 'basic weakness' of perpetual adolescent chaos that is the result of growing up in an unstable society: 'Where I grew up, there was no uniform gesture, no social code, no clear rules for behavior at table. Practically every person I met was different, not because of his own special self, but as a representative of some group, class or nation. One lived in the twentieth century, another in the nineteenth, a third in the fourteenth.'

The Miłosz family's fourteenth-century neighbours could well have been my great-grandparents; people who found their own refuge from statelessness in an intense commitment to medieval rituals and whose exterior form was so easily recognisable it became a caricature and then a shooting target. Miłosz is no doubt idealising early twentieth-century Eastern European formlessness – a borderland identity – because of the extremity of the formalism to which his own people were subsequently subject: Stalinism, Nazism, ethnic nationalism. As we drove through Lithuania, I thought constantly about how we map our identities onto landscapes and what the form of my own identity was as a twenty-first-century South African Jew, now expanding his own imagination outwards across these spires poking up through these woodlands of my forebears.

*

My father's mother, Granny Janie, left the logging town of Dwinsk – now the unutterably bleak Latvian city of Daugavpils – as an infant with her mother, following her tobacconist father, Jacob Moshal, who had gone on a year previously to Durban. It was the last years of the nineteenth century, when the collapse of Jewish communities in the Russian Pale of Settlement coincided with the gold rush and the South African economic boom. My paternal grandfather, Grandpa Morris, arrived in Durban five years later, a talmudic scholar in his twenties from a family of leather-workers, fleeing both the poverty of his *shtetl* and conscription into the army during the Russo–Japanese War. My own father often used to have me rapt with stories of this '*yeshiva-bocher*' arriving stupefied off the boat in steamy, subtropical Durban, in the bustle and hubbub of one of the British Empire's busiest ports, filled with redcoats going home after the Boer War, indentured labourers who had been shipped out from India to work the sugarfields, and Zulu workers in their traditional skins and beads.

Lithuania lost around 90 per cent of its Jewish population during the Holocaust, the highest percentage of any European country, and I had read and heard many stories of roots-tourism to this part of the world that had turned up nothing but killing-fields, desecrated cemeteries, and derelict synagogues. I think I was expecting the topography to reflect this desolation. And so I was taken aback, now, at the beauty of Podzelve (now Želva), the Gevisser *shtetl*, 65 kilometres north-east of Vilna (now Vilnius), nestled in a river valley in undulating wooded countryside, its low-roofed timber houses jauntily painted in yellows and blues and greens, and its gardens bursting with flowers and vegetables. There were only a few Soviet additions to this bucolic landscape: these included the derelict concrete-block offices of the Soviet Collective, with a stucco angel inexplicably poised for flight off one corner, and the incongruously grand, Stalinist-era high school, where we were headed, to meet its retired director, a woman named Zita Kriaučiūnienė, who ran the village history museum.

Zita was waiting outside for us in the 35° midday heat, a stout and bluff older woman in a calf-length skirt, her apparent grumpiness at having been called out at such short notice ill-concealed by large tinted glasses. The approach to the museum was equally unpromising – a dingy school corridor – but when she unlocked the room we were transported into an intricately carved jewel-box, meticulously finished with wooden cabinets and shelves covered in folkloric objects, clothing, photographs, and agricultural implements, around a work table on which a tea had been arranged under doilies.

My dispatcher's eye was drawn, immediately, to a large-scale, handmade map by the window, on which small irregular blocks of coloured construction paper had been pasted onto a hand-drawn street guide

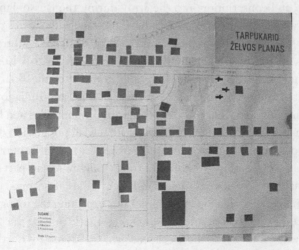

to the village. Zita noticed my interest and pulled me over to the map to explain it to us, through our guide and translator, a large and gentle man called Simon Davidovich, one of Lithuania's few remaining Jews. Zita told us that she had made the map after conducting research into the demography of the village in 1941 at the time of the Nazi occupation. According to the legend on the side of the map, 'Lithuanian properties' were green and there were about thirty-five of them; 'Jewish properties' were blue and there were double the number.

'Do you understand what this means?' Zita asked severely, her hands on her hips, in a way that suggested that very few Jewish roots-tourists had passed through Želva before us, and that the purpose of this museum was, rather, to educate her ignorant fellow compatriots. Before we could respond, she continued: 'It means that Želva was *Jewish*. *Jewish* and Lithuanian; they lived here together, in peace, for centuries.'

And with this, in an unexpectedly theatrical flourish, she opened the map. Literally: I had not noticed the carved latches on the side of it, and she now unclasped them and swung open the board on which the map was pasted so that a series of hinged wooden leaves was revealed behind it, like pages of a book, each one exposing another aspect of the town's hidden Jewish history. Zita removed her glasses to show a face planed with sharp Slavic contours and illuminated by intense pale blue eyes. Her taciturn welcome now melted into an unstoppable torrent as she led us through the story, with xeroxed photographs and documents of Želva's Jews, delivering it with such intensity that it seemed she had been waiting all her life to tell it.

Some of the story of my own family is documented in Zita's museum too. I have a relative, Aaron Klug, who was born in Želva; he won the 1982 Nobel Prize in chemistry and is consequently the *shtetl*'s most famous son. Klug left Želva as an infant with his family to join their Gevisser relatives in Durban in 1926, and he stands, for Zita, as a symbol of all that was lost when its Jewry was obliterated. One can imagine her in her classroom: 'If a boy from Želva achieved this – the Nobel prize! – you can achieve anything; so long as you are diligent and hard-working, like the Jews of Želva were . . .'

Zita arranged for a memorial to Klug to be erected in the town square and we walked over to look at it after our visit to the museum. It is a sleek constructivist sculpture, unexpectedly literate and playful: an oversized magnifying glass resting on a cylindrical plinth, designed by a local art student. On the way to the memorial, Zita paraded us through the town, shouting my cousin's name – 'Here are the relatives of Klug!' – to the bemused villagers sitting on their porches. An elderly man, tinkering in one of the wrecked old cars that litter the village, gestured down to the river: 'Oh, some Jews,' he said. 'Take them to see the *mikvah* [the ritual bath].' We gasped yet again, this time at the everydayness of the response, as if a half century of brutal history had not blotted out the Jewish presence in-between.

In the museum, Zita had told, with the intimate precision of a villager's consciousness, the stories of what had happened to each and every one of the *shtetl*'s Jewish residents who were rounded up in Mottel Heller's barn before being murdered by the Lithuanian *SS Einsatzgruppen* in 1941. She could even provide the exact number of killers: thirteen. I had grown up with stories of the Holocaust, but it had always seemed too vast to assimilate into my consciousness; now I imagined it happening in a place so close it could be mapped onto just one sheet of Zita Kriaučiūnienė's classroom poster board.

The museum had been going since 1959, Zita told us, but when she took it over in 1998 she had been shocked to discover that there was no mention of Želva's Jews, and so she had set about rectifying this.

Why, I asked her, had the museum become her passion?

Her answer had the moral clarity of a fable. She had been born in prison, in 1935. Her mother, held on charges of illegally distilling vodka, had been released when Zita was three weeks old, and was walking home through the woods around Želva when night fell. Her infant was in danger of being snatched by the wolves, but a Jewish family of the *shtetl* took them in.

'How long were you sheltered here', I asked, 'by this Jewish family in Želva?'

'One night,' she responded. 'They gave us food and a place to sleep and then drove us home in their cart the following morning. And they refused to be paid anything for this.'

I sensed that this story was shorthand for a deeper and more complicated set of emotions and motivations, but it was no less moving for that. A single night is a slender thread indeed on which to hang a life's work, but for Zita it seemed to represent nothing less that than the thread of life itself; of continuity and accountability, and humanity. These are the values she has pasted onto her map of Želva, in blue and green construction paper, with her students: a map of people who lived together until evil blew the village apart.

*

We ended our Želva visit at the Jewish graveyard, opposite the school, overgrown and untended, and I thought of Czesław Miłosz's description of what remains of Jewish culture in this part of the world: 'A foot brushes against a carved stone ...' On our way out of the town, at dusk, we noticed inebriated youths gathering in open spaces and tearing through the village in pimped-up old cars: there was an air of menace to them, that negative energy that comes from having nothing to do and nowhere to go.

It was a matter of some consternation to my hosts that Aaron Klug – by this point in his eighties – had not accepted an invitation to return to Želva. As we left the village joking about the prospect of his triumphant yet unlikely return, our guide Simon motioned dryly to the drunk youths kicking a can about in front of the derelict Collective offices: 'When Klug finally comes to visit, they'll round up all the *shikkered goyim* [drunk non-Jews] to come and welcome him.'

Simon had a wry, sad sense of humour; the *bittere gelechte* – bitter laughter – that is the fount of Yiddish comedy. At one point, lumbering through the woods (he drove his van with immense caution), he had us in such fits that we suggested he give up his day job and become a stand-up comic: 'But who will come to listen?' he asked. 'One Jew in a van and a thousand killing fields. Some joke.' His comment about the *shikkered goyim* was his only slight lapse into recrimination: perhaps because he was Zita's inverse – the child of

Jews who had survived the Holocaust by being hidden by Catholic neighbours – he continually countered our impulse to imagine Lithuanian society as irrevocably brutish and anti-Semitic. I know that my Grandpa Morris and his brothers never felt fully at home in South Africa and hankered all their lives after *di heim*, where they had left their mother. One of them actually went back, to settle in the city of Kovno (now Kaunas), in the 1920s. Now, because of Simon and because of Zita – and most of all because of her map – I felt that my own 'central privileged space' had expanded northward, from page 77 of the *Holmden's*, to a place that represented not only the trauma and dislocation so intrinsic to the narrative of Jewish migrancy, but an attempt to heal this rupture, too. When Zita Kriaučiūnienė opened up her map-book she opened up another childhood to me – that of a grandfather I had never known – and, with it, a perspective on my own South African childhood nearly a century later.

Grandpa Morris's mother – my great-grandmother Beila Gitl – was spared Mottel Heller's barn. She died in Želva of old age, mercifully just before the war began. The property on which she raised my grandfather and his siblings, in a low-roofed house with a tannery on the side and a *matzoh*-oven in the back, is represented on Zita's map by a block of blue construction paper, along the Wilkomir Road, up against the stream that Zita has ruled in two artless straight lines. Its direct neighbour is blue, too, but across the road is a green block and just across the stream another green one. Thus has Zita's map of Želva become my counter-*Holmden's*; an image, perhaps, of the formless borderland identity that Czesław Miłosz idealises and that I – as a child who grew up in apartheid South Africa with no possible way of crossing page 77 onto page 75 – continue to idealise too.

'Ulysses is About Us'

Johannesburg's 'Old Cemetery', on page 3 of the *Holmden's* alongside the Fort and my Granny Gertie's suburb of Hillbrow, was one of the landmarks of urbanity I hankered after in my early dispatching days. I went there for the first time only recently, after having been told by my cousin Adrian that Granny Gertie's maternal grandparents, Zalman and Minnie Blum (sometimes spelt 'Bloom'), were buried there. When I called the Chevra Kadisha, the Jewish Burial Society, to confirm the numbers of their graves, the woman there warned me that it was not safe and suggested I come by 'the new cemetery' at West Park to pick up a worker to protect me. Adrian, who lives in Israel, issued the same warning.

West Park has actually been in operation since 1942. My father is buried there in the Jewish section, as are Granny Gertie – my maternal grandmother – and her parents, Marcus and Ida Freedman. I know West Park well. But the Old Cemetery at Braamfontein is another story. Although it occupies a rectangle of land just off the M1 freeway and across the road from Wits University, it is passed unnoticed by most Johannesburgers and hardly ever visited. Until my visit in search of Zalman and Minnie, it had been entirely foreign to me, despite the fact that I once had an office at the university overlooking it. It had been as much a vacuum in my urban consciousness as the fort-turned-prison down the road.

Armed with my ancestors' tombstone numbers but not with an escort, I went off on a wet summer's afternoon in February 2012 to find them. Having struck off the Smit Street exit of the M1 past the carrion tow-trucks that skulk at the gates of the cemetery, I was immediately seduced by the voluptuous beauty of the place, laid out as a

funerary parkland in much the same way as Highgate in London or
Père Lachaise in Paris but far less dense, and meticulously kept by the
Johannesburg Parks Department. There were paved pathways and
statuaries, war memorials and mossy tombstones, lawns and low stone
walls and a handsome redbrick crematorium, and most of all there
were trees, grand old oaks and planes and blue gums, fed by decades
of composting flesh.

Such fulsomeness was, of course, only to be found in the white
parts of the cemetery. As I stumbled northward in the rain, looking for
the Jewish section but finding myself instead in the section where
black people had been buried, I was startled by the contrast. Here
there were grassy fields, a few derelict mounds and a forest of blue
gums; but few signs of the dead.

*

Johannesburg's civic fathers set boundaries in death as in life, I discovered as I came across more early maps of the city. On first glance
it had, quite reasonably, to do with religion. The southern portion of
the Old Cemetery, established in 1909, had been consecrated for
Christian denominations – 'Dutch Reformed', 'Nonconformist',
'Roman Catholic', and 'Church of England' – while the northern por-
tion seemed to be reserved for other faiths: 'Chinese', 'Coolies', 'Cape
People', 'Mahomedans', 'Kaffirs', and – my favourite – 'Christian
Kaffirs', this last exposing the fiction that it was about religion at all.
It was, of course, about race.

Separating the two portions was a large buffer, running to almost
the full extent of the cemetery: 'Jews'. This was evidence not only of
the size and significance of the Jewish community in Johannesburg,
from mining magnates to pimps, but of official ambivalence towards
them. Zalman and Minnie Blum had arrived in South Africa in 1918
from Dublin, fleeing the Irish Civil War, following their children and
grandchildren (including my Granny Gertie), who had arrived earlier
in the century. If they had tried to immigrate a few years later, it would
have been more difficult. As nativism and *herrenvolk* ideology began to
spread in the 1920s and 1930s, the South African government imposed

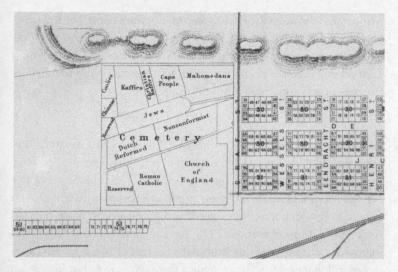

immigration quotas on Jews, along with other swarthy not-quite types, the Italians and the Portuguese, the Greeks and the Lebanese. Exploitative capitalist Jews, in particular, were blamed for exacerbating the 'poor white' problem following the Great Depression and scapegoated as a cause of Afrikaner misfortune. The pro-Nazi, anti-British Ossewa-Brandwag movement attracted mass support during the Second World War: thousands of its followers, including the future prime minister John Vorster, were interned for opposing South Africa's participation on the Allied side, and anti-Semitism was an inevitable by-product of the movement.

After the war, the government of Jan Smuts did not allow Jewish refugees from Europe to come to South Africa: Palestine was expected to absorb them. But in 1948, once the Afrikaner National Party came into power and realised it needed all the whites it could get, Jews and Southern Europeans were welcomed once more; any doubts these groups might have previously had about being members of the master race were dispelled by the institution of apartheid.

The virulent anti-Semitism of the early twentieth century receded, too, as the post-war economy boomed and as Jews left the country-side, removing themselves from direct competition with the

Afrikaners, who were themselves becoming more confident and prosperous under the National Party's rule. The rapprochement was helped, in no small part, by the way South Africa and Israel found each other in the late twentieth century, two pariah states founded by two sets of self-appointed 'chosen people'.

*

I turned around and walked southwards in the Old Cemetery that rainy day, looking for the Jewish buffer zone that I seemed to have missed despite its apparent size on the map. I stumbled over a few derelict Muslim graves and through a gap in a barbed-wire fence found myself, at last, 'at home', so to speak, in a granite forest of six-pointed stars and Hebrew characters. The Jewish cemetery was dense, and intense, an extraordinary memorial to the density of the Jewish experience in Johannesburg. It was only a few metres wide but long as an avenue, and bordered by rows of huge old blue-gum trees. It swept up the gentle rise of the cemetery in its own gentle arc, the tombstones so close together that they appeared, as you looked up along them towards the setting sun burning peach and violet into the thunderclouds, to be cobblestones of the dead along some eternal avenue.

It was not easy to find my great-great-grandparents: most of the copper number plates on the tombs had been pillaged, so I had to make my way chronologically through the early years of the century. Zalman and Minnie Blum had died in the great flu epidemic of 1918, just months after arriving in Johannesburg. Not surprisingly, this was a busy year for Johannesburg cemeteries: it took me a while to locate my ancestors and when I did find Zalman and Minnie, a row away from each other, I was struck by how illegible the tombstones were to me, despite the names carved in English at their bases; how undistinguishable they were, too, from those around them, all those Cantors and those Kravitzes, those Harts and those Perelmans set in solid black granite or the more flecked and porous reddish-brown variety that South African Jews seem to prefer. Zalman and Minnie's tombstones held little, for me, in their specificity. Their power was in their context; their presence among so many others.

Later, a friend of a friend, a gifted classical Hebrew poet, liberally translated the enchanting rhyming couplet on Minnie's tombstone inscription for me:

A woman whose soul was one of a kind
Pure, untainted, supremely refined
Menuha Feige, daughter of Reb Simcha
Passed away aged 69
On 29 Sivan 5769

Although I knew little about them, I grew up with the images of these two fine people, crowning the ancestor-wall of photos in the study, and I often fantasized about their lives during the reveries of my childhood. They could not look more distinguished, his full white beard alight with gunpowder-flash, providing luminous counter-weight to the sculpted bun swept up in perfect symmetry above her head. The portraits were made in a Johannesburg studio, probably shortly before Zalman and Minnie took ill and died, and although they were not wealthy, the couple exude the confidence and poise of the Jewish bourgeoisie. Zalman's Jewish identity is manifest in the beard and hat but nonetheless pulled into order – not unlike his wife's

thick black hair – by the photographer's tight composition; worlds away, certainly, from the postcards of thickset Gevissers in Lithuania from the same time, stashed in a shoebox at the bottom of one of the cupboards in the study, messages scrawled on the back in Yiddish to faraway loved ones at the outer edge of an unknowable continent.

Like my Gevisser relatives, Zalman and Minnie Blum were Litvaks, natives of Akmene, to the north-west of what is now Lithuania. They had immigrated to Ireland with their children in 1890, at a time when Queen Victoria's Britain welcomed Jews fleeing the collapsing Russian empire, and became part of the small Jewish community in Dublin, settling in 'Little Jerusalem', the warren of streets around Lower Clanbrassil Street. Zalman was registered as a 'draper', as was Marcus Freedman, my namesake, an immigrant from Akmene too, who lodged with the Blums and married their oldest daughter, Ida. The term 'draper' was a catch-all term for petty traders, or 'weekly-men' – as the Irish put it – who provided credit through a weekly tab to the local population, beginning with religious and political pictures and then graduating to dry goods and the rag trade once they'd established a regular clientele. They were, in short, moneylenders, and their services were much solicited in a poverty-stricken country.

My Granny Gertie was born to Marcus and Ida Freedman in 'Little Jerusalem' in 1901. The full romance of her Irish roots hit me only in my adolescence, when I developed an obsession with James Joyce's *A Portrait of the Artist as a Young Man* and was told by my grandmother – as I remember it – that *Ulysses* was 'about us'. This, of course, was on the basis of the common name: Joyce's Jewish–Irish anti-hero in *Ulysses* is named Leopold Bloom. I harboured this romance for many years and hatched it, finally, in 2010, when I made a visit to Dublin to trace the history of my Irish Blum relatives. I discovered that Granny Gertie was born at 5 Lombard Street West, and that she lived there with her mother, Ida, and her older brother, Toby, in the home of her grandparents, Zalman and Minnie Blum. The address is significant: we learn in *Ulysses* that Leopold and his wife Molly had begun their married lives just down the block, at 57 Lombard Street West, a little closer to Lower Clanbrassil Street.

Marcus Freedman had given his wife, Ida, two quick children before leaving for the colonies in 1902. He and his brother Israel immigrated to the former Boer republic of the Orange Free State as part of a British resettlement scheme just after the Anglo-Boer War ended. On Bloomsday, 16 June 1904, the day James Joyce sent Leopold Bloom on his day-long odyssey around the city, Marcus and Israel were behind the counter in one or other of the many enterprises they attempted to set up along the railway lines the British were laying from the vanquished Boer capital of Bloemfontein to the port of Durban. On that day, Granny Gertie, aged three and a half, was at home in Dublin, at 5 Lombard Street West, with her mother and grandparents.

Marcus sent for sent for his wife and children a few years later, and by 1908 they had joined him in the highlands settler-village of Westminster, near the Basutholand border. My grandmother spoke of a bountiful childhood on a farm called Childerley – although the records I found, in the Free State archives, track so tenuous an existence of vagabondage and bankruptcy, well into the 1920s, that the journey of my Granny Gertie's family toward becoming settled as South Africans strikes me, too, as worthy of the description 'odyssey'.

The literary Bloomists, and there are many, disagree about how James Joyce settled on the name and religious background of his everyman protagonist in *Ulysses*. What is certain is that Joyce knew little about Dublin's insular Jewish community, in which it would have been impossible to marry out of the faith and remain part of the community the way the fictional Leopold did. To the extent that Bloom and his co-religionists are modelled on any Jews at all, these are the more cosmopolitan mittel-European Jews of Trieste, where Joyce wrote his book.

I choose to follow those Bloomists who think Joyce got the name for his character after reading in the Irish papers of the scandalous 'Wexford Murder' of 1910, in which a Jewish photographer named Simon Bloom killed his Irish assistant in what appeared to be a staged suicide-pact-gone-wrong because she would not marry him. There is a trace of this, too, in *Ulysses*: the Blooms' daughter, Milly, is a photographer's assistant in Mullingar, a provincial town like Wexford. And then, of course, there is the clinching Lombard Street West clue: Joyce would have seen Zalman's name, spelt 'Bloom', while he was playing Dispatcher with the *Thom's Directory* in the Dublin Public Library, his primary research tool for mapping his protagonist's odyssey through the city.

The photographer Simon Bloom would be found guilty of murder and would spend a few years at the Dundrum Lunatic Asylum for the Criminally Insane. After his release he would change his name and move to the United States to become a genial Jewish patriarch of the Chicago suburbs; his descendants were horrified when an overly assiduous Irish–Jewish genealogist contacted them to spill the beans. Simon's brother was Benny Bloom, a peddler who fought with the British in the Boer War and came back claiming he owned a gold mine in South Africa. Benny later became a familiar figure in Dublin, trawling the suburbs up until his death in 1969, selling religious pictures to devout Catholics, his daily wanderings were not unlike those of his fictional namesake, and he is also sometimes claimed as Joyce's inspiration. I have verified that the brothers Simon and Benny were Zalman Bloom's cousins. And so my Granny Gertie was correct: we are related to Leopold Bloom.

In 1939, just after the publication of *Finnegans Wake* and just before the outbreak of the Second World War, James Joyce – in a penurious financial condition – was told by his friend Samuel Beckett that there was a position for a lecturer in Italian at the University of Cape Town.

Joyce planned to apply for the job, but in the end did not follow through because he was mortally terrified of thunderstorms. He was, of course, confusing Johannesburg – which has notoriously fearsome summer storms – with Cape Town, which has gentle winter rain, not unlike what Joyce would have known well in Trieste. The uncharacteristic rain that was falling when I went to visit the Old Cemetery was more Adriatic than Highveld, and as I stood in it over the tombstones of my great-great-grandparents it pleased me to think that even if Joyce did not make it here, some of his fictional anti-hero's relatives did, and that they are buried in the Jewish section, eternally weathering the Highveld's thunderstorms as they keep the Christian Christians away from the heathen ones.

Forests of the Dead

At the Old Cemetery that wet summer's afternoon, I said goodbye to my great-great-grandparents, Zalman and Minnie Bloom, and moved back, under the row of blue gums and across the barbed-wire fence, into the non-European north of the cemetery. After so dense a forest of commemoration, the lack of any sign marking graves here was all the more striking. Save for a few derelict tombstones belonging to Chinese, Hindu or Muslim graves, there was only a large granite block, laid in 1996 by Nelson Mandela, to commemorate the burial place of Enoch Sontonga, the composer of South Africa's liberation anthem, *Nkosi Sikelel 'iAfrika*.

For the first few years of Johannesburg's existence there had been a democracy, at least, of death. Because of the lack of any central government, people buried their dead wherever they saw fit, regardless of race or creed. But once the city's first administrators took control, there was the inevitable 'hierarchisation of death' along racial lines, as the historical geographer Garrey Dennie puts it. By 1907, the cemetery had been mapped racially and the white section landscaped into a garden. In contrast, the decaying black sections, screened from white mourners by the line of blue-gum trees I had just crossed, would later be described in a church report as 'a slum of the dead'.

In Johannesburg's early years, black migrant miners were generally dumped into unproductive mine property, in unmarked communal graves, because their families were unable to afford the costs of transporting their corpses back to their homes and because the mines did not, of course, provide burial policies for them. Thus were tens of thousands of mineworkers interred at their place of work for reasons that had everything to do with sanitation and efficiency and nothing to do with ritual and commemoration; thus were the remains of dead miners never returned home, leaving them eternal migrants in the afterworld. Those black labourers – or urban artisans or professionals – who could afford it would obtain a plot at the cemetery as a sort of halfway house to the ancestors: at least your bones were in the ground and could be visited, even if they weren't actually physically with your ancestors. Still, for purposes of efficiency and economy, the graves were usually communal, and marked only by flimsy wooden crosses.

Alan Buff, a senior City Parks official, has made it a personal mission to excavate the histories of Johannesburg's cemeteries: it was he who found Enoch Sontonga's bones at the Old Cemetery. He told me that he had used infrared X-ray photography to scan the earth beneath the seemingly empty northern non-European part of the cemetery to confirm that it was, indeed, full of bones. He believed that the reason why these grave sites seemed to be unmarked was because the cost of purchasing a tombstone was exorbitant, and so most black mourners had simply used the wooden crosses, which had decayed and disappeared over time. The copse of blue-gum – or eucalyptus – trees, he told me, was all that remained of a dense forest that had grown all across the northern reaches of the cemetery and had been cleared by the 1970s because it was perceived to be a security risk. It had grown, he was certain, from the fragrant blue-gum twigs that black people traditionally set on the graves of their deceased – taken, no doubt, from the line of trees planted to screen their messy affairs from the white burial park beyond. This practice had developed to mark the graves or, perhaps, to ward off the stench of rotting flesh, as most black burials were undertaken without coffins. The custom of placing blue-gum twigs on a grave survives today and is believed to ward off evil spirits. It is a fascinatingly syncretic tradition, the product of migration itself, given that eucalyptus was an Australian native originally brought to the Highveld to provide timber-props for the mines.

*

Walking through the remaining copse of blue gums at the Old Cemetery that late afternoon, the air fragrant with the sap released by the rain and by my feet crunching against the twigs and pods strewn beneath the trees, I found myself thinking about the Ponary forests outside Vilnius. We had visited Ponary on our trip to Lithuania in 2010. My father's Aunt Pessah and her family had been killed here, alongside 100,000 others, sometime between 1941 and 1944, by the assassins of SS *Einsatzgruppen* 9. They were marched from the Warsaw Ghetto to the forest and herded into spherical pits originally built to store the city's winter heating-oil, before being shot like fish in a barrel.

I had not known about Pessah until the early 1990s, when my father received a family tree from his cousin Julius. Meticulously laid out across several pages and generations, it culminated in a display – with headshots affixed – of the three 'Gevisser Boys' of Podzelve, who had come to Durban from Lithuania in the first years of the twentieth century, and their progeny. I was duly noted with my brothers, along with all the cousins I knew. But to the left of the tree was a

BEREL—LEIB   ISSY   MORRIS
+- 1906/?

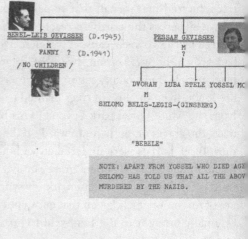

BEREL-LEIB GEVISSER (D.1945)
M
FANNY ? (D.1941)
/ NO CHILDREN /

PESSAH GEVISSER
M
?

DVORAH LUBA ETELE YOSSEL MO
M
SHLOMO BELIS-LEGIS-(GINSBERG)

"BEBELE"

NOTE: APART FROM YOSSEL WHO DIED AGE
SHLOMO HAS TOLD US THAT ALL THE ABOV
MURDERED BY THE NAZIS.

branch I had never heard of. The Gevisser Boys had had a sister, this Pessah, who had stayed in Lithuania, married and borne five children, and a grandchild identified in the family tree only as '*Bebele*' ('little baby'). There is a grainy photo of Aunt Pessah – she has the doughty no-nonsense demeanour of many of the women of my father's family – and a note: 'All the above were murdered by the Nazis.'

We asked my father whether he knew about these people, his aunt and cousins, and he professed to a vague memory of their mention when he was a child. There is some correspondence accompanying the family tree, illuminating this amnesia: in 1965, the sole survivor of this wing of the family, one Shlomo Belis-Legis, writes to my father's Uncle Issy from Warsaw, to say that he married Pessah's eldest daughter, Dvorah, that they had a child in 1936, and that he had escaped death by fleeing Vilnius after the German occupation, crossing over into Russia and joining the Red Army. Returning to Vilnius after the war ended in 1945, he found no one alive, including his daughter, his wife and all of her family. It was 'difficult', this relative continued in his letter to an unknown man thousands of kilometres

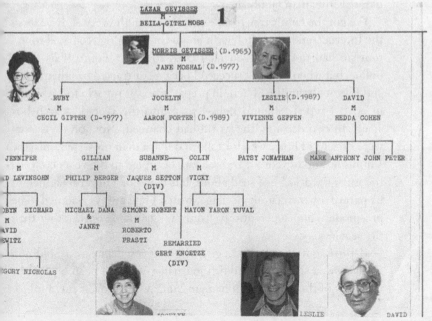

away in Durban, 'to realise from so far away what it means to a man to come home and find he has lost his whole family, to a soul. It is a miracle that I didn't go out of my mind. Even today, I cannot understand how I overcame my grief. Their faces were always in front of me, especially at night, I could not fall asleep. And then I developed an obsession to find out what happened to every single one of them up to their last day and how each one of them died. I made extensive inquiries from survivors and gathered details of each member of the family and how they met their end. Each detail hurt, but I undertook the task as a labour of love.' He ended the letter: 'Should I tell you everything I learned? Are you prepared to hear it all? You were so far away from the war – would you understand?'

The answer was no. Uncle Issy received the letter at the end of May, 1965. Six months later, his wife Aunt Jennie wrote back to Warsaw asking her correspondent 'not to tell us any more and not to open the wounds of the past'. Issy and Jennie sent Belis-Legis annual gifts for a while, along with an occasional *Shana Tova* card, but he got the message. He was never heard from again. Thus did the memory of our Lithuanian family die.

We got the family tree from cousin Julius in the very early years of the Internet, and the twin Jewish booms of genealogy.com and roots-tourism had not yet kicked in. I tried to find Shlomo Belis-Legis online, but when I did not succeed I became distracted by other things and forgot about him. Then, in preparation for my trip to Lithuania in 2010 I typed 'Shlomo Belis-Legis' into the Google search box again. In two decades, the world had changed. Now on my screen were dozens of links, which I followed like a man possessed, into the Vilnius he and my cousin Dvorah had occupied in the years between the wars; a world I had read about, but that I had never imagined to be part of my own family heritage, which I had always assumed to be pre-modern and superstitious, from the Orthodox *shtetl* rather than the secular city.

It turns out that Belis-Legis, whose given name was Solomon Beylis, was a significant Yiddish journalist. He had been one of the founders of the left-wing bohemian Yung Vilne movement, a minor poet, and the theatre critic for *Folksztyme*, the post-war Polish-communist Yiddish newspaper. By the time I went to Eastern Europe in 2010, he was no longer alive (he died in 1995), but in Vilnius I found an elderly Yiddish-language journalist who had known him, and who put me in touch with his second wife, a retired doctor named Wiktoria Czernobielska, whom I went to meet in Warsaw. Dr Czernobielska was lame and well into her nineties, but once she got over her initial suspicion (was I one of those Jews coming 'home' to claim Polish property?), she was charming and delightful, vivacious in a bright orange kaftan and bracelets that jangled up and down her emaciated arms as she told me a story that spanned Tszarism, Stalinism, Nazism and nationalism in one life.

She had been born in the Ukraine into a wealthy assimilated Jewish family. A fervent member of the Communist Party, she was posted as a doctor to Vilnius after the war, where she met Beylis, recovering from his war wounds in a hospital. They had moved to Poland to escape the post-war anti-Semitic purges of the Soviet Union, and had decided not to move to Israel with Poland's other surviving Jews in 1968 because she remained a true Marxist–Leninist believer. Beylis, devastated by the anti-Semitism of communist Poland, had spent the last two decades of his life in deep depression and, ultimately, the confusion of early-onset dementia.

He had barely spoken about his pre-war family to her, but she did have the story of how he survived, while they did not: 'When the Germans came to Vilnius,' she told me, through a translator, 'Beylis and wife decided to go east to Russia, because they were in danger due to their left-wing ideology. They left their baby daughter in his brother's house, because she was very ill. The brother seemed safe, because he was a tailor, and he made clothes for the Germans. But while Beylis and wife were walking through the forests towards the border, his wife decides to come back, because she feels she cannot leave the child. So they agree, in the woods, that the one will go on to Russia and the other will return to Vilnius ...'

After Beylis had died, Dr Czernobielska told me, she had found some photographs of his pre-war family. She now gave them to me.

One in particular compels me, today, as it held me when I first saw it, in the Beylis apartment. The image is shot in a Vilnius yard in

summertime, and I cannot but compare it to all the photographs in my family archive, of summers in the garden, of those seemingly contradictory sensations of freedom and containment that a garden brings to a child. The young family emerge, almost edenically, from the foliage, Beylis and his toddler daughter 'Bebele' shirtless, my cousin Dvorah in a sleeveless dress. You can feel the little girl's sense of security as she sits between her parents, propped on her father's broad left shoulder.

It is the summer of 1939.

*

When we visited the Ponary Forest in 2010, where Dvorah and Bebele had been killed together with my father's Aunt Pessah and the rest of her family, the fragrance had been pine and birch rather than eucalyptus, and the forests had felt as infinite and unbounded as any attempt I tried to make to wrap my head around the scale of the atrocity. Here, in downtown Johannesburg, walking through the Old Cemetery in 2012, there was something pathetic about this little blue-gum glade, so bounded by the city around it, so unequal to the burden of memory it was required to carry.

The present day's callousness toward history was writ large at Ponary. As we were walking back to our guide's car, stunned by the vision of the now grassed-over spherical depressions in the forest, the birdsong was shattered by gunfire. Shocked and distressed, we hastened to find the source: a couple of kids had set up some tin cans in the parking lot of this forest on the outskirts of town, for target-practice.

The insouciance at the Old Cemetery in Braamfontein was more banal and in that way perhaps more distressing: a hadeda ibis shrieked, a beggar accosted me for some change, two men in City Parks overalls piled sodden blue-gum branches into the back of a truck, and the cars zoomed past on Enoch Sontonga Avenue.

Wall of Ancestors

Hanging beneath Zalman and Minnie in the family study is a series of portraits of my father's dynastic family, the Moshals and the Gevissers, from the arrival of my Grandpa Morris and his brothers shortly after the end of the Boer War up to my father's own infancy in the late 1920s.

My great-grandfather Josef Gevisser was a tanner who had settled in Želva sometime in the mid-nineteenth century because it was the region's largest horse market. After his early death and the family's destitution, my Grandpa Morris and his siblings were farmed out to family to support them; Morris and his brothers eventually ended up living in prayer-houses in Vilnius, informal *yeshivot* which allowed destitute young scholars to sleep on the prayer benches and arranged for them

to eat daily meals with congregants. Unlike his brothers, Morris actually became very religious, and my father always said he would have far preferred a life in a *yeshiva* than the bustling tropical trading-house that the family business became. Morris was the last to arrive in South Africa; soon after his reunion with his brothers, the three Gevisser Boys posed for a photograph, which hangs on the wall of ancestors. The image projects all the worldly refinement of three young men-about-town, transmitting the message back to their mother Beila-Gitl in Želva and forward unto the future generations: 'We have arrived.'

They had not, of course. Not yet. At the time this photograph was taken, the brothers lived together in a little room behind the shop leased by the oldest brother, Bere-Leib, which sold basic goods to black dockworkers on the Point Road. Morris gained a quarter-share of a '*kaffir*-eating' (or '*kaffir*-eatnik'), as it was known, where he and his partners provided the morning meal to 'rickshaw-boys' at their station on the Point Road. Originally from India, rickshaws were the two-wheeled hand-drawn carts that were the primary means of moving people and goods around Durban; the cart-pullers began work at 4 a.m., which meant that they needed to eat at 3 a.m. So my grandfather and his partners worked from midnight through to the morning, assisted by fifteen-year-old Issy – his face so fresh in the photograph beneath a self-conscious cowlick – before he went off to school.

The Gevisser brothers ate many of their own meals at a kosher boarding house on Windermere Road, run by the Moshals, then one of Durban's most prominent Jewish families. A dynastic marriage was arranged when Grandpa Morris offered a half of his quarter-share in the 'kaffir-eating' for Granny Janie's hand. 'This', writes my father in his own memoir, 'was the foundation of the Moshal–Gevisser partnership that became one of the three or four great wholesale trading houses which dominated South African commerce from the mid 1930s to their post-war demise in the 1960s.'

The Moshals had status, in the small Jewish community, but not much capital; the Gevissers, on the other hand, were orphan boys with entrepreneurial flair, who had stashed a fair bit of cash under the bed and who had identified a gap in the market: bottles, bones, boxes and bags. It was, in short, a waste-recycling business: bottles would be cleaned and resold to the dairies, bags would be restitched and sold to ice-companies, boxes would be salvaged and refitted, and bones would be ground down and sold to fertiliser companies. 'The all-pervading smell of rotting bones still haunts me,' writes my father of his childhood in Durban in the 1930s. 'Purchases and sales were all for cash,

and there was a constant traffic of Zulu and Indian hawkers pushing home-made hand-carts piled high with bottles, bones, bags and crates.'

On the page opposite the description in my father's memoir is a photograph of the Moshal–Gevisser wedding in 1912, a large print of which also hangs on the wall of ancestors. The men in the portrait are stiff in morning suits, the older women upholstered like plump Victorian couches. The younger Moshal children are got up as shepherd boys and girls, and the studio photographer has chosen the backdrop of an abstracted landscape to complete his pastoral. Weddings are, of course, dress-up occasions by definition, but so far is the Moshal–Gevisser wedding portrait from the frenetic and earthy trade on Victoria Street it would facilitate, that it makes explicit, it seems to me, an equation between photography, memory and desire: the nostalgia that drives us to hang photographs of ancestors on our walls tells us more about who we would like to be than where we have come from.

*

It would take the Moshal–Gevissers less than a generation to grow into the substantial outfits they rented from the studio photographer. The Indian and Zulu scrap-hawkers were unable to meet the demands of the company's customers for new boxes, so my father's Uncle Sol Moshal, a visionary entrepreneur, gave a contract for new timber to the Acme Box Company. Unhappy with the output of the factory, Uncle Sol bought it. Like all smart industrialists he soon saw the benefits of travelling even further upstream, so he bought a forest in northern Natal and set up a lumber empire that he would control for the rest of his professional life.

There was one problem with this rapid expansion, however: notwithstanding the family's roots in the woodlands of eastern Lithuania, they knew nothing about trees. At around this point, my father – a shy, studious boy who loved history and literature and had a terrible stutter – was coming to the end of his high-school career. Uncle Sol had no male heirs and the future was clear: Dovidl, as he was known in the family, was to study forestry at the University of Stellenbosch, the fulcrum of Afrikaner nationalism, the only institution in the country to offer such training.

'It was', my father records in his memoir, which he called *The Unlikely Forester*, 'a mad choice for a small, unworldly, unsporting Jewish boy from English-speaking Natal.' His torment began on the two-day train ride from Durban to Stellenbosch, when it became known that there was a Jew on board: he was, at first, 'a curiosity, an intruder, and a good opportunity to convert [the other students'] youthful unformed theoretical anti-Semitism into something more

real and practical and satisfying. They had a Jew all to themselves.'
But the 'mild anti-semitic folk-lore', shocking as it was, gave way to
bloody harangues, pushing and shoving, and then more brutal initiation: 'my months of purgatory had begun, although I had no clear
idea what was in store for me'.

At the university, his assigned roommate refused to share with a
Jew, as he had been brought up believing that Jews did not bathe.
Once word spread that there was a Jew on the campus, 'I became an
object of extreme interest to be interrogated, shoved, poked, humil-
iated. Much of this was in fairly typical cruel adolescent vein, but some
of it was openly racist. I was told in clear and threatening terms that
Stellenbosch should be *Judenrein* ['clean of Jews'], and that I was
regarded as the first of an unwelcome wave of Jewish infiltrators, that
I should leave forthwith, and that if I had any doubts about all of this
I should be aware of what was happening to 'my people' in Germany.'
On his first day in the Botany class – his first ever university lecture –
the professor, a prominent pro-Nazi Afrikaner, strode in and said,
'There's a Jew in my class. Can this be true. I wonder what he looks
like. Jew – stand up ... Come and sit here in the front row under my
eye. I must watch you.' When my father wrote his first Botany test,
he was failed. When he went to ask the professor why, 'he looked at
me coldly and said slowly – "*Jode moet weet dat hulle nie in Stellenbosch
welkom is nie.*" ("Jews must know that they are not welcome in
Stellenbosch")'.

The initiation process, my father writes, was 'a nightmare': he
describes being paraded around the university with a placard round
his neck proclaiming '*Ons is die kak van die land*' ('We are the shit of
the land'). All he records of the nights is that the initiation high jinks
would 'degenerate into physical attack, bruising and pain' – so much
so that he set himself up in a shelter on the banks of the Eerste River,
close to the hostel, and sometimes slept there.

'I should have left after that first horrible week,' he writes. But he
stayed, and quickly made a few friends who took it as their 'personal
crusade to persuade me to persevere' and who protected him at great
personal cost to themselves. Through them, he came to see that

'Afrikanerdom was not irredemediably racist', even as he came to 'the very clear conclusion that at that time in South African history, a local Hitler could awaken the same disregard for humanity and acceptance of brutality that had become evident in Nazi Germany'.

It was here that my father discovered his particular power and his singular vengeance: he could befriend anyone. It was a matter of great pride to him that '*die fokken Jood*' ('the fucking Jew') soon became '*Onse Joodjie*' ('our little Jewboy'), that he became one of the most popular students in his year, and that – by the time he graduated – he was dating the daughter of the professor who had given him zero and was supping at his table. It was at Stellenbosch, too, that he discovered his politics: 'I have no clear recollection of what turned me [so] strongly and vehemently anti-nationalist and pro-liberal,' he writes. 'It was probably a mix of revulsion to student/Afrikaner attitudes to "non-whites", to their growing adherence to the embryonic apartheid doctrine, and to Afrikanerdom's blatant racism of which I had become so clearly aware as a handy victim.'

Because of his experiences at Stellenbosch and his lifetime of work in the forestry industry, which was Afrikaner-dominated, my father both loved Afrikaners and loathed 'Afrikanerdom'. Notwithstanding his clear affection for many of the individuals he had studied and worked with, we grew up, almost imperceptibly, with the self-satisfied notion of Afrikaners as 'bad' whites and 'English' people – as we called ourselves – as good ones. Indeed, the very first derogatory words I heard in my life – on the school playground rather than at home – were about Afrikaners, not blacks: 'crunchies', 'hairybacks', '*chatteses*' or '*chataysim*' (a Yiddish word, the roots of which remain obscure). It was only in my adulthood that I got over this.

'Venus de Milo "Suspect"'

I was born on 11 November 1964, in the Florence Nightingale Nursing Home on Kotze Street in Hillbrow, in a room that looked north over the Fort's ramparts. My parents had met two years previously, introduced by mutual friends. My father was, at this point, a dashing bachelor in his mid thirties, dividing his time between the plantations on the Eastern Transvaal escarpment and his head office in Johannesburg. My mother, ten years younger, was a gifted pianist and a high school English teacher, renowned for her beauty and her very sharp wits. Theirs was a passionate love, and after a couple of months he proposed marriage. When she became pregnant, they bought a suburban ranch house in the new suburb of Atholl, along the Sandspruit north of Johannesburg in what was then known as the Peri-Urban Areas, a semi-rural chequerboard of farms, small-holdings and new developments.

After graduating from Stellenbosch, my father had joined the novelist Alan Paton's anti-apartheid Liberal Party, but he had broken with the party because he believed, unlike Paton, that liberal whites should remain in parliament and fight the system from within. By the time I was born, he had become a 'Prog', a member of the Progressive Party represented by Helen Suzman, the lone anti-apartheid member of parliament. My mother's father, David Cohen, had been a furniture manufacturer of modest scale, a communist and a self-taught intellectual of the 1930s. A passionate bibliophile, he had been a member of the Left Book Club, that extraordinary venture set up by the publisher Victor Gollancz and others to publish and disseminate left-wing literature; thus had Grandpa David – who died before I was born – bequeathed a voluminous orange-jacketed library to his only daughter: George Orwell's *The Road to Wigan Pier*, Edgar Snow's *Red Star over China*, Sidney and Beatrice Webb's *Soviet Communism*.

By November 1964, at the time of my birth, Nelson Mandela and his co-defendants in the Rivonia treason trial had been sentenced to life imprisonment on Robben Island. Bram Fischer, Mandela's lawyer and the leader of the South African Communist Party, had just been arrested with eleven other white activists, all awaiting trial for having contravened the country's anti-communist laws. A bomb had gone off in the central concourse of the Johannesburg Station, killing an elderly white woman and injuring dozens more people; the bomber, a white man named John Harris who was part of the African Resistance Movement, had just been sentenced to death.

After the station bomb, the illusion that the country's political instability could be contained in the black townships was shattered. Between June and December 1964, eighteen white activists found themselves in the dock in three separate political trials; many were Jewish, and part of my parents' broad, liberal, professional world. Their friends were emigrating in droves. On the brink of starting a family, my parents feared for the future but were loath to leave South Africa. The police apprehended a close associate of theirs; he had typed a 'subversive' letter, but had managed to throw the incriminating typewriter into Hartbeespoort Dam and so was not charged. A handyman working for them turned out to be a moonlighting policeman, and they feared a raid. They wanted to make the world safe for their new family and so, one balmy Saturday night, they set a fire in their living room fireplace and fed my grandfather's library to the flames. Books do not burn as easily as you might think; it took them all night. A few days later, I was born.

*

'VENUS DE MILO "SUSPECT"' read the headline of the *Rand Daily Mail* on the day that I was born. The newspaper told the story of how the Customs Department had instituted a new practice of 'embargoing' books pending judgment by the censorship board. 'It has become so silly now,' opined the *Mail*, South Africa's flagship liberal daily

RAND
Daily ✠ Mail

MORNING FINAL

JOHANNESBURG, WEDNESDAY, NOVEMBER 11, 1964.   Price 3 cents

JOY PACKER — 'The Glass Barrier'
LEON URIS — 'Armageddon'
LORD RUSSELL — The Trial of Adolf Eichmann

EMBARGOED

2 drown after 'danger' board removed

VENUS DE MILO 'SUSPECT'

S.A.'s book squad has new plan

By MICHAEL LORIMER

THE latest move to control the reading habits of South Africans is a new Customs Department pick-a-title plan, which aims at controlling the sale of "undesirable" literature.

According to booksellers, a "suspect" word or a cover picture can be sufficient to warrant a visit from the "paint" squad.

It has become an ugly story that we must work a picture of the Venus de Milo on its cover could be forbidden to South African readers.

Still no head— death pan may be emptied

By CHRIS VERMAAK
Crime Reporter

A DUMMY RUN FOR POLICE

WAS HUNG ON DOOR, DEATH NOW MAN SAYS

Breaking news

Suspect list

'Absurd'

Venus de Milo

Farmer and wife shot by gunmen

EFFECTS OF U.D.I. PROBED

From JOHN WORRALL

FREAK STORMS HIT TRANSVAAL

NEXT BIG ADVANCE AGAINST DENTAL DISEASE

Slick coatings to guard teeth

newspaper, 'that a book with a picture of the Venus de Milo on its cover could be forbidden to South African readers.'

A Customs Department spokesman explained the decision to the newspaper: 'Customs officials haven't the time or the qualifications to censor books. If a book is doubtful, for whatever reason, it is embargoed.' What made a book 'doubtful'? Because books on Nazism had been embargoed, Lord Russell's *The Trial of Adolf Eichmann* was no longer for sale. Neither was Leon Uris's *Armageddon*, along with books, unnamed, by Fyodor Dostoevsky, Emile Zola, Iris Murdoch and Joy Packer. According to a high-end bookseller who suddenly found he could not sell much of his stock, 'the books appear to have been embargoed because they have a suggestive word in the title, like "bikini", or a suggestive cover, like a picture of the Venus de Milo, or the word "black" or the word "sex".'

*

In 1964:

- 48 people were placed under house arrest, 11 of whom fled the country
- 173 people were placed under 90-day detention
- 671 people were found guilty of political offences, five of whom were sentenced to death
- 303 South Africans were banned, 22 of whom left the country
- 141 white men and 110 'Bantu' women were convicted of inter-racial carnal intercourse, as were one white woman and four 'Bantu' men
- 56 men were convicted of bigamy, 42 of them 'Bantu'
- 21 women were found guilty of illegal abortions, 12 of them 'Bantu'
- 13 people were convicted of keeping a brothel, five of them coloured women
- 643 men were convicted of 'public indecency', 309 of them 'Bantu'
- 41 people were convicted of being in possession of 'indecent publications'

- 504 publications were banned
- 216 people were convicted of 'other indecent, immoral or sexual offences'
- 57 people were convicted of bestiality, 42 of whom were 'Bantu' men
- 20 white men were convicted of the 'unnatural act' of committing sodomy with other white men
- 186 'non-white' men were convicted of committing sodomy with other 'non-white' men
- 2 white men and 2 'Bantu' men were convicted of committing sodomy with each other
- Over 200,000 black people were convicted of pass offences, most of which were contraventions of curfew regulations.

*

At the time I write this, in 2013, South Africa is without question a freer country than the one into which I was born: the Venus de Milo is no longer suspect, abortion is legal, sodomy is no longer a crime. I am married to my husband, a man of a different race to me. Whether my native land is a more equal place is another story, another book. Whether it is a more violent place is, surprisingly, debatable: the murder rate has risen from 27 per 100,000 people only slightly to 31 over the course of my life to date, and the rate of assault with grievous bodily harm has actually decreased by 25 per cent. Rape rates have doubled, but this might have to do with better awareness and reporting. What is indisputable, though, is that South Africa is a more armed place: while common robberies – those without weapons – are down by half over the course of my life to date, armed robberies are up, exponentially, from 14 per 100,000 in 1964 to 203 per 100,000 in 2012.

I have become one of those statistics. 'My life to date' might well have become 'my life', on the 11th of January 2012. I would have been forty-seven years old.

Yidden

My earliest memory of conscious imagination is that of deciding that a corner of our garden in Atholl, down some stone steps and next to a flower bed and the huge furniture that held big people, was called 'Yidden'.

This was, I think, my attempt to say 'England' – a word I must have heard from my parents and which I evidently associated with place – rather than any reference to my Jewish ancestry, of which I would then have been unaware. Or maybe I was looking for a place to lose myself, a place in which I wanted to be 'Hidden' so that I could – like all toddlers who drive us to distraction with endless hide-and-seek play – be found by adults in an enactment of their responsibilities over me. The thrill of being invisible, when you are a child, of being lost, is eclipsed only by the pleasure of being found: you need, perpetually, to enter the territory of the former so as to test the efficacy of the latter.

I named 'Yidden' when I was acquiring language, so I must have been two or three, the same age as 'Bebele' in the Vilnius garden. Even before the *Holmden's* came along, my imaginative pastime was to plot houses, streets, suburbs, cities and countries – to plot other lives, really – across the topography of whatever space in which I found myself: the garden, the summer holiday cottage, the beach, the gnarls and knots in the extraordinary pitched-pine ceiling of my bedroom, buttressed by huge whole logs from my father's forests, in which I could lose myself for hours while lying on my bed. Once or twice I would find a fellow traveller who could be seduced into this fantasy geography, but usually I journeyed alone.

At roughly the same time as I had become involved with the

Holmden's, I had discovered the maroon *World Book Atlas* in my parents' study. I struggled to open it and turn its pages: more of a world than a book, it was the biggest volume I had ever encountered, a scale that seemed entirely appropriate. An adult must have explained to me the relationship between the star representing the capital city and the expanse of single colour that enveloped it: every precocious child has a party trick, and mine became World Capitals. 'Upper Volta?' someone would shout out, and I would respond, 'Ouagadougou!' Bhutan? 'Thimpu!' Nicaragua? 'Managua!'

More significantly, I developed second lives for myself in some of these places. For reasons that were probably no deeper than the exotic sound of it, I found myself, at the age of six, drawn to the town of Wonthaggi, outside of Melbourne, on the edge of the pink expanse of Australia's state of Victoria. I began generating the necessary documentation – township outlines, street maps, house plans – and in a class presentation, I gave a detailed account of my life there. I was rumbled on Parents' Day, as one inevitably is, and although I do not recall being punished, a stern reminder was issued about the frontier between fact and fantasy. From then on, I knew to keep my second lives to myself, and there are still journals – the black card-covered schoolbooks with red or green spines and blotchy blue-ink lines ruled across very cheap paper that all South African students used – filled with my maps and plans, stashed somewhere in the cupboard of my old room, beneath the pine universe, in the family home.

*

There is a common story heard among South African Jews, often told with a wry self-deprecation: 'Our parents got on the wrong boat.' Or: 'There wasn't room on the boat to New York.' Or: 'They got off at the wrong port. They were actually meant to be going to Australia.' I have wondered, as an adult, whether my second lives in Wonthaggi and elsewhere were an infantile expression of a familial discomfort with being South African; perhaps, as well, some kind of atavistic diaspora consciousness, received from generations of itinerant Israelites.

With the exception of Grandpa Morris, my grandparents came to

Southern Africa as children with their mothers, following pathfinding men who had gone ahead several years previously to investigate the possibilities in this faraway country. Granny Gertie, Grandpa David, Granny Janie: all three met their fathers for the first time after long sea voyages, disembarking at Port Elizabeth and Beira and Durban respectively. They were, then, pretty much the same age I would be seventy years later, when I began tracing their routes in the *World Book Atlas*. I have played global Dispatcher with them ever since, bringing them home from Dublin and Dwinsk, from Podzelve and Port Said, and I have often wondered about the places they left as they were dispatched outward from homes to which they would never return; so unlike my imaginary couriers who, no matter how far they roamed across the *Holmden's* or the *World Book Atlas*, would always be back in time for supper and a bedtime story.

*

In the handwritten Yiddish memoir he penned shortly before his death, my father's Uncle Issy describes the journey he undertook in 1904, when he came alone to South Africa at the age of thirteen. The memoir captures the terror of having to cross the Russian border illegally under gunfire in thick snow; of having to face being turned back because he forgot to lie to the Prussian authorities about his destination; of arriving, finally, in Durban and finding nobody waiting for him because of the kind of miscommunication we could not begin to imagine in this age of digital connection. A letter he sent to his mother back in the *shtetl* describes the joy of his eventual reunion with his brother, the oldest Gevisser boy, Bere-Leib; how they drove home to his room behind the shop on Point Road in a rickshaw 'and now I was in Africa. And immediately on the second day, he [Bere-Leib] had already made me into an "Afrikaner" [with] a pair of yellow shoes and short trousers and long socks and a straw hat. And this is South Africa! In one minute you become [illegible].'

What words has time scratched out? 'A native'? 'At home'? 'A South African'? My Grandpa Morris, the *yeshiva-bocher*, would join his 'Afrikaner' siblings a few years later, but he would be the only one of my four grandparents who never really made South Africa his home. He had a thick Yiddish accent, a faraway look in his eyes and, according to my father at least, a perpetual befuddlement at the life in which he found himself, in Africa, in commerce, and in the English language. But after difficult beginnings, my other three grandparents settled into their new identities almost as easily as Uncle Issy donned his safari-suit, and by the time I began describing myself a half-century later, I could not have imagined calling myself anything other than 'South African'.

I knew where to find myself i then *Holmden's*: in a triangular set of roads so familiar to me that it conjures a nostalgia as sickly-sweet as the smell of springtime jasmine.

And I knew where to find myself in the *World Book Atlas* too: South Africa was that cradle-shaped curve in the southern seas just across from the icy white of Antarctica; a paradoxical island itself, because the rest of the continent, full of exotic names ('Ouagadougou!', 'Lubumbashi!'), was so inaccessible and unknowable that it might as well have been a sea itself, separating us from more familiar territory to the north.

There was the occasional African name in the *Holmden's*, but our lives were generally lived on roads called Oxford and Coronation, at shopping centres called Hyde Park and Rosebank, and on holidays at resorts called Clifton and Sheffield; the other pink bits of the world were thus familiar not only culturally but cartographically too.

When our parents went away, they were going 'to Overseas'; when friends' families emigrated during the tough years of the 1970s, they were going to live 'in Overseas'. This has become rooted in the South African lexicon: even today, when I return to Johannesburg, my housekeeper will ask, 'how are things there, in Overseas?' Once I was able to establish that overseas was not a place, I had to grapple with it as a concept. Why were places like London and Paris, which my parents visited, described as 'over seas' when there was, really, a huge expanse of land between them with no seas over which to fly but for the splash of Mediterranean? I think it might have been explained to me that South African planes were not allowed to fly over Africa because the black people there did not like the way we treated our own black people, but this only entrenched the notion of the rest of Africa as somewhere else, a literal no-fly zone.

Early on, I learned it was wrong for us to call ourselves 'Europeans' and black people 'Non-Europeans', as stipulated by the race classification laws. The adults in my liberal English-speaking world preferred the word 'African' to 'black' or 'Non-European', perhaps in the mistaken assumption that this accorded more dignity. But this only strengthened my sense of African as other. I surely knew that South Africa was on a continent called Africa – I would have learned this at school and seen it on the map – but I already had many years as a global dispatcher under my belt before it hit me that the continent was actually part of my country's name and thus my identity. That if I was 'South African', I must be 'African' too. It struck me with the force of revelation.

*

Although I might not have known that I was African, I never doubted that I was South African, or that I was a Gevisser. I belonged to my country and I belonged to my family. But I never fully belonged to my childhood. This might have been because I was out of kilter with my peers: I read very early, wrote very late, apparently left the potty late too. I was at ease with my own company and that of my brothers, and content to have just one or two fellow-romancers for companions – until a witless teacher on playground duty tainted (perhaps I mean to write 'taunted') my solitude by asking what was wrong with me, and instructed me to play with the other children.

I was in Grade One, my first year at school, at Sandown Primary, the local whites-only government school. As I remember it, the boys and girls were separated at break, and week by week we alternated between two sides of the playground: while the boys were on the swings and the jungle-gyms, the girls would be in the sandpit and on the field, and then vice-versa. I had terrible motor coordination and did not like to compete physically with other boys; I also had a phobia that if I went too high on the swings, I would swing over the crossbar like a cow jumping over the moon and the world would end. I was thus far more comfortable making worlds in the sandpit, or lost in the wilderness at the edge of the field while the other boys were kicking a ball around, and I dreaded the simian swinging-and-climbing weeks.

It must have been during one of these, while I was lingering around the runnel of sorts that formed the frontier between the two sides of the playground – my reverie might have even carried me across the boundary – that Mrs M pounced. I am sure she meant well, and even if she didn't, I probably should be grateful to her, for it was as vital a moment in my socialisation as Mrs K's discovery the following year that I didn't come from the Australian town of Wonthaggi. I learned that if I was going to fit in, I needed to appear to accept the boundaries set for me while transgressing them silently, underground or in the ether, beyond the patrol of adults.

Who is able to say, of his childhood, what was a cause and what a symptom? We explain ourselves – to ourselves and others – by constructing emblematic moments which we cure in formaldehyde and onto which we mount our adult identities like so many butterflies in the cabinets of our childhood. Here, then, is one: my Sunday afternoon escapes to the Mercedes with the *Holmden's*. And here another: Mrs M snaring me in the runnel and making my truth manifest. I was not like other boys.

Sandspruit

Our home in Athol, on East Avenue, was a block away from the Sandspruit, five or so kilometres downstream from The Wilds and the stream's headwaters, now buried beneath the concrete of Hillbrow. The Sandspruit is a tributary of the Jukskei River, which also rises in central Johannesburg and flows along the eastern perimeter of the city and through Alexandra township. Once joined, on the grounds of Leeuwkop Prison north of Johannesburg, these waters find their way into the Crocodile, which joins the Groot Marico, which becomes Rudyard Kipling's 'great grey-green greasy Limpopo' at the Botswana border before describing the vast arc of South Africa's northern border and then emptying itself into the Indian Ocean in Mozambique, whence our manservant James came.

James lived, of course, across the yard in the servants' quarters, together with the other staff. When my white suburban South African ears hear the word 'yard', my mind imagines not an enclosed space of outdoor green behind a house the way an American does (we would call that a 'garden'), nor an industrial enclosure, the way a European might. Rather, I see the expanse of paving between the kitchen door and the servants' quarters, perhaps a bit cracked with some weeds growing through and a washing-line pulled across it. I see a borderland, a place that is part of my world but also inexplicably beyond it, a passage from the known certitudes of my childhood to something mysterious and unknowable.

From the 1930s, South African municipal by-laws required every white residence to include servants' quarters. In apartment blocks, these were typically built as low-budget rooftop appendages nicknamed 'locations in the sky', inverted penthouses not dissimilar to the *chambres de bonne* of Paris; evocative, too, of Rio's favelas, where the city's poorest residents have the most fabulous views. For individual white residences the law was very specific: the servants' quarters were required to be across the yard (there were to be no shared walls between white master and black servant) and were typically mean little rooms with a sink and a toilet; the law, of course, proscribed shared ablution facilities across racial lines, even within the private space of a residence.

Thus was the other, the outsider, woven structurally into the Johannesburg of my childhood; thus could interchange happen across the suburban backyard, a place of encounter across race and class, no matter how much the laws and the authorities of the country tried to deny it or patrol it. The yard was the place where my brothers and I, as children, heard other languages and played with the words of these languages ourselves, and where our aural landscape expanded to include the jaunty squashbox-melodies and fusillade of tongue-clicks of the Radio Bantu stations; where we played, too, even if very fleetingly, with the servants' children when they came to spend the school holidays; where we were permitted to eat with our fingers, which we dug into the plates of sour mieliemeal *pap* slathered with the piquant sausage and gravy we called 'Soccer Meat', as our Sunday morning treat. I recently asked our nanny Bettinah, who still works for my mother, where the term came from: "It was your name for it," she said, "you must ask yourselves." I imagine it must have had something to do with those black faces on the foamy undersides of the Coca-Cola bottles: did we imagine, dipping our fingers into the *chakalaka*, that we were heroes like Jomo Sono and Kaizer Motaung?

The laws of apartheid meant that the servants were not allowed any visitors, conjugal, familial or otherwise, and the architecture of suburban South Africa meant that even if the servants had a separate entrance off a common driveway, their goings-on could be strictly monitored. My own parents were lax with these rules, but even in the more regimented households of some of my friends I intuited, from an early age, the ways that the winds of the outside world blew across the yard, bringing the danger or the thrill of a broader urbanity into the very confines of the white suburban laager.

*

We all loved James. He worked for us until 1975, a year after Mozambique's independence, when he went home to try to sort out his land, collectivised by the new revolutionary government. He never returned. I am not certain when he came to work for us, but I have memories of him from my early childhood, and I can conjure his odour merely by closing my eyes and thinking his name: a working man's sweat cut by antiseptic Sunlight soap and Vaseline. Is it the rustle of James's starched khaki workclothes I can feel against my skin or someone else's? It does not much matter: I can still feel it, still feel too the softness of his hands – a consequence, surely, of the Vaseline, given his hard manual labour.

When I look at the photographs of my father holding me – his first child – in my early years, I am moved by his tender, careful touch; there are images of him enfolding me with his love, on a beach or a lawn. Still, some of my strongest early memories of being held by a

male adult are by the man I remember as 'James', seen here on the day he took leave of us to return to Mozambique. James would lift me onto his shoulders even when I was too big to be carried, and of all the adults around, he seemed most willing to indulge the dispatching side of my personality. Do I mean, I wonder, having read the above sentence, that he seemed most willing to be dispatched by me? What is map-reading and route-finding if not a form of mastery; a traveller's attempts at negotiating unknown territory, a child's attempts to gain purchase over adult terrain?

In my liberal childhood home, the language of racial supremacism was elided so artfully that when classmates sang the juvenile taunt, 'I made you look, I made you look, I made you kiss the kaffir-cook,' I had assumed they were saying 'café-cook'. Similarly, I took those large black boiled sweets we loved so much to be 'liquor-balls', in some way associated with their liquorice taste rather than their colour. They were actually called 'nigger-balls', a word I don't think I knew. But I certainly knew the word 'Master': this was what James and the other servants – I knew that word too – called my father.

Was there a moment of consciousness, I wonder now, when I came to understand that I was the master of the man I loved as a little boy, and that he was my servant? Or do children who grow up in such feudal environments assimilate such knowledge of their status even before they are able to reason? And if this is so, what did it do to my understanding of love to learn primal affection from a man whose job it was to serve me; whose race made him inferior to me?

*

East Avenue was aptly named: this was pretty much as far east as you could go before you hit the Sandspruit and the edge of page 77 of the *Holmden's*. In the late 1970s, the M1 freeway was laid along the bed of the river, but at the time we lived there the stream was edged by veld, traversed by the domestic workers of the Northern Suburbs as they made their way eastward, through the industrial buffer-suburb of Wynberg and across the Old Pretoria Main Road to their homes in Alexandra. The eastern boundary of my world was the fence at the bottom of Peter Pan Nursery School, behind the swings, against which I would stand and watch black people picking their way along the river bed. I remember, vividly, a naked man washing himself; I remember groups of women clustered on the rocks, gambling with the Chinese *fahfee* man. I have the recollection, too, of spotting the man who worked for us, James or his predecessor, sitting by the side of the river with his friends, smoking cigarettes and talking to each other in their strange-sounding tongue.

The river was one of those gaps in the urban stitching of apartheid. It seemed, to the very young me, to belong to black people, and this no doubt heightened my anticipation when, having graduated from Peter Pan, I found a similar gap in the regimented surveillance over my childhood and slipped occasionally down its banks with a neighbourhood gang to play at being Lost Boys on the rocks and in the reeds. The waters in those days were still clean and shallow, and besides, there was little fear of drowning: we had learned to swim in our suburban pools almost before we had learned to walk. But still, the river was forbidden, and the adults' choice deterrent was bilharzia, a disease which would kill us quickly and very painfully through the entry of a microscopic snail into our bloodstream via the holes of our penises.

Was it one of my parents who levelled this horrific threat? A friend's parent? A nanny? James? Whoever: it stuck. When I went to look at the Sandspruit in Atholl recently – now strewn with litter and lined with palisade security fencing that prevents access along the trails laid by the city in the 1970s – I felt a burning sensation in my groin, a tenderness that took me right back to the thrill and fear of being five or six and on that dangerous frontier just beyond Peter Pan Nursery School: that naked bathing man, those invisible snails.

Bird's-Eye View

The way to Neverland, Peter Pan famously told Wendy, was: 'Second to the right, and straight on till morning.'

But, comments the narrator in J.M. Barrie's *Peter and Wendy*, 'even birds, carrying maps and consulting them at windy corners, could not have sighted it with these instructions. Peter, you see, just said anything that came into his head. At first his companions trusted him implicitly, and so great were the delights of flying that they wasted time circling round church spires or any other tall objects on the way that took their fancy.'

What is the flight to the Neverland if not a game of Dispatcher, pulling the Darling children out of their comfortable beds of bourgeois respectability and sending them swooping over London's spires towards a feared and fabled destination? If running away into the world of fantasy – a world unregulated by adults – is one of the primal urges of childhood, then the terror of getting lost, or being misled, is its accompanying anxiety. Like Hansel and Gretel, we have to learn to find our way home. If not, we end up as the Neverland's Lost Boys, those 'children who fall out of perambulators when the nurse is looking the other way', as Barrie has it, doomed to the perpetual youth that is, of course, death.

But before adults come along and erect boundaries and draw routes, the map of a child's mind is just like that of the Neverland, says Barrie, 'always more or less an island', but paradoxically unbounded, often with 'another map showing through'; 'all rather confusing, especially as nothing will stand still'. The Neverland is somewhere you dream of flying off to, but it is not – as Wendy and her little brothers discover – somewhere you would want to stay for ever. And even if

Peter Pan shows characteristic contempt for such mortal concerns as route-finding, his own seemingly insouciant parody of directions ('second right and straight on till morning') plots a wonderful path through the world of dreams and nightmares to the moment that the sun begins to creep through the curtains to rouse you back to consciousness. They are directions that actually bring you home, rather than lose you in Neverland.

But how, of course, can home ever be the same after you've been one of the Lost Boys yourself, even if just for a night?

*

In *West with the Night*, Beryl Markham's luminous memoir of her life as an early African aviator, the author writes that a map in the hands of a pilot 'is a testimony of a man's faith in other men; it is a symbol of confidence and trust. It is not like a printed page that bears mere words, ambiguous and artful, and whose most believing reader – even whose author, perhaps – must allow in his mind a recess for doubt. A map says to you, "Read me carefully, follow me closely, doubt me not." It says, "I am the earth in the palm of your hand. Without me, you are alone and lost."'

Writing her *A Field Guide to Getting Lost* half a century later, on a very different kind of flight, the essayist Rebecca Solnit describes the world from an aeroplane as she criss-crosses North America by passenger jet: 'From miles up in the sky, the land looks like a map of itself, but without any of the points of reference that make maps make sense. The oxbows and mesas out the window are anonymous, unfathomable, a map without words ... These nameless places awaken a desire to be lost, to be far away, a desire for that melancholy wonder that is the blue of distance.'

The early aviators were often flying over uncharted territory, and thus read the topography of the planet as the map beneath them as they steered a course into the blue of distance. As Antoine de Saint-Exupéry's fictionalised pilot begins his journey in France in *Southern Mail*, he reflects on the 'well-ordered world' beneath him, 'neatly laid out like a toy sheepfold in its box. Houses, canals, roads – men's playthings. A sectioned world, a chessboard world, where each field touches its fence, each park its wall. Carcassonne, where each milliner relives the life of her grandmother. Humble lives happily herded together, men's playthings neatly drawn up in their show-case. Yes, a showcase world, too exposed, too spread out, with towns laid out in order on the unrolled map and which a slow earth pulls towards him with the sureness of a tide.'

But as the pilot flies southward on his mail-delivery run to Dakar, gravity itself seems to unlock its hold. The earth presents him noth-ing more, as a wayfinder, than the thin white line of surf between the Sahara Desert and the Atlantic Ocean until he lands, exhilarated and exhausted, in Senegal. In the same years that Saint-Exupéry was pio-neering flight over Africa, two Portuguese aviators, Gago Coutinho and Sacadura Cabral, made the first aerial flight over the South Atlantic, in 1922. Once they left the African shore, they lost their map, in effect: all that they had to guide them, for five hours that must have seemed an eternity, was Coutinho's sextant, adapted for air-nav-igation. Like the early ship-navigators before them, they found themselves in a blue infinity, as they turned the page from one map – the West African shore – to the other: that of Recife, America's east-ernmost protuberance.

Thus does a border – a thick red line at the edge of the page pre-venting free passage from page 75 to page 77 in the *Holmdens'* – expand, as the pilot flies across the sea or the dispatcher across the edge of the page, into the thrill, the terror, of infinite blue. Thus does a line open up into a territory, a liminal space, a borderland.

*

In early 2013 I went to see an exhibition called 'The King's Map', at the South African Museum in Cape Town. The centrepiece was a vast map of southern Africa made for King Louis XVI by the ornitholo-gist François le Vaillant just before the French Revolution. Le Vaillant was a celebrity of his time for having brought a giraffe specimen to Europe, and for his bestselling *Travels into the Interior of Africa*. The map, three metres by two and painted onto percale, tracks Le

Vaillant's explorations and is remarkable for its aesthetic beauty, particularly the painted drawings of flora and fauna pasted onto appropriate places – a fish eagle at the Keurbooms River mouth, a giant aloe in Namaqualand – and his larger ethnographic *cartouches*, or panels, of indigenous human life.

Le Vaillant is sometimes described as a proto-anthropologist, deeply influenced by Jean-Jacques Rousseau, and he was sharply critical of the way the colonialists treated South African indigenes. The exhibition's curator, Ian Glenn, makes much of the way Le Vaillant depicted Africans with humanity and grace, seeing in them reflections of civilisations described by the Greeks and the Romans in the classical era. Le Vaillant treated his guides and his hosts alike with unconventional respect, and there is the strong

suggestion that he had a romantic relationship with, and idolised, a young Gonaqua woman he named Narina.

The South African Museum has made the wise decision to keep its infamous apartheid-era ethnographic displays of 'Bantu Tribes' and 'Bushmen' intact, as artefacts of their time. As I wandered around the museum, the fusty and unfashionable *grand dame* of Cape Town's Company Gardens, filled with its dioramas of indigenous animals and tribes, I could not but compare Le Vaillant's classicist humanism with the cold, pseudo-scientific calipers of apartheid's ethnographers. It was as if nothing had changed for these people over the two centuries of colonisation and urbanisation, except perhaps the chilling of their beholder's gaze.

Le Vaillant made what is claimed by the curators of the exhibition to be the world's first travel map: he plots his journeys with red and blue lines, inscribing copious notes about what happened where. As is the convention, he writes the words 'PAYS INCONNU' on the white space across the map's north-eastern reaches. As I lost myself in his map, it came to me that all mapped territory is in fact *pays inconnu*, or at least partially known, or perhaps one should say imagined, not just for its viewer but for its creator too. What to make, for example, of the annotations of encounters with the 'tribe of a *sorcière*', or witch, or the 'tribe of white woman' somewhere up the west coast, reminiscent of the fables of a white Queen of Africa that Rider Haggard would later exploit in the Victorian era? And why is the coastline so accurate, yet so startlingly mismatched with the interior, giving the impression that Le Vaillant made it nearly all the way up to Delagoa Bay in what is now Mozambique when he did not, in fact, go much farther than the Great Fish River?

Ian Glenn believes that this is because Le Vaillant was overreaching himself, literally, showing off to Louis XVI about the depth of his penetration into Africa. The effect of this mismatch, whatever its roots, is that it removes from the South African map the entire populous south-east frontier area, the home of the Xhosa-speaking tribes, which were providing the greatest threat to white settlement at the time due to the Frontier Wars, which had already begun by the time Le Vaillant travelled there.

In other contemporary maps of the Cape, the known world ends abruptly at the natural border provided by the Great Fish River, with the word 'Kafirs' providing the only detail on the far side, in marked contrast to the density of the detail within the bounds of the settled Cape. Looking at Le Vaillant's map, I thought about the way he prefers, instead, to elide the unknown world, or simply to let it fade away at the limits of his experience. Whether deliberately or not, this has the effect of representing the frontier between the known and the unknown – the understood and the misunderstood – as a borderland rather than a border.

*

With the *Holmden's* as the map of my world, my own notion of boundaries was innate. How different it must be for my nephews, I imagine, as I watch them zoom around the globe on their computers. I am moved by the boundlessness of their enterprise. The apartheid world of my childhood was chopped up into a series of discrete maps with no route through, but the world of today appears to be one infinite chart. Political borders simply do not show up on the satellite photographs of Google Earth; you can go anywhere you like, so long as you have a destination. Just as we have outsourced memory to our gadgets, so too have we outsourced route-finding: just punch in a destination and follow the directions. Using Google Maps, I can give my imaginary courier the directions all the way from my father's birthplace at 87 Madeleine Road in Durban to his tombstone in the West Park Jewish Cemetery in Johannesburg, and can even predict that the journey will take not 82 years, but 6 hours and 23 minutes: turn second left and carry on till nightfall.

If I ask the Google Maps programme to find me a route between Želva in Lithuania and Durban– the journey my Grandpa Morris undertook a century ago – I am told that it will take 9 days and 18 hours to cover the 16,075.737 kilometres by car, and the only warning of the obstacles that might be presented to me is through a computer-generated travel advisory in the form of a poem:

This route has tolls.
This route includes a ferry.
This route crosses through multiple countries.
This route has restricted usage or private roads.

On the map itself, the computer has drawn a chunky blue line from point A, up near the Baltic Sea, to point B, down on the south-east tip of Africa. It jags through Europe before striking decisively across the Mediterranean ('This route includes a ferry') and then meanders down the spine of Africa. The accompanying fourteen pages of directions, broken down into 293 instructions, tell me to 'Head north on A. Smetanos Gatve,' which was, in fact, the road on which Grandpa Morris was born, although in those days it was simply known as 'The Wilkomir Road' according to Uncle Issy's memoirs. It then dispatches me through a history of the twentieth century. I bypass Warsaw, Berlin and Nuremberg on autobahns which sweep me down the Rhine and Rhone valleys to the port of Marseilles before I am put on the ferry to Algiers. After tortuous turns through the casbah I am on the Trans-Sahara Highway, which leads me across the desert into northern Nigeria (instruction 144: 'Turn left onto A3, go through 1 roundabout. Pass by Health Care'), and so on through Chad, the Sudans, Uganda, Tanzania, Zambia, Zimbabwe and across the Limpopo River onto the familiar South African N1, which sweeps me down through Johannesburg to the Buccleuch Interchange (page 89 of the *Holmden's*, just three pages from my childhood home) and onto the N3 to Durban, eventually depositing me on Mahatma Gandhi Avenue, which is how the seedy Point Road is now known, and where Grandpa Morris shared a room with his brothers behind their trading store when he arrived in 1905.

Why, I wonder, does Google Maps' dispatcher not route me more directly down Africa's west coast? Is he worried that the Congo remains a 'heart of darkness', or that landmines might still be strewn across Angola's roads after three decades of violent civil war? Doesn't he realise that, at the least, I will make up valuable time crossing Namibia on the superb roads built by the South African military to transport its materiel and troops (among whose number I was not: I evaded conscription) to fight the 'communist onslaught' up at the border? And why, if Google Maps possesses such capacity for judgement, am I being sent through South Sudan, the world's newest country, a territory the size of France with only a hundred kilometres of paved road and a war on its border?

Google received criticism that its directions were 'car-centric' and so it added a pedestrian routing option that you can generate by pushing the icon of the walking man rather than the car. When I click on this icon for Grandpa Morris's route, I am told that the journey will take me 118 days and three hours on foot, and I am issued the following travel advisory: 'Use caution – This route may be missing sidewalks or pedestrian paths.'

I'll say.

Mysteriously, the dispatcher has decided that if I am to do the journey by foot, I am to be routed through Britain, taking ferries across the North Sea and the English Channel, thereby more closely approximating my grandfather's actual journey, which required him to spend a few nights in the Poor Jews' Temporary Shelter in London's East End, before finding his way to Southampton to board the ship to Cape Town.

I can, of course, zoom in on any part of the route and look, in detail, at the terrain I will be passing through: the dense topography of Northern Europe, chequerboards of woodland scored with tracks and settlements; the medieval cartographic spirals of Marseilles and Algiers and then the nothingness of the Sahara; the illusion of order in the sophisticated network of roads and settlements across central and eastern Africa. In an echo of my childhood experiences with the Map Studio *Street Guide* to Johannesburg and Soweto, I am struck by how deceptively similar it all looks, given how different it really is. Notwithstanding the massive advances in cartographical technology, the map, of course, tells me little about the actual journey my Grandpa Morris would have taken; I cannot glean much more than I would have been able to through the *World Book Atlas* in which I first traced his journey as a child.

But even as I write these words, the representational possibilities of maps are undergoing a revolution, with Google Earth and its seamless fusion of map and satellite photograph. Now I can simply switch from 'plan' function to 'photo' function, and look at the landscape, from above, zooming in on satellite images to actually examine the terrain I will be passing through; to make my own judgements about the condition of a road, or to give me more of a sense of what it must be like to live there, or pass through there, than drawn maps have ever been able to.

Thus have maps become artless and empirical. Le Vaillant's map of South Africa was subjective ('this is what I know) and Tompkins' map of Johannesburg was speculative ('this is what I want'); even in the maps of the *Holmden's*, with their handdrawn lines and quirky lettering, one discerns the spoor of the men who made them; not just their labours, but their worldviews too. All the cartographer does today is trace the lines he sees on a satellite photo and colour them in. How different this is from the original relationship between map and mapmaker, captured by Beryl Markham in *West with the Night*: '[I]t is a cold thing, a map, humourless and dull, born of calipers and a draughtsman's board ... This brown blot that marks a mountain has, for the casual eye, no other significance, though twenty men, or ten, or only one, may have squandered life to climb it. Here is a valley, there a swamp, and there a desert; and here is a river that some curious and courageous soul, like a pencil in the hand of God, first traced with bleeding feet.'

*

Global-positioning technology may well have triggered a revolution in spatial consciousness in the early twenty-first century, much as the 'birds-eye view' of aviation did in the early twentieth century. The architect Le Corbusier writes about the day in 1909 when a colleague burst into his Paris atelier brandishing a newspaper: "'Blériot has crossed the Channel [in his plane]!'" cried his colleague. "Wars are finished: no more wars are possible! There are no longer any frontiers!'"

Would that it had been so. Le Corbusier is the first to admit that the new metal bird, given its omniscient eye over the planet, could be 'dove or hawk', and that with the Great War it became an agent of great destruction over Europe. Still, something profound had shifted, and not only because cartographers could now work off aerial survey photographs (how did they ever manage before, with nothing more than sextants and mirrors?). Le Corbusier published an eccentric book called *Aircraft*, in 1935, in which he juxtaposed his trademark aphorisms with photographs of planes, or the views you saw from them. '*L'avion accuse!*' was the book's battle-cry: ('The airplane indicts!'). 'The eye of the airplane is pitiless,' he wrote beneath aerial views of London and Paris. 'This time we have the actual record of reality. What an appalling thing! Do human beings live here? Do they consent to do so? Will they not revolt against it?'

I have thought often of these words as I looked at aerial images of endlessly horizontal Soweto from when the township was developed in the 1950s and 1960s, images that give the lie to the fiction of the Map Studio legend that they are made of the same stuff – the yellow roads, the green parks, the gold schools – as the suburbs. Some might say Le Corbusier has a lot to answer for: he was one of the inspirations for apartheid's urban planning. He would have approved, at least, of the townships' geometry: thousands of identical little 'matchbox' houses plotted onto the parched greyish landscape of monochrome aerial photographs, with a hand so comfortable with its mastery over other souls it is chilling.

About a decade after the end of apartheid, the photographer David Goldblatt – whose cool eye has been the conscience of Johannesburg for over six decades – has taken to flying over Johannesburg in a small plane. He makes aerial images of townships, of  squatter-camps and of the vast new security cluster-developments that are an eczema on the surface of the city. These images deliberately echo those township-from-above photos from the Fifties, iconic documents of apartheid's roll-out, but unbalance them, too, with oblique low angles that suggest a fundamental urban alienation in the architecture of Johannesburg. For me, the most distressing of these images is his 'Women's Hostel, Alexandra Township, 26 June 2009', which, by its angle, accentuates just how much the township is dwarfed by the gargantuan migrant-labour hostel the authorities built in the 1980s. Shot in colour, it feels like one of those childhood nightmares where the source of distress is, literally, too big for the landscape of your unconscious.

The artist Bongi Dhlomo has lived in Alexandra since 1988. She comes from rural KwaZulu-Natal and she told me about her very first visit to Johannesburg, which was also her very first plane ride: 'I looked down as we were landing, and tried to figure out what was where. The thing that confused me most were those blue squares and circles all over the place. What could they be? What weird and bizarre thing did Joburg have that I had not encountered before? I had never seen a swimming pool before: certainly not from above. Now I know, when you look out of a plane over a South African city, how to tell immediately where the suburbs are as opposed to the townships: look for the blue squares and circles.'

As a boy I would splash around in one of those blue squares – well, actually it was a rectangle – on a hot afternoon. I would sluice away the blue-gum pods so that I could warm myself by lying on the hot, wet bricks surrounding the pool. The fierce sun would evaporate the water around me, so that when I got up there would be an impression left of me on that part of the bricks my little body had covered, a water-painting of my silhouette, as at a crime scene. I would look up at the sky and try to decipher the vapour trails written by jets across the blue dome of my universe so as to imagine where they might transport me.

Fringe Country

My Grandpa David Cohen had a significant library beyond the Left Book Club, and the remains of it settled in the upstairs study of the house my parents built when I was a little boy. Like all libraries frozen at the moment of their collectors' deaths, this one captures in printed amber not just the tastes of its owner but the fashions of his times, and so alongside the collected works of Ibsen and Shaw there are yards of forgotten names from the mid twentieth century on shelves soaring up to the room's steeply pitched slatted-pine ceiling, buttressed – like the rest of the house – with massive, lacquered pine logs from my father's forests. The bookshelves are made from simple varnished pine, as are the slatted cupboards, giving the room a woody, booky harmony, particularly when a winter fire is burning. With its photographs of ancestors on the walls and a couple of couches that have been allowed to sag, the study was the hearth of my childhood, the place where a large, unruly family threaded itself together every evening over my father's two twilight Scotches before unspooling into the night. But the study was also a place of solitary quest, in the middle of the day, when everyone else was otherwise occupied. As a child I would often get lost up there, barefoot on a chair, running a finger along the expanses of my grandfather's library, maroon and ochre and royal blue.

Grandpa David died before my parents met, and I knew very little about him – save the irresistibly romantic fact that he had been born in Port Said, a piece of information which had me poring over the Levantine pages of the *World Book Atlas*. I would later come to find out that his family was among the pre-Zionist Ashkenazi settlers in Palestine who had moved there from Vilnius in the early nineteenth

century to work as priests in the synagogues of Jerusalem. My great-grandfather Samuel Cohen was trained as a wooden scroll-worker, and allegedly did the inlay work of many of Jerusalem's churches; at the turn of the twentieth century he followed the tentacles of the Ottoman Empire down the east coast of Africa and eventually set up shop as a general trader in Pretoria, north of Johannesburg. There were few photographs of Grandpa David about – he seemed rumpled and kind, with an air both distracted and intense that is often just the consequence of being very short-sighted and with which I, in spectacles from the age of seven, instinctively identified.

My mother told me that he loved George Bernard Shaw, and so I pulled out *Major Barbara* from his library – it seemed the most promising title – and spent months with it by my bedside. Many years later, when I cleared out Granny Gertie's room after her death in 1991, I found a shoebox containing his courtship letters to her, and a three-act play he had written, entitled 'Crossroads to Nirvana', about a concert pianist. I was struck, in both, by an arch modernism that seemed of a piece with his library in the study, and I felt the strange pull of nostalgia: a sense of loss about someone I had never known.

Many of the books in Grandpa David's library carried inside their covers a little rectangular pink sticker for Vanguard Booksellers, and I came to harbour the secret fantasy of a visit to this place. As an adult I would discover, to my delight, that Vanguard had belonged to an indefatigable Trotskyist intellectual named Fanny Klenerman who had run her shop out of several locations in downtown Johannesburg from 1927, when my grandfather would have begun collecting his library, through to the mid 1970s. It was Klenerman who introduced the Left Book Club to South Africa and, while they were still legal, Russian newspapers such as *Pravda* and *Izvestia*. In the early 1930s, she imported the first copies of James Joyce's *Ulysses* into South Africa, defying an effective worldwide ban on the book. This was exactly the time Grandpa David was courting Granny Gertie, and he would most certainly have read *Ulysses*, although I cannot find the volume in his library; I like to think that he wooed her with Leopold Bloom, and gave her the idea that Joyce's book was about her family.

By the early 1960s, Vanguard had become 'a haven of nonracial creative energies in a fiercely segregated city', writes the historian Jonathan Hyslop in his essay 'Gandhi, Mandela and the African Modern'. It was here that the young Nadine Gordimer had her first encounter with literary cosmopolitanism and fell in love with literature, according to her then boyfriend, Philip Stein. Stein, who worked at Vanguard, recalls that the fiercely modern Klenerman used to keep two piles of 'subversive' literature for distribution beneath the counter – one political and the other pornographic – and that the bookshop made space for encounters not only political and literary but amorous too, across the colour bar: 'Curious and interesting things used to happen in the stockrooms upstairs ... I can remember some well-known South African black writers who were having love affairs with the female assistants in the shop and they used to write songs and poetry upstairs and rush downstairs and read them!'

Several of Johannesburg's black intellectuals worked at the bookshop too: they were part of what became known as the '*Drum* Generation', after the magazine many of them wrote for. *Drum* was a mass-circulation black title captivated by beauty queens and gangsters, but it also engaged South Africa's finest black writers and photographers to document anti-apartheid politics to the extent that this was possible. One of these was a shooting star named Nat Nakasa, who would throw himself off a New York skyscraper while on a Nieman Fellowship in 1965. A few years earlier, in March 1961, Nakasa published an article in *Drum* entitled 'Fringe Country: Where There is No Colour-Bar.' I keep on returning to it. It documented

DRUM 23

24 **WHERE THE C**

ART Modern Art fans, black, white an "beatnik" bookshop in Johannes tures. Some had strong views to g

THEATRE Non-whites got their first in white theatre when the kens, arranges auditions

BLACKS AT A WHITE WEDDING There were many African guests among the crowd of white socialites who attended this wedding in Dunkeld. The groom (left) is a lecturer at Roma. He invited two African students along from Roma.

'FRINGE COUNTRY': WHERE THERE IS NO

COLOUR - BAR

Nathaniel Nakasa tells of life between two worlds—between pure white society and the all black townships. He calls it "fringe-country," that social no-mans land, where energetic, defiant, young people of all races live and play together as humans. Yes, even under the racial skies of South Africa!

AUNT SALLY'S shebeen was doing excellent business, customers spending lavishly. Two white journalists, perched nervously on a bench, looked like business executives in a brothel.

Suddenly, from outside, Aunt Sally pulled the door with all the might in her round, fat arms. "Make quick," she screamed. "The police! Lock top and bottom!" Someone jumped for the door and bolted it.

The man let out a shout announcing that he had locked. "All right," answered Aunt Sally, "then shut up, close your mouths." The man returned to his drink. The two journalists couldn't help laughing, although somewhat terrified by the prospect of being marched to a police station.

After a while the doors were flung open,

and in stepped Aunt Sally with a thin, naughty-girl's smile on her face. Apparently she had spotted a 900lb. police sergeant propelling himself in the direction of her place. "But it's all fixed up now," she assured us all.

For my two journalist friends, this was their first taste of life on "the fringe." Life is a "No-man's Land" where anybody meets anybody, to hell with the price of their false teeth or anything else.

My two white mates had not seen such things happen before. Yet they happen, all over the Union. In Johannesburg and Bloemfontein, Durban and Cape Town. In the swanky homes of white suburbia, as well as in the slums of Cato Manor, District Six or Alexandra Township.

PLEASE TURN OVER

WHITES LISTEN BLACKS PLAY Music knows no colour bar. When Kwela kids whistle, all races stop and listen to them.

Some people call it "crossing the colour line." You may call it jumping the line or wiping it clean off. Whatever you phrase, Those who live on the fringe have no special labels. They see it simply as LIVING.

Eating a girl. Inviting a friend to lunch. Arranging a party for people who are interested in writing or painting, jazz or boxing. Or even apartheid. For that matter, I once organised such a party for talks with Afrikaner nationalists from Pretoria University. Among them was the son of a very senior Cabinet Minister. We talked apartheid and religion. We were just talking and drinking, not "crushing" anything. We didn't see it that way, anyhow.

"It's a question of having friends who are white when you are black," Henry Sono

DS: WHITE AND BLACK MEET, PLAY AND ENJOY FRIENDSHIP

place is less race conscious than the Jazz nd. The Goodwill lounge in Durban was a d venue, so was Crescent in Johannesburg.

There are many whites, like this lady, who take their problems to a black witch doctor. Must think the black man has a monopoly on magic!

TENNIS When American tennis stars visited South Africa they insisted on playing non-whites.

FOOTBALL Joseph Biasi asked, and was allowed to play, in African league football.

BOXING People were surprised at the good standard of boxing and the sportsmanship when Gerry Brits met Blas Tshabalala in Basutoland. This interracial boxing match could mark a turning point in South African sport.

sengers of justice rushing about. Not a grouse from the neighbours. We even got blessings from Father Dennis Sabji who had, earlier, conducted the wedding service with two African altar boys helping. Yes, there are men of God as well on the fringe. Father Huddleston was one.

Some outsiders look at the fringe-dwellers and wonder "what is the world coming to." Others blink and twist their faces in disgust. There are those who take a look and decide, "It is not any of my business how other people choose to live."

Until recently, the Crescent Restaurant in Fordsburg, Johannesburg, ran jazz sessions every Sunday night. Jazz cats from the University of Witwatersrand and from every quarter of Johannesburg gathered there and

listened to some of the best jazzmen at work. Jonas Gwangwa, Kippie Moeketsi, Lenny Lee and others. Every session at the Crescent was a delicious experience. Like getting a bit of sunshine on a winter day, — with the knowledge that soon, very soon, it would all be gone.

Fringe men knew that sooner or later officialdom would stop the sessions on the grounds and there's a strange irony here — that "there is bound to be trouble when blacks mix with whites." But it was good while it lasted. Good — and quite without trouble!

It was reminiscent of the jazz nights at the Goodwill Lounge, in Durban. The Goodwill opened its doors once or twice a week and jazz addicts piled into the back rooms

where Dalton Khanyile and other Durban jazzmen belted their instruments.

One Sunday night an Afrikaner policeman came to a session at the Crescent. Brul draped in uniform, this cop sat pounding the piano to a background of mild, black and white hand-clapping. On the following Sunday, the man of Justice brought his sister along to sing while he played the piano. "Dig those cats," yelled a member of the crowd, "they're real gone, man, real gone. There's a cop who digs us real deep!"

Once, an American film producer visited Sophiatown shortly before it was demolished by officialdom.

It was during one of those evening when "Soft-town" listened to jazz, and Shakespearean plays. There were a few young citi-

zens of Sophiatown and several young women from the white suburbs. Suddenly, the police materialised with their heavy knocks at the door.

"One minute, Sergeant," Bloke said, turning to his gram to put on Shakespeare's play, Julius Caesar. Immediately after, he opened the door with a smile which looked perfectly normal, although it was a put-up job.

"Do come in Sarge," Bloke said. "Can I help you at all?"

The Sergeant's face turned pink instantly. The floor was covered with liquor. He stammered at last, "We're searching for drink, you're not keeping any liquor illegally here, are you?"

Realising the helplessness of the man, Bloke

PLEASE TURN OVER

what he called 'that social no-man's-land, where energetic, defiant, young people of all races live and play together as humans. Yes, even under the racial skies of South Africa!' Some people, wrote Nakasa, 'call it "crossing the colour line". You may call it jumping the line or wiping it clean off. Whatever you please. Those who live on the fringe have no special labels. They see it simply as LIVING. Dating a girl. Inviting a friend to lunch. Arranging a party for people who are interested in writing or painting, jazz or boxing, or even apartheid, for that matter.'

Over a five-page spread, *Drum* took its readers on a tour of Fringe Country: black guests at a white wedding, a white pianist in a black jazz band, blacks and whites on tennis courts and in swimming pools together – and an image of a bespectacled black man, earnestly and passionately addressing a white woman in front of a painting of a female nude balanced against the ramshackle bookshelves of Fanny Klenerman's shop. The caption to this photograph reads: 'Modern Art fans, black, white and brown, packed the "beatnik" bookshop in Johannesburg to see the pictures. Some had strong views to get off their chests too!'

The man with strong views in this image is the *Drum* writer Bloke Modisane, who worked at Vanguard and describes the bookshop in his memoir *Blame Me on History* as the only non-racial space he ever knew in Johannesburg. Klenerman, he writes, was a polymath who 'spoke with the temper and the rat-a-tat repartee of a sergeant major, flared with the tantrums of a Hollywood film star, a fanatical perfectionist who became hysterical in the face of carelessness and ignorance'. Her temper 'was non-racial, it was zeroed at the staff irrespective of color or sex, and those of us who made up the African staff loved and admired her sense of fair play . . . I think she mothered me somewhat, and I loved her for what she did for me as a person, for making me feel and believe myself equal to the white staff' – even if the law required Klenerman to pay her black employees less and give them their tea breaks in a separate room.

'Psychopathia Sexualis'

It did not take long for me to find, among my Grandpa David's books on the very top shelf of the study, a thick brown volume with its title embossed, in gold, on a faded maroon strip: *Psychopathia Sexualis*, by one 'Dr. R. v. Krafft-Ebing'. The author's name alone was enough to snare me; the presence of the word 'Sex' in the title, and the pink Vanguard Booksellers sticker on the inside cover, sealed my fate.

Pulling the book out, now, from exactly the same place I had originally found it over three decades ago on the top shelf, I remember immediately its structure: a series of case studies organised under different categories of pathology, such as 'Torture of Animals Dependent on Sadism', or 'Unnatural Abuse – Sodomy'. Under 'Homo-Sexual Feeling in Both Sexes', I find the following testimony from one '*Sch.*, aged thirty, physician': 'One evening in the opera-house, an old gentleman sat near me. He courted me. I laughed heartily at the foolish old man, and entered into his joke. *Exinopinato genitalia mea prehendit, quo facto statim penis meus se erexit.* Frightened, I demanded of him what he meant. He said that he was in love with me. Having heard of hermaphrodites in the clinics, I thought I had one before me, and became curious to see his genitals. The old man was very willing, and went with me to the water closet. *Sicuti penem maximum ejus erectum adspexi, perterritus effugi.*'

Krafft-Ebing's *pudeur* (deployed, no doubt, precisely to discourage juvenile offenders such as myself) sent me rushing, breathlessly, in search of a Latin dictionary. I think I found one somewhere on my parents' shelves, but the words I needed were not there. No matter, their import was clear: the event turned poor '*Sch.*' into a homosexual himself: 'This man followed me, and made strange proposals which

I did not understand, and repelled. He did not give me any rest. I learned the secrets of male love for males, and felt that my sexuality was excited by it.' Elsewhere in the chapter, I came across a passage I remembered vividly from my childhood: 'nothing is so prone to contaminate – under certain circumstances, even to exhaust – the source of all noble and ideal sentiments ... as the practice of masturbation in early years. It despoils the unfolding bud of perfume and beauty, and leaves behind only the coarse, animal desire for sexual satisfaction. If an individual, thus depraved, reaches the age of maturity, there is wanting in him that aesthetic, ideal, pure and free impulse which draws the opposite sexes together.' For such an unfortunate there was only one destiny, and it seemed to be mine.

I find it extraordinary to think, in retrospect, that in an enlightened home in the 1970s, this Victorian horror – enlightened though it might have been in its own time – was to become a primary source of information about my sexuality. Thank God I also found, on the more recent shelves of my own parents' collection, the somewhat more forgiving sexuality bible of their own generation, *Everything You Always Wanted To Know About Sex (But Were Afraid To Ask)*, with its counsel to concerned parents that boys who engaged in mutual masturbation between the ages of twelve and fourteen would grow out of it. I would spirit the book out of the study and into my room – often in tandem with its close bookshelf neighbour, *The Happy Hooker* – and rush it back to its spot as soon as I heard the Mercedes straining up the drive. By this point lingering tentatively at the portals of my own puberty, I used the passage to convince my friend Adam that what I wanted us to do was normal. But once our terrified locked-bedroom-door sex spilled over into our adolescence, way beyond the stipulated cut-off point, I had to accept – with two broken girlfriend hearts behind me too – that I was not going to outgrow my homosexual desires. I would, instead, need to find a way to clothe them, which I did, with all the cocky braggadocio of Uncle Issy and his first safari suit: I was gay. The suit didn't fit perfectly then and neither does it today, but I understood that I needed to be dressed in some identifiable way in a society that polices the runnels so rigidly, and so I made it my own.

I have often wondered about the links between my budding under-standing of my sexual difference and my early experience of being stifled by the whiteness, the privilege of my childhood. I do not remember making any connection, even into my teens, between my illicit sexuality and the inferior conditions of the black people who worked for us and lived around us. I likewise have no insight into how my early sense of the injustice of apartheid, sparked by my liberal father, might have found further kindling in my own lived experience of other forms of discrimination. But as I think about my cartomania, and, particularly, the queen of my obsessions, the Dispatcher game, I realise that it plotted outward journeys both sexual and social; routes leading me out of atomised suburbia and into the troubled world of Johannesburg of the 1970s; ways of crossing the impermeable bound-aries that were set around the life of a white suburban boy.

Or perhaps it was the opposite: a flight from these troubles, social and political and sexual, into a cartography that could not even begin to represent them. I do not believe my cartomania was flight fantasy, though: I always talked my couriers home. I did not want to leave for good, so much as get beyond the confines of my childhood.

My nostalgia for the *Holmden's* might be a wistful longing for the certitudes of its bounded cartography. But it also triggers a thrill: the thrill of transgressing these boundaries that is the very definition of desire.

Xai-Xai

When I tired of books in my solitary afternoon meanderings through the study, I would move across to the family photo albums. They are, I think now, looking at them again, a very South African record, a record of gardens and swimming pools, and of the growing white suburban family that filled them.

There is a particularly lucent quality to the family photographs of white middle-class suburban South Africans in the 1960s and 1970s. This is not just because of the Kodachrome technology of the day or the excess of Johannesburg's sunlight, but because of the ease of childhood too: that perfect balance between containment and freedom that comes, when you are a child, from being in a garden; the promise in so much firm, tan skin; the trays of lemon-barley squash and tennis biscuits; the unthinking certainty that there will always be people to look after you.

The photographs were stuck into the adhesive pages of mass-produced albums with garish plastic covers. One album, however, was different. Bound in red leather with a leather bow, and embossed in the bottom-right-hand corner with a gold springbok, it had black card pages onto which its holdings were secured with silver photo corners. It was, in the grammar of my childhood, the past perfect: before-I-came. This special album begins with my parents' wedding in 1963, and then pages through the first few years of their life together and the birth of their first two sons, myself and my brother Antony.

My favourite image from the wedding sequence remains that of my mother outside the synagogue, cupping my father's chin in her hand and preparing him for a kiss, between the foreground of a white man in a suit bending down to unlock the door of a car – his body obscuring the figure of a black man in a chauffeur's cap standing rigidly to attention – and the background of the catering truck. At this moment, neither of them knows – or cares – about the ever-vigilant camera, and so the resulting image is the elusive soul-memory  of the event, that moment when the primary players are captured spontaneously inhabiting the emotions elsewhere so self-consciously performed. A white man bends down to unlock a car while a black man stands to attention. One imagines the black man will now drive the couple away from the public performance of their love and into the privacy of married life while the caterers pile the remains of the day into their truck; out of this shift-change the couple steals a kiss.

Recently, paging through that red leather-embossed album, I found myself compelled by a photograph a few pages after this record of my parents' wedding. It is an image of them, from their first holiday alone, a few months after my birth, in what was then the Portuguese colony of Mozambique, the favoured weekend getaway for people of their class and station. They are in Xai-Xai, suspended in the tepid and translucent tropical water, their legs entwined and clearly visible beneath the surface as they hold each other. They are a human conch; a heart drawn in the water, so beautiful that their son forgives them their solipsism, as he imagines how he must have been abandoned to facilitate this moment.

I thought, immediately, of this submarine photograph of my parents' love when I found myself looking at an image illustrating Nat Nakasa's article on 'Fringe Country' in *Drum*, published exactly a year before my parents met. This, too, is an image of a young couple in the water, a black man and a white woman this time, in a suburban swimming pool, eyes ecstatically closed, held by the silvery late-afternoon

sun on the rippling water. 'Where's this?' reads the caption. 'Surely not South Africa, with white and black in the same swimming pool? If that's what you thought, you are wrong, this picture was taken in one of the smartest suburbs of Johannesburg.'

The laws of apartheid made all the other activities illustrated in the piece – such as, for example, arguing over 'modern art' at Vanguard Books – a challenge, albeit not criminal. But physical intimacy across the colour line was a different matter: sex between people of different races was strictly proscribed by the Immorality Act. And so what is particularly compelling about the swimming-pool photograph is the way it works, so neatly, as an analogue of its subject: unlike in the photograph of my parents at Xai-Xai, there is no visible physical contact between the man and the woman. And yet I know, by the positions of their bodies and the looks on their faces, that beneath the surface of the water they are entwined, their desire expressed by the silvery whirlpool of water around them.

I wanted to see more images of this transgression, and so I went to the Bailey's African History Archive, where *Drum's* legendary collection of photographs is held. Here I was given a manila folder entitled 'No Colour Bar: 1961'. It was the raw archive for the 'Fringe Country' story, and as I poured it out onto the inspection table I watched a genie unbottled, the stardust of what might have been: dozens of prints of blacks and whites playing, jamming, working and loving together in the Johannesburg that just predated my birth. I found another image of the white woman and the black man in the swimming pool, taken from a wider angle, shot just moments before the clinch in the image eventually chosen for publication. Standing in the shallow end is a coloured man, locked in intimacy with a white woman who is sitting at the pool's edge, dangling her feet in the water. Behind them, receding back to a house and a row of sun-dappled trees, are untidy clusters of semi-naked white families, doing what white families do on a Sunday afternoon in suburban Johannesburg. All form a halo of human activity around the focal point of the photograph: a powerfully built, strikingly handsome black man, wading through the pool at nipple-level toward the white woman who will – we know, from the following photo – pull him down into the water with her.

As a child of suburban Johannesburg, I look at this photo and feel a hunger that ripples down the sides of my tongue and gathers in my throat, for the sycamore berries and the blue-gum pods beneath bare feet, caught in the grooves between the slats; for that tray of lemon-barley squash and Tennis biscuits on a glass-topped iron table; for the

sun reflected off a zinc roof onto beds of Namaqualand daisies; for the insane, prehistoric shriek of hadeda ibises piercing the sky, the purple violence of a cloudburst, the lengthening shadows, the inevitable nightfall quick as a gangster's knife. I was born three years after these photographs were taken, just as Nelson Mandela and his Rivonia co-defendants were beginning their life sentences on Robben Island. There were no such poolside gatherings any more. I look at these images and see my childhood, blanched, with the focal point – that black man advancing through the water – removed. I see what might have been.

*

The crop of the photographs accompanying Nakasa's 'Fringe Country' article in *Drum* is self-conscious and polemical: the point, in the swimming-pool photograph, is precisely to demonstrate just how normal it is for a white woman and a black man to be in the water together by having the people in the background, unbothered by the waves the couple is making. And yet – in the logic of photographs – it has something of the opposite effect: because the others are not looking at the couple and no one at all is looking at the camera, our own view of them seems stolen, illicit. Why should we be bothering – or even remarking – about these lovebirds if no one else in the frame is?

Despite a similar transgression into intimacy in the photograph of my parents at Xai-Xai, there is something in the way my mother and father are looking at each other, with such beatific composure, that welcomes the viewer. Perhaps this is because the photographer is a friend; perhaps because the image is destined for a family album rather than a magazine or newspaper.

Of course, in the end, both couplings are staged: my parents are posing for the camera, while the couple in the pool are studiously *not posing* for the *Drum* photographer. Still, the photographs sit on my desk as counterweights today. In the image of my parents I see blissful transparency; in that of the couple in the swimming pool I sense hidden desire. In the relationship between the two I find my place, contained by the former and compelled by the latter.

The Fischer Pool on Beaumont Street

Pam dos Santos was a denizen of 'Fringe Country', one of its poster girls. And so I took the poolside photographs from the 'No Colour Bar: 1961' file to show her, in the hope that she would be able to identify the pool and the people. She did, immediately: 'It's the Fischer pool on Beaumont Street,' she said. The SA Communist Party leader Bram Fischer and his wife, Molly, were famous for their Sunday afternoon pool gatherings at their home in the suburb of Oaklands, where activists of all races gathered. 'And that's me,' Pam added, pointing to the white woman sitting on the edge of the pool, flirting with the coloured man: 'With Joe.'

My parents were already courting, in May 1962, when a Johannesburg newspaper blared the headline, '19-Year-Old Typist in Skin-Tight Red Jeans Held on Morals Charge with Coloured!' Pam – then Pamela Beira – was the typist in question, and her lover was Joe Louw, a photojournalist who told their story in *Drum*. Joe worked for *New Age* and had captured the first photographs of the slave-labour potato farms in Bethel; Pam, a rebellious Jewish teenager, had found a way out of suburbia by striking up friendships with the musicians who would play at venues like the Nightbeat or the Barclay Hotel in town. 'First we white girls met the musicians,' she told me, 'and through them the journalists, and through them the activists.' In November 1961 she and Joe were staying at an acquaintance's flat in Hillbrow when the police, informed by the caretaker's wife, broke through their door. They found a woman draped in a red towel, in bed behind a beaded curtain, and a man sitting at the table, fully clothed, his arm in a sling. Pam threw on some bright red jeans and a red, green and white top, and the two were taken down to Hillbrow

Police Station, where Pam was subjected to an intrusive medical examination.

The medical officer found, as he was later to testify, that 'one would tend to think there was no intercourse', and so the couple was finally found guilty of having 'conspired to commit immorality' rather than the perpetration of the act itself. This verdict hinged on two key items missing from Pam's person at the time of the arrest: her hymen and her underwear. The magistrate asked: why would a woman, no longer a virgin, be wearing nothing but a red towel in the presence of a coloured man at fifteen minutes to midnight if she did not have

...JOURNEY'S END IN LOVERS' MEETING

HAND IN HAND, ON THE BEACH AT DAR-ES-SALAAM, PAM AND JOE ARE TOGETHER AND HAPPY AGAIN

immoral intentions? The arresting officer testified that he ordered her to 'put on panties ... She looked half asleep, but I couldn't say with accused number two because he is a Coloured and it is more difficult.'

Pam fled into exile before sentencing, and Joe spent six months in jail, where he underwent severe harassment from the warders for having sullied the honour of a white woman. After his release, he joined her in exile, and wrote an article called 'My Flight To Love' for *Drum* in June 1962, alongside a photograph of the two of them walking along the palm-fringed shore in Dar es Salaam, in Julius Nyerere's newly liberated Tanganyika. Even by *Drum*'s standards, Mahomed Amin's rear-view photograph of them on the beach at Dar was racy: a black man and a white woman, on a beach together, holding hands. The straps of Beira's bathing suit have fallen suggestively off her shoulders, and her hand assertively clasps that of Louw, who is clad in a scant pair of bathing trunks. There is something unmistakably victorious about it all: their clasped, outstretched arms actually form a triumphant 'V' at the centre of the image, beneath the headline, 'Journey's End in Lovers' Meeting'.

*

At the time that the photographs of Bram Fischer's pool were published to illustrate 'Fringe Country' in the March 1961 edition of *Drum*, Fischer was presenting the concluding arguments in the showpiece Treason Trial. This trial had pulled 156 African National Congress leaders into court and had kept them tied up in litigation since the mid 1950s, even though it had been superseded by the dramatic events a year previously: the pass-burning defiance campaigns, the Sharpeville massacre, and the banning of the ANC and the first State of Emergency. In response to its banning, the ANC had resorted to underground armed struggle, about which Fischer knew and approved, and which would be launched through a countrywide series of bombings in December 1961.

Fischer was an affable, ruddy man from one of the country's grandest Afrikaner families. Fischer led the defence for Nelson Mandela and his fellow accused in the Rivonia Trial in 1963 and when he himself was arrested in September 1964, there was a particular heartlessness to the vigour with which the state pursued him. Three days after the sentencing of the Rivonia trialists, an exhausted Fischer was driving his wife down to the Cape when he lost control of his car, which plunged into a dam on the side of the highway. He escaped but she drowned. Two weeks later, devastated and disoriented, Fischer was detained on suspicion of being a member of a banned organisation and two weeks after that he was charged.

The trial began on 16 November, five days after my birth. As my mother nursed me she would have read about it every morning in the *Rand Daily Mail*: the allegations made against the accused by Piet Beyleveld, a Communist Party member who had been turned while under interrogation and who now seemed to take up his Judas role with a passionate vengeance, and by Gerard Ludi, an undercover agent who had infiltrated the white left in the guise of a radical journalist. Ludi was introduced to the court as a dashing if somewhat ridiculous homegrown James Bond ('Agent Q018'). Although his core evidence alone was damning, he embroidered his narrative for dramatic effect, painting a picture of a world of sexual dissolution and moral torpor through salacious accounts of on-the-job seductions across the colour bar to prove his struggle credentials, and wild Sunday romps at the Fischer swimming pool. '*Naked?*' asked Fischer's counsel, sarcastically. 'Of course', Ludi replied.

I had first read about the Fischer pool, without realising it, in Nadine Gordimer's novel *Burger's Daughter*, inspired by Fischer's life, which I had found in its iconic purple and gold Jonathan Cape cover on the shelves of my parents' study. This must have been in 1980, when I was sixteen (it had been banned for four months shortly after its publication the previous year), and I had been instinctively drawn to its theme: a daughter's dissection of her relationship with her communist father, jailed for life for remaining true to his ideals. Gordimer gives us the Fischer pool: 'Many people came on Sundays, it was a tradition. They came when she and her brother were little, they came when her mother was detained ... [and] they came when her father was out on bail during his trial. Nothing the secret police could do more than interrupt. Life went on; Lionel Burger, in his swimming trunks, cooking steak and boerewors for his comrades and friends, was proof.'

Fischer's biographer, Stephen Clingman, writes that for Fischer's friends and comrades, 'together in that pool, a new kind of South Africa could be represented, all the more outrageous to white puritanism for its refusal to be anything more than ordinary. Though the pool altered no obvious dispensations, stopped no removals of communities, gave voting rights to none, it became its own kind of enchanted domain.' With their Sunday swimming parties, the Fischers were reinterpreting – through the prism of their activism – the utopia, the bounded paradise, represented by the suburban swimming pool. Later, when he was in jail serving his life term and his daughter, Ilse, was forced to sell the Beaumont Street house, he wrote to her that one day, 'in the new city of Johannesburg', the pool would be at the centre of a children's playground the size of two blocks. Through this poignant idealism, he seemed to be trying to reconcile the undeniable privilege of being a white pool-owning South African with the egalitarian ideology to which he had given his life.

Ilse and her husband now live around the corner from me in Johannesburg; they swim every morning in their pool, a ritual that she believes she inherited from her father. The Fischer family was extraordinary, in the literal sense of the word: many years before the phenomenon became quite common in post-apartheid households, Bram and Molly informally adopted the niece of their domestic worker, a little girl named Nora, who had been orphaned in infancy. As we drove, one morning in 2012, to visit her adoptive sister in the township of Soshanguve, north of Pretoria, Ilse told me that she and Nora had shared a bedroom all their childhood. She explained the ways her mother had tried to protect the black child from the harshness of racism: most days, Nora ate with the family, but when Bram's conservative mother came to visit, Molly would instruct all the children to eat together in the kitchen, so that Nora would not feel ostracised.

Ilse and Nora had grown somewhat apart in adult life, and had not seen each other in several years. When we got to Nora's neat little home in Soshanguve, the two women embraced gently and very affectionately, whispered to each other in Afrikaans, and wept a little. We settled down to talk and Nora brought out some prized mementos; one of these was an example of the many articles in the Afrikaner press that slurred Fischer at the time of his trial. '*Bantoedoegter Was Soos Eie Kind In Fischers se Huis,*' blared one headline, repeating some of the incriminating evidence which the prosecution had led in court: 'Bantu Girl Was Like Their Own Child In Fischer's House.'

Ilse had brought along some family photographs too. One of these captured yet another afternoon at the Fischer pool, a juvenile Fringe Country. A group of kids are splashing about the pool, as one does in the suburbs on a summer's afternoon; some of these kids are black. 'Your garden,' sighed Nora as we looked at the image. 'My magic place. Remember the hopping game we used to play under those trees, hey?'

There were, of course, no schools for Nora in the northern suburbs, and so Bram and Molly sent her to a mission school in the countryside, bringing her back to visit during holidays. What Nora remembers as an idyllic childhood ended cataclysmically when, only seventeen, she got pregnant at exactly the time that Molly was detained in 1960. She moved back to the township to become another teenage mother.

*

Bram Fischer jumped bail in January 1965. Rather than fleeing into exile to join his fellow comrades, he elected to go underground, and did so by hiding out in a house on Corlett Drive, not more than a mile from Beaumont Street. He was eventually tracked down and arrested on 11 November 1965, my first birthday. He was tried and sentenced to life imprisonment; inside, he was singled out for exceptionally harsh treatment because he was seen by the warders to be a 'verraaier', a traitor to his race. In 1974 he developed cancer and became terminally ill; he was released into protective custody just before his death.

Why had Fischer not gone into exile? There was no tactical benefit to be gained by going underground – the armed struggle had already been effectively snuffed out – but he had been determined to risk martyrdom, or perhaps, feeling culpable in the death of his wife, self-destruction. Mandela, a black man, had been willing to sacrifice everything for the struggle, why shouldn't he? He had observed Mandela closely, as his friend and counsel, for two decades, and he had come to understand the value of performative gesture: he needed to show the world, show his fellow countrymen most of all, that a white man, too, was willing to put himself into outlaw shoes, the Fringe Country identity, that was the daily lot of black South Africans. When his lawyer George Bizos – who was also Mandela's lawyer – asked him whether it was worth sacrificing everything for the struggle, he snapped back: 'George, did you ask Nelson Mandela the same question?'

Bram Fischer's cell-mate Hugh Lewin addresses the same issue in his memoir, *Stones Against the Mirror*: 'It was a perilous step to take,' Lewin writes of his decision to become a saboteur, 'and there weren't many whites who took it. My fellow-dynamiters were totally unsuited for their clandestine, quasi-militaristic role. But it was the only way we could escape our whiteness. Apartheid had crippled us.' Lewin and his comrades found a limit to their ability to cross the boundaries imposed by apartheid: 'Even where the barriers were breached, the differences remained. We were white and therefore privileged, and this gave us protection. However much we tried to ignore it, we were wrapped in our magic cloaks of whiteness. To deny it was dishonest: we could always retreat into our impenetrable privilege and exclusivity. The worst would always happen to *them*, not to us. If it did happen to us, it required only a quick flick of readjustment to reassert our separateness.'

The Fort

The opening scene of Nadine Gordimer's *Burger's Daughter* is for ever branded on my consciousness. A fourteen-year-old schoolgirl in her brown-and-yellow uniform is queuing in the winter chill outside the Johannesburg Fort prison, having gone there directly after school the day her ill mother has been arrested, waiting patiently in line to bring her an eiderdown and a hot-water bottle. 'It was a bitter winter day,' comments the unnamed narrator. 'Little Rosa Burger knew her mother, that courageous and warm-hearted woman, was under doctor's orders. The child was dry-eyed and composed, in fact she was an example to us all about how a detainee's family ought to behave.' The only reason why Rosa was there in the first place was that her father, the lawyer Lionel Burger, 'had put others' plight before his own, and had been tirelessly busy ever since his own wife had been taken in the early hours of the morning, going from police station to police station, trying to establish for helpless African families where their people were being held. But he knew that his schoolgirl daughter could be counted on in this family totally united in and dedicated to the struggle.'

Today these last words seem flat for so fine a writer, but at the time they stirred my imagination deeply. Although four years separated the 1960 State of Emergency, when Molly Fischer was detained at the Old Fort, and my birth in 1964 at the Florence Nightingale, I imagine my mother looking up from nursing me, across Kotze Street and back four years in time to little Rosa Burger in her brown-and-yellow dress. Ever since I read those opening words of Gordimer's book, I have found myself drawn to the accounts of my contemporaries – Jewish, middle-class, northern-suburbs kids – whose parents happened to be activists, and who thus put the struggle first. It goes without saying that the accounts of black families are more harrowing, but it was the white ones that gripped me: not just because I could identify with them, but because of the way I could quantify – due to my own experience – what had been forfeited, alongside the gains of moral purpose.

Did I fantasise, as I read *Burger's Daughter*, that I could be a stoic, heroic teenager like Rosa? If so, I indulged such fantasies from a suburban home which had been made safe for me, in which any incriminating literature had been burned, and where my teenage political activism extended no further than campaigning alongside my parents for the 'Progs' in all-white elections, or getting my school principal to agree not to have us sing the national anthem during the Republic Day twentieth-anniversary celebrations of 1981 by threatening to lead a walk-out of my fellow students.

Hilda Bernstein, whose husband Rusty had been one of Mandela's co-accused in the Rivonia Trial, told me about the frontier her children had had to cross every time they left home: 'We couldn't live in townships, of course. So they had to go to white schools and participate in white activities. As soon as they stepped outside the front gate, they had a different sense of social attitudes and moralities than they had when they were inside our home, and it became more and more noticeable as they grew up.' Like the Fischers, the Bernsteins also had a swimming pool, 'and on Sundays we very often had a lot of friends, Indians and Africans, who would come for lunch, we had these big open braais, lots of people all round the swimming pool and servants to clear up afterwards, so it wasn't a great hassle for us. At some time at the beginning of the week Toni would say to me, "Are you expecting friends on Sunday?" The inference of that remark was: "Because if you are, I can't ask *my* friends to come and swim on Sunday." These things were very uncomfortable for her, and uncomfortable for the other children, very hard for them to understand . . .'

Ilse Fischer told me how much she and her siblings cherished the odd Sunday morning when Bram and Molly piled them into the car to take them off for a picnic by the banks of a river in the veld, so as to avoid the weekly deluge of comrade-visitors invading their swimming pool; for the rest of the time, their lives were public property. Robyn Slovo, the daughter of Joe Slovo and Ruth First, prominent communist leaders of the liberation movement, has said that her parents were 'totally absorbed' in the struggle, 'and I always interpreted that as being my fault, because I wasn't interesting enough, or I wasn't important enough ... The problem was with feeling any kind of pain, or expressing any kind of loss, or even missing my mother when she was in prison, or feeling frightened when we suddenly got woken up in the middle of the night and found ourselves in another country. Not only was it extremely weak to say, "I'm scared" or, "Please. What about me?" But it was actually injurious to Ruth and Joe, that what I was doing was weakening their struggle, and the struggle was clearly the most important thing.' Her own pain 'had no validity ... I was taught that pain is relative. There are others always worse off than you are.'

How different it was for me. My parents burnt the books. They secured the perimeters of my childhood. I rebelled against these boundaries and would come to define myself against them. But I also thrived within them.

*

In 2003 I was appointed to the team charged with transforming the Johannesburg Fort into Constitution Hill, the new home of South Africa's Constitutional Court, forged out of the old prison buildings. When the prison was moved to Soweto in 1987 – it no longer seemed safe to keep so many black offenders in the very heart of the city – the fort had been given to the army and had subsequently become derelict. Black Johannesburgers call it 'Number Four' – historically the name of the black male jail in the complex – and these two words still send shivers down the spine. For generations it represented horror – the black members of our team remembered being threatened with it if they misbehaved as children – and it was perhaps the most acute symbol of dispossession. It was where you ended up if you were caught in the city without a valid pass or in contravention of any one of a number of other laws that criminalised your very existence, forced into horribly overcrowded communal cells with gangsters, murderers, and other criminals.

My black colleagues on the project spoke about how crossing the threshold into the abandoned Number Four was both terrifying and liberating, and we all felt the restorative power of the natural world, in the way wild grasses and rampant invasive tree species were reclaiming the space, cracking the concrete of the courtyards and separating the bricks from the mortar of the communal cells. For all of us, the initial impulse was to leave it to decay. But nature and time itself would have to be arrested, here at Number Four, if the history of the place was to be conserved.

The Johannesburg Fort had been built in 1892 by Paul Kruger, the president of the Transvaal Boer Republic, to keep watch over the troublesome *uitlanders* ('outsiders') – the Brits and Jews and 'Coolies', and also, of course, the 'Kaffirs' – who had flocked to the mining camp below it, in the last two decades of the nineteenth century. In a deft metaphor of Boer insularity (and perhaps insecurity, too, up against British imperium and capital), Kruger had inverted the fortress. Its grand façade, carrying the Boer coat of arms, faced inward, while the outer ramparts were piled with earth and planted with grass to resemble a hilly outcrop at the top of the ridge. The sole entry into the Fort, off Kotze Street, diagonally across from the Florence Nightingale, appeared as a gash in the landscape. I grew up knowing that something bad was on the other side, without knowing exactly what it was – or once I did know what it was, without having the faintest idea of what it might look like.

The notion now was to fill this dark hole in the middle of the city with civic space, a 'campus for human rights', with museums, green space, retail and commercial development, and offices for all organisations dealing with the rights protected by the Constitution. The court itself is post-apartheid South Africa's signature public building: with much glass and exuberant craftwork, it marries the architectural and constitutional virtues of transparency and diversity. Most compellingly, the actual court chamber is built on the footprint of the original, awaiting-trial prison, fashioned out of the very bricks of this dismantled prison, as if to model the way that South Africa has begun building the possibilities of the future out of the difficulties of the past. But the development itself has been fraught with difficulty: in part because of politics and poor management, but also because the kind of civic space it envisaged was just not possible in a twenty-first-century inner-city Johannesburg given over to dirt-poor peasants and refugees.

While researching the Fort's history, I would spend much time looking at the images *Drum* published in 1956 by the photographer Bob Gosani, an exposé of the dehumanising practice of '*Tausa*' that took place within the Fort, whereby black prisoners were forced to dance naked in front of each other and the warders to demonstrate that they had nothing hidden up their anuses. Gosani shot the images by pretending to be a 'flatboy' in one of the apartment blocks that overlooked the Fort and sneaking onto its rooftop. What is most

shocking about the photographs is that if Gosani could see what was happening inside its ramparts, then so could all the white residents living in the Hillbrow flats around the periphery, if they cared to look.

I would also work, in my adult life, on a film about the gay white communist theatre director, Cecil Williams, whom Nelson Mandela was 'driving' when the two were arrested outside Howick in 1962. Mandela's cover, while he was underground, was that he was Williams's chauffeur in the latter's gleaming black Austin Westminster. Williams liked to tell the story of how, when he was detained at the Fort during the 1960 State of Emergency, he glanced up from a courtyard to the flat of a friend overlooking the prison, and observed a 'queer' party in progress with people hanging over the balcony as they sipped their *parfaits d'amour*. The partygoers themselves occupied their own partitioned space in society, somewhat invisible to the mainstream. And yet here they were, white people, in a neat analogy of the blindness mapped by the *Holmden's*, looking straight at Cecil Williams but unable to see him. He had crossed into the void.

Town

From the age of about ten or eleven, I was dropped off occasionally in Hillbrow to spend a morning or an afternoon with my Granny Gertie.

She was unlike other grannies I knew, although I would only later discover why. She had married late and been a working mother, a music teacher married to a communist husband with bohemian friends. She clocked me quickly: 'You and me, Marky,' she would say, 'we're *agin'* the government.' She was, in fact, a good deal more conservative than my romantic image of her allowed; a product of her race and class and time. But when I look at photographs of her as a young woman, I detect in her style and her features a modernity that I think I intuited in the woman whose gentle humour and love of reading beguiled me.

When I visited her at her residential hotel, we would have tea and anchovy toast in her room, or, occasionally, lunch with the hotel's other residents in the dining room, and then we would take a walk up Claim Hill to the bustle of Pretoria Street. Here there were Viennese balcony cafes and Greek pavement restaurants, bookshops and record stores, hippies and an underground flea market; here were perfumed men in tight trousers who attracted my attention for reasons I would only come to understand later. I loved the way Hillbrow, such a modest little triangle in the *Holmden's*, opened up vertically when explored: its hills, its skyscraper apartment blocks, the brooding Hillbrow Tower itself. I loved the way those tall buildings spilled such humanity out into the canyons they made. You could spy the Fort's ramparts through these canyons, at the end of Pretoria Street. Once, my grandmother walked me as far as the Florence Nightingale, but she seemed unwilling to walk me down Kotze Street towards the Fort to investigate any further. I think I was relieved.

*

As children we went to 'town', that territory on the other side of Hillbrow and the Fort, only occasionally: to the grand old domed Wolmarans Street *shul* on Jewish holidays, to shop at the John Orr's department store on Eloff Street, to see children's plays or concerts at His Majesty's or the Colosseum; later, to go shopping at the Carlton Centre and ice-skating at the new Carlton Skyrink, or to go to the doctor in one of the skyscrapers filled with consulting rooms on Jeppe Street. There was little possibility, on these outings, for independent discovery, beyond sneaking out of *shul* during Yom Kippur and dipping into Joubert Park or buying sweets from the Greek cafe on Claim Street, or lingering on Jeppe Street while waiting for my mother after a doctor's consultation. I had two rituals, during these waits, which my mother was happy to facilitate by arriving a little late to collect me: I would visit the Totem Meneghelli Gallery on the street level of the building, which sold African art, and I would buy a brandy ball from the German bakery next door. I can still taste today the brandy-soaked cake rolled in chocolate sprinkles; it conjures up the thrill and slightly illicit promise of the city.

In the Seventies, the white city was still safe for white kids. Despite the fact that my strict parents denied me the freedom to ramble that many of my friends had, I began discovering, for myself, the routes I knew so well from the map-books. As young teenagers, my friends and I would walk the few kilometres to Rosebank, the suburban shopping and commercial district, on Saturday afternoons; we were tolerated around the pool tables of the Rosewold Club, beneath the Post Office, despite being under-age. A little later, we would catch the red-and-white double-decker trolley-bus that sparked and sputtered down Oxford Road and Jan Smuts Avenue into town, to wander around the huge new Carlton Centre. This meant the terrors of ice-skating: not just on the rink but at the food concession too, for there were rumours that drinks were spiked with 'drugs' to get kids hooked.

More enticing was Hillbrow: the bus deposited you on Pretoria Street before dropping down Claim Hill into town. When I was with friends, we would get a schwarma on the pavement at Mi-Va-Mi before spending many hours at Hillbrow Records or trolling through the hippyish, incense-redolent underground flea market, where there were also rumours of drugs, but somehow more alluring. When I went to Hillbrow alone, I got off the bus at the corner of Edith Cavell and Pretoria and went directly to Exclusive Books, where I would install myself for most of the afternoon. This was Johannesburg's best bookshop, a gathering place not just for the city's intellectuals but also for somewhat alienated young suburbanites such as myself looking for kindred spirits; I imagined it to be something like Vanguard. In later years, I have discovered that so many of the friends I made during adulthood took exactly the same bus into town to spend exactly the same sort of time at Exclusive's, but I never met them then, indeed, I never actually met anyone there, so busy was I with the stuff between covers.

Or, perhaps more accurately, with the covers themselves. Ahead of its time, Exclusive's had reading tables, to which I would take a selection of books that might typically include Gerald Durrell, Leon Uris and André Brink, out of which I would select the one I would buy. I could have got these all at the Children's Bookshop in Rosebank, a wonderful place that had an extensive adults section too, and where I held a part-time job that afforded me a discount. But I was drawn to Exclusive's by something else: the gay shelf, around which I would hover guiltily, but from which I would not, for years, be brave enough to pull something. There were some novels there, but – in my memory, at least – most of it was given over to mild erotica, glossy art and photo books shrink-wrapped in plastic.

After some hours of frustrated desire I would wander across the street to Estoril Books, a long and narrow L-shaped storefront that was crammed with literature and magazines in many languages, catering to Hillbrow's immigrant communities. It also had, in the same spirit of worldliness, extensive shelves of erotica, gay and straight. Its cramped layout meant you could bump up against someone else also pretending to be interested in German novels or Italian football magazines while actually eyeing the erotica. It was here that I discovered *Equus*, a South African publication, which typically had on its cover a bare-torsoed man who looked like an Afrikaner policeman on his day off, riding a horse. Once or twice in Estoril, someone brushed a hand against my crotch or rubbed his own against me. My heart racing, I would flee downstairs into the flea market, and find refuge discussing scents with a hippyish incense-merchant, or buying – on one occasion – a purple chiffon Indian scarf with gold appliqué dots that would drive my parents to distraction; a poor substitute for *Equus* or *Wixer*, as I think a German publication was called, but a trophy to take back to the suburbs, nonetheless, of my thrilling brush with cosmopolitanism.

As my adolescence progressed I began roaming wider, carried over my innate obedience by more adventurous friends and by *zol*, as we called marijuana. We hitched to bohemian Rockey Street in Yeoville, where we hung about a shop called So Modern which captured the New Wave style of the times, or snuck beneath the age-limit into Café Casablanca; sometimes, we would hitch into town and spend the night at a club, Blue Beat or DV8, and take the first bus back to the suburbs in the morning. My friends were influenced by Anthony Burgess's *A Clockwork Orange*, and we translated it into thoughtless suburban nihilism: we called ourselves 'Clockwork' and would gather in the more permissive parents' living rooms, getting stoned and talking about revolution while listening to Queen, and then Pink Floyd and then David Bowie. We listened to Bob Marley and Peter Tosh, too, but I am not sure if we ever connected any of this, in a sustained way, to our own society.

If a friend's parents were out, we might steal a car for a joyride; a few times, we drove through the suburbs half-heartedly trashing lamps, but I don't remember us ever going much beyond Yeoville. By this point I had moved from King David to Redhill, a secular private school; I had a Portuguese classmate with a much older boyfriend, and with them I got to explore a little bit of the working-class Mediterranean south of Johannesburg, the mythical territories of Bez Valley and La Rochelle whence the fearsome 'Porra' and 'Leb' gangs came to disrupt our Northern Suburbs parties. But there was a line I never crossed: I never went into a township. There was a group at school, called Interact, that did some kind of good work in Alexandra, but I rejected it with the callow ignorance of a nerdy kid who wants to be in with the cool set; Interact seemed churchy, too much the preserve of the goodie-goodies.

Certainly, being in Hillbrow or in town gave me the opportunity to rub shoulders with black people who were not in maids' uniforms or workmen's khakis. They would not, at this point, be sitting at tables next to us at Mi-Va-Mi or skating next to us at the Skyrink or, later, dancing next to us at Metal Beat. But there were always nattily dressed black people on the streets in town: there were black shoppers at Hillbrow Records and black readers at the shelves of Exclusive Books; later, there were black spectators on the seats right next to us when we went to the Market Theatre with our history teacher Miss Schulman.

Two theatrical events at the Market opened my teenage eyes, at least as profoundly as reading *Burger's Daughter*. The first was *Woza Albert!*, the extraordinary piece of physical theatre made by Barney Simon, Mbongeni Ngema and Percy Mtwa, which imagines Christ's second coming in apartheid South Africa. The second was *Ain't We Got Fun?*, a camp Twenties-style ensemble cabaret with Robert Whitehead, David Eppel, Vanessa Cooke and Fiona Ramsay. If the first afforded me my first real understanding of what life must be like on the other side (and how creative resistance could be), then the second helped me see that the expression of homosexuality need not be furtive and fraught. That both were imbibed among a mixed audience that exemplified urbanity to me only heightened the experience.

It was the thrill of having shared an afternoon with such people, even if I never said a word to them, that I carried home, in the distinctive brown-paper Exclusive Books bag alongside ee cummings' *in just spring* or Oswald Mbuyiseni Mtshali's *Sounds of a Cowhide Drum*.

Black Bells

Do you remember those times when you looked up from a page and the world was different?

That is what happened to me, sitting at a table in Exclusive Books, reading *Sounds of a Cowhide Drum*. 'I am the drum on your dormant soul,' beat Oswald Mtshali in his title poem, and I felt he was awakening my own very soul from its suburban slumber with his lyrical word-paintings of black South African life, both in the countryside and in the city: a newly born calf 'like an oven-baked bread steaming under a cellophane cover'; 'scavenging dogs draped in red bandanas of blood' fighting fiercely for the 'squirming bundle' of an abandoned baby on a slag-heap in Soweto. And, most memorably, 'Boy On A Swing', precisely because of my ability to identify with it – up until the blow-to-the-guts of the last verse:

> Slowly he moves
> to and fro, to and fro
> then faster and faster
> he swishes up and down.
>
> His blue shirt
> billows in the breeze
> like a tattered kite.
>
> The world whirls by:
> east becomes west,
> north turns to south;

the four cardinal points
meet in his head.

Mother!
Where did I come from?
When will I wear long trousers?
Why was my father jailed?

Sounds of a Cowhide Drum and its companion volume, Mongane
Wally Serote's *Yakhal'inkhomo*, were among my very first purchases
from Exclusive Books. I still have them today, slender volumes with
thick pages, rough woodcut cover designs by the artist Thami Mnyele
(he would go into exile and be killed in a South African raid on
Botswana in 1985), and binding that has not worn particularly well.
They attracted me because they carried an authenticity lacking in the
other books on the shelves: they seemed hand-made, and to be
addressing themselves directly to me. I could not have known, at the
time I bought them, that they held immense cultural and political
significance: the first efflorescence of black creativity since the clam-
pdown of the early 1960s; the first public herald, too, of the Black
Consciousness movement, the energy of which would spark the 1976
Soweto Uprising.

The books were published by Renoster Books, set up by the young
white poet Lionel Abrahams, and Mtshali's book alone sold fourteen
thousand copies in its first year, 'a wide readership for any poet, anywhere,' wrote Nadine Gordimer the following year in the *New York
Times*. Gordimer offered a beautiful image for why these volumes
remained available when even a T-shirt bearing the legend 'Help
Cure Virginity' had been banned by apartheid's censors: 'Poetry is a
dragonfly released,' she wrote, 'whose shimmer censors must find difficult to pin down to any of the Publications and Entertainments Act's
ninety-seven definitions of what is undesirable.'

Reading Serote's poems in *Yakhal'inkomo* now, I find it an extraordinary wonder – once more, one of those gaps in the stitching of
apartheid – that this dragonfly was not yet pinned down by the time

I found it on the shelves of Exclusive Books: if Mtshali's words were soothing in their own way – they spoke a universal language of poetry – Serote's were deeply shocking to me. I had never, previously, encountered black anger, and now here it was, in his sour anthem to our shared home town, 'City Johannesburg'. Here it was, too, in 'What's in this Black "Shit"', creating a metaphor of the 'steaming little rot in the toilet bucket' that Alexandra's residents had to leave outside their doors every night to be collected because there was no sewage system in the township, and connecting it to the lived experience of oppression of black people, before putting the word 'shit' into the poet's own mouth as a form of rebellion against a policeman.

Serote came from Alexandra. From a relatively well-off property owning family, he was radicalised in 1969 by nine months of brutal detention linked to participation in Lionel Abrahams' writing workshop; this, he has said, 'opened up [something] in my writing'. A decade later, after publishing three volumes of poetry, he received a Fulbright scholarship to study creative writing at Columbia University and stayed outside the country, becoming an exile and joining the ANC. He would return to South Africa, one of its most celebrated writers and the ANC's head of arts and culture, in 1990. The poem that affected me most, when I first read *Yakhal'inkomo* (which means, 'the crying of the cattle when they go to the slaughter'), was its last one,' Black Bells'.

It began:

> AND,
> > Words
> Make pain
> Like poverty can make pain.

And ended:

> Words,
> > WORDS.
> Trying to get out

Words. Words. By Whitey.
No. No. No. By Whitey,
I know I'm trapped.
Helpless
Hopeless
You've trapped me whitey! Memm wanna ge aot Fuc
Pschwee e ep booboodubooboodu bllll
Black books,
Flesh blood words shitrr Haii,
Amen.

Not only did this appeal to my teenage modernism – my thrill at the discovery that you could break the rules – but it spoke to the writer in me. I would have to wait until my discovery of Steve Biko at university to understand the theory driving this poem – how white words disempowered black souls by preventing them from speaking for themselves – but what I got, as a sixteen-year-old, was the understanding that words could cause pain, that words could express anger, and that writing against oppression (in this instance, represented by 'Whitey', by *me*) could be liberating: out of the turmoil of inchoate rage or frustration banged out on a keyboard came 'Black books', came 'flesh blood words', which I understood then – correctly, I think – as action. 'Amen'.

'Jim Comes to Joburg'

There is an image of the street by David Goldblatt that best captures, to my mind, the drama of arrival in Johannesburg. In 'Arriving family, King George Street (circa 1955)', a man steps ahead holding his young son's hand, his urban aspirations expressed by a shabby buttoned jacket and the shoes on his feet. His son is unshod, as is his wife, a few steps behind, wearing traditional blanket and headwrap and carrying all the family's belongings in a cardboard suitcase. The landscape into which these innocents have stepped, as if into a moral fable, is the archetypical modern city – it could be Moscow or New York – painted with shadow and light as these play against the planes of an art deco skyscraper, brought into context by two rickshaw carts parked on the side of the street. The building is not insignificant: it is the headquarters of Eskom, the electricity utility. There could be no brighter symbol of modernity. Even as the carts bring the pre-modern into the frame, their formal qualities paradoxically suggest the cogs of a Chaplinesque machine which will now entrap the newly arrived peasants. It is hard not to fear for them, and particularly for the woman: my gaze returns, repeatedly, to her step, pressing her bare toes white against the hot, hard tarmac. And yet one hopes for them too: on a street lamp pole, just to the side of the man's blank, determined face, is a litter-bin with some advertising signage: 'Learn to Write'.

*

> Oh I came to Jo'burg, the Golden City
> Oh what did I come here for?
> I'm a long way from home in Joburg City
> So far away from my kraal.

These 'Golden City Blues' are sung by Sophiatown siren Dolly Rathebe, Nelson Mandela's one-time girlfriend, in the 1949 film *Jim Comes to Joburg*. Rathebe had adapted them from Lena Horne's 'Salt Lake City Blues' in *Cabin in the Sky*, a film that attained such cult status in the South African townships in the Forties that it gave us the word '*tsotsi*' for 'gangster' – a vernacularization of Cab Calloway's signature 'zoot suit'.

The 'Golden City Blues' – or their sentiment, at least – riff through much of twentieth-century South African consciousness: '*Jim comes to Joburg*' has entered the lexicon as a phrase to describe the central moral fable of black life in a world dominated by migrant labour – that of the decent country boy who comes to the city from his safe, coherent tribal world, to enter a world of sin and possibility.

Perhaps the most famous literary 'Jim' is Alan Paton's hero from *Cry, the Beloved Country*, the Reverend Stephen Kumalo, who comes to the city to find a lost soul and whose utter incomprehension is signified by a neon advertisement he sees upon arrival: 'Water comes out of a bottle, till the glass is full. Then the lights go out. And when they come on again, lo the bottle is full and upright, and the glass empty. And there goes the bottle over again. Black and white, it says, black and white, though it is red and green. It is too much to understand. He is silent, his head aches, he is afraid.'

Nelson Mandela's own 1941 arrival in the Golden City was filled with similar apprehension, but in counterpoint to Paton's somewhat worn account of the descent of a noble savage into Sodom, it is powered by wonder rather than dread, possibility rather than incomprehension. Fleeing the constraints of his feudal society – an arranged marriage, to be precise – Mandela was entranced by the city's modernity. He describes how, when he arrived by car at night, 'we saw before us, glinting in the distance, a maze of lights that seemed to stretch in all directions. Electricity to me had always been a novelty and a luxury, and here was a vast landscape of electricity, a city of light… Johannesburg had always been depicted as a city of dreams, a place where one could transform oneself from a poor peasant into a wealthy sophisticate, a city of danger and opportunity … It all seemed tremendously glamorous.'

The flipside to Mandela's fantasy is expressed by the *Drum* journalist Nat Nakasa, for whom the city was 'a depressing mess' precisely because it did not – it could not – live up to such expectations: 'too many Africans sweating away on company bicycles or lingering on pavements in search of work' in a city where 'newly recruited mine boys walked through the town with blankets on their shoulders and loaves of bread under their armpits, to be housed in the hostels of the gold mines ... They spoiled my image of Johannesburg as the throbbing giant which threw up sophisticated gangsters, brave politicians and intellectuals who challenged white authority.'

By Nakasa's time, the apartheid city was a place of manifest oppression. Even if they had lived there for two or three generations, black people were 'temporary sojourners' who had to leave by curfew if they were not barracked in servants' quarters. Very few men went through life without a visit to 'Number Four' on a pass offence. And yet, like all cities, this city could also be, paradoxically, a place of liberation. You could lose yourself in the crowd, away from the prying eyes and constraints of your community; you could spend your money on something other than beer – the only commodity available in the township. I will never forget the bittersweet story an older black man once told me, about how exciting it was to strut down Eloff Street, buying clothing by pointing at what you wanted through the shop window: black people, obviously, could not try on 'white clothes'. Never mind: you returned home on Saturday afternoon to the smoggy township – Soweto was electrified only in the late 1970s, Alexandra a decade later – with the proof of your urbanity in your hand and you felt a man of the world.

From the 1940s onwards there were street photographers in South African cities who would capture you as you went about your business and then approach you to pay a shilling or two for this memento. These were not posed studio shots, and there is something modern not just in the street scenes they capture, but in their candour; the way they release their subjects from the studio-photographer's trove of props, from the earnest and severe gaze his slow shutter required. There are several of these in my family archive, and I am struck in all of them by the way these first-generation immigrants claim the street, as in this image of my Granny Janie and her sister-in-law Zelda:

One of these images compels me particularly, from the collection of Michele Bruno, a cross-dressing man I interviewed for a 2009 exhibition I was curating about the lives of gay, lesbian and transgendered people in Johannesburg.

In this photo, taken in 1963, Michele is captured walking down Rissik Street with his friend Louis; two young, white, gay men in their early twenties. Louis is wearing a suit, but Michele told me, when showing me the photograph, that his friend has subsequently undergone gender reassignment, and now lives as a woman. Michele himself, in the photograph, is code-switching, and doing it quite joyously on the streets of Johannesburg at the height of apartheid's darkness: he is wearing a tapered feminine pantsuit and has, hanging from his mouth to go with it, a long thin feminine cigarette.

With his woman's handbag and gamine per- oxide hairdo, Michele is undoubtedly the focus of the street-photographer's gaze. And yet there is a woman on the pavement behind him that I keep coming back to: an older woman in a cap and somewhat shapeless coat, holding the hand of her man, out of the frame. Looking at the photo- graph, I imagine her experience in the city, as opposed to that of Michele's. This is 1963: she would have had to carry a pass. She would have to leave by the last train. She had no cause to be on these streets,

save to come and go to work. And yet she, too, like Michele and Louis, is finding space in the city; claiming her ground. She is holding her man's hand.

In the Third Basement

My obsession with route maps to the city of my birth, and with what came before the *Holmden's*, inevitably led me underground. I found myself beneath the streets of the city, in the third basement of the Johannesburg Public Library, a handsome, neoclassical, sandstone building dating from 1935 opposite the old City Hall, now the Gauteng Provincial Legislature. Because the library was closed for major renovations in 2011, I needed to get special permission to look at its map collection. I was instructed to enter not up the steps and beneath the grand portico, but rather through a basement door, a hole in the wall, leading off from a corner of the Harry Hofmeyr public garage, where I had parked after having had 10 rand extorted from me by an access guard who lied that parking was only available for visitors to the legislature.

Before the library had been closed, any visitors driving in from the suburbs would have used this basement entrance, and in his book *Portrait with Keys* Ivan Vladislavic describes 'the makeshift reversal at the Public Library' as 'refreshingly ingenuous: while the black children who are now the main users of the facility stroll arm-in-arm up the broad staircase from the library gardens or gather in the grand lobby to giggle and whisper, the few white suburbanites who still venture here park underground and slip in up the back stairs'.

In I thus slipped. I found myself on a landing with a linoleum floor, on which a reading-room desk had been commandeered as a makeshift kitchen table, and around which at any given time library employees on break would gather. Johannesburg is famous for its outdoor cafes that spill out of shopping malls onto parking lots that choke their patrons with petrol fumes, but this took it down to another level,

I thought, as I watched the workers taking the basement-parking air while they drank their tea or ate their lunch.

I stated my name and quest, and with a nod toward the stairwell from a woman picking her teeth with a shard of chicken-bone, I fell down a hole into the stacks. I found myself free to roam in a wonderland of leather and paper from which regular users are usually barred. I wandered among the shelves, lost in arcana – the records of, say, the Johannesburg Silvicultural Society – that I came to realise would soon have no place in our world: the renovation of the library includes the digitisation of much of its paper holdings, the result of a huge Carnegie Foundation grant. As I followed an idle conveyor-belt that wound through the stacks, I wondered how it would sound on a normal working day down here, clanking and belching books through this vault and spitting them up into the reading room. Would the conveyor belt ever move again, or would it lie here like a declawed leviathan, a silent reproach to the digital age?

I found myself at the newspapers, and pulled out the bound volume of editions from November 1964, losing myself in the news around my birth. There I read not only that the Customs Office was embargoing books with the words 'black' and 'sex' in the titles and that Bram Fischer was about to go on trial, but also of the ongoing dredging of the Wemmer Pan for more deposits made there by the 'suitcase murderer', who chopped up his victims and put their body parts in suitcases before throwing them into the dam. Even though I turned the pages with as much care as I could muster, the paper disintegrated at my touch: how we destroy the things we love. I would probably be one of the very last people to browse these old bound volumes.

As I wandered through the stacks I would, every now and then, come across a little island of settlement in the shadows of the shelves, a desk with some framed family photos and stationery set upon it and, perhaps, a reading lamp casting a pool of friendly yellow light and a tinny radio tinkling. 'Hello!' a pleasantly surprised voice would say, happy for the diversion, greeting me as if I were a traveller from another dimension. I almost expected to be given an invitation by the Queen of Hearts to tea, but most of the time I was simply offered directions, which is how I found my way to the map cabinets.

Amazed, and a little disturbed by the trust put in me, a stranger, albeit with a *laissez-passer* from the chief librarian, I was then left alone to pull out drawer after drawer of maps, some of them sheathed in plastic but most of them stashed in careless and random piles; Johannesburgs by the hundred, drawn and printed, folded and discarded, against the northern wall of the third basement beneath the streets of the city.

*

Perhaps it was because I was underground myself that I was drawn immediately to the maps of Johannesburg's subterranean world. I had been down mines a couple of times, on assignment, and these were experiences I would never forget. Looking at these vertical projections of Johannesburg's underground, I remembered the experience: of how, even after you are deposited by the cage at what appears to be the centre of the earth, you have to begin the long commute to work, a trudge of up to four kilometres along the crosscut to the gold reef. Following a team to the reef, I remembered how I had been engulfed by a stream of silent, overall-clad figures; shadowed faces beneath helmet lamps, drained of all emotion, as if the drop into the earth had pulled a mask of blankness over them. The passageway itself had the look of Victorian industrial fantasy: overhead pipes sputtered and hissed with the water and air that make the underground habitable. Strangely, the accretion of so many years of activity in such a narrow space evoked not so much claustrophobia as another civilisation, in which the components of surface life – space, time, sound, light, climate – had been rearranged unintelligibly.

I was struck, now, in the third basement of the library, by how these meticulously plotted vertical projections of the subterranean civilisation resembled the plans of life above it. The passages, or 'levels', are laid out at right angles to the lift shafts, creating a grid-like impression of civilisation. Nature flows through this grid in the

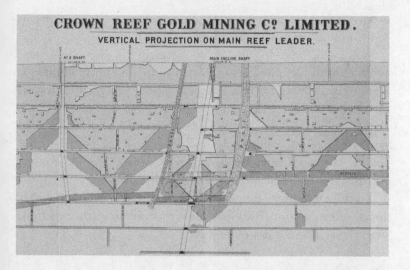

CROWN REEF GOLD MINING Cº LIMITED.
VERTICAL PROJECTION ON MAIN REEF LEADER.

form of dangerous rock-faults or the diagonal ore-bearing reefs which the passages bisect and which are, of course, their *raison d'être*.

Drafted by engineers and surveyors rather than poets or moralists, these maps do not offer us a cross-section of the underworld – and the human impulses that drive that us there – that one finds, for example, in Botticelli's *Chart of Hell*, illustrating Dante's *Inferno*. Neither do they bear any resemblance to the infernal lives that miners led down there, particularly in the early days. When I interviewed miners a few years ago, one older man recalled for me his first experience under-ground: 'People were naked. There was no privacy, no dignity, everyone shouted. It was hell – no other word will do.' Others spoke of the fear that woke them every morning of their working lives: more than 70,000 men died in mine accidents in South Africa in the twen-tieth century, and the current accident fatality rate in gold mines, down dramatically, still averages more than one per every three thou-sand miners. These numbers do not begin to account for the hundreds of thousands who have died from tuberculosis, which spreads rapidly in the underground's closed climate, or silicosis, which results from prolonged dust inhalation, or HIV, which has infected an estimated 30 per cent of South African miners, a consequence in part of their socio-economic conditions.

I squinted, now, looking at the aesthetically pleasing vertical projections of Johannesburg's mines, and tried to imagine them as plans of battlefields, for I remembered from my interviews how the miners had defined themselves as soldiers. The team leader I was shadowing had told me: 'Every morning, I put on my hard hat and I go to the cage that will take me underground. I tell myself: "I am a soldier. Maybe I'll come back and maybe I won't."' An older miner had used similarly martial imagery: 'Your drill becomes your AK-47, and you are fighting, fighting – blasting your way to freedom. But of course it is an illusion. Because there is no freedom on the other side of the rock. There is just more rock.'

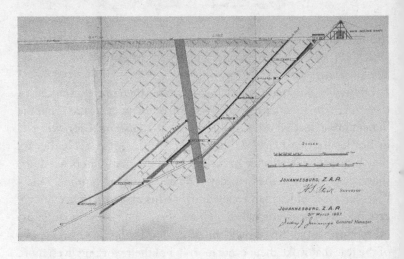

The vertical projections of the mines do, in fact, suggest this existential truth. Above the 'datum line' – as the surface is labelled – in one of the 1897 maps there is a little line-drawing of the reception buildings and the headgear that houses the machinery used to winch the miners down into the earth and the gold ore back up; known, recognisable objects, sharply sketched. The map plots the mine down to the ninth level, 200 metres beneath the earth's surface: here detail gets hazy, and the main incline shaft, cutting deep into the earth at a diagonal, does not end at a point or a cul-de-sac; it just peters out, open ended, into the *terra incognita* of the blank page. And here is where the underground maps declare their difference from those of life above the datum line: there are no southern boundaries down here. The rock is as infinite and unknowable as the uncharted sea was to early navigators; it has no end and there is consequently no destination. There is, rather, promise, or terror, or numbing hopelessness, in the journey to the centre of the earth.

*

Like other mining boom-towns in the Americas or Australia that sprang out of the wilderness, towns that were populated by migrants and powered by mammon, the hardscrabble mining camp of Johannesburg gave birth to a different kind of underworld above the earth's surface too. According to an 1896 census of the approximately 100,000 people who had streamed into the city in its first decade, there were two white men to every white woman in the new city, and ten black men to every black woman. These figures do not even begin to account for the tens of thousands of black men who were housed in single-sex migrant-labour hostels on the mines themselves. Unsurprisingly, given these demographics, commerce in the above-ground city was driven by vice. In fact, the whole central precinct of Johannesburg fanning out around Market Square – where the Public Library is now – became known as 'Frenchfontein' because of the number of brothels established there. There was a criminal under-world run largely by Litvak Jews with the same origins as my antecedents, who played their role in the city's booming economy, as did their more upright co-religionists who ran the mining houses.

There is a continuum in the city's narrative of lawlessness from its beginnings to now: the centrality of vice to its identity. But what makes Johannesburg's history specific, different from other lawless frontier boom-towns, is that it has not only a figurative underworld but an actual underground too: the subterranean world dug out by the mines. More than that, this second, literal underground is the place where the grossest criminality actually occurred: the slave conditions of black mine labour.

Thus developed Johannesburg's vertical equation: the deeper down the workers dug, the higher up the bosses could build their modernist Manhattanish skyline. As I sat in the third basement, I thought about how this literal underground becomes figurative too, representative of the underworld that black South Africans were forced to inhabit by their second-class citizenship and unwelcome status in the city: they were underground in more ways than one.

Underground Underworld

I don't remember where and how I first heard the expression 'in the closet'; it must have been when I was still quite young, as at the time I did not yet know what 'closet' meant; in South Africa we said 'cupboard' or 'wardrobe', as they did in all the pink parts of my *World Book Atlas*. I might have found the phrase in my voracious search for any literature that might cast some light on my condition, perhaps in one of my mother's women's magazines. Or maybe I heard it eavesdropping on adults describing the double life of someone they knew. Whichever: long before I knew a closet was a place where you put things away, I thought of it as a place where you hid something. And I thought of it, spatially, as being underground. This gave it an infernal dimension, although I cannot remember whether I thought it was homosexuality itself which put you in hell, or the concealing of it, or both.

And so, from the beginning of my perception of my difference, I made the entirely rational conflation of underground and underworld: my sexuality was concealed because it was illicit, and so I was a denizen of both. Thinking about it now, I wonder how this perception of myself opened me to an understanding of other undergrounds, other underworlds, in my city so defined by subterranean geography, and whether the routes I plotted along the surface of the *Holmden's* were not covers, themselves, for more vertical voyages of discovery.

The games of sexual Dispatcher I played in my teenage years often carried both the same promise and the same frustrating limitations as the cartographical ones I continued to play with the Map Studio *Street Guide* and any other road atlas that came my way. My ever-present notebooks of street plans and floor plans became interspersed with elaborately coded tables that, for example, graded the boys in my class sexually across a variety of categories. If snooping parents had come across these notebooks, they would have dismissed these tabulated fantasies as just another map-like diversion of their geeky child.

My early teenage Darling children were *The Rocky Horror Picture Show*'s Brad and Janet, Peter Pan updated into FranknFurter. A little later, I found a suitable Jim Hawkins in Michael York's Christopher Isherwood character in *Cabaret*, accessing through him the terror and thrill of a *Treasure Island* set in decadent Weimar Berlin: Joel Grey plays Long John Silver? Even now, over three decades later, I feel the vise of longing as I remember Michael York's ménage à trois with Liza Minelli and the Nazi aristocrat.

More so still, the swimming-pool scene at the climax of *Rocky Horror*: 'Don't dream it, be it' became the anthem of my desire, even if I could not actually live up to its injunction, and I lost myself for hours in those underwater shots of polysexual pleasure. If even the 'Venus de Milo' was suspect in South Africa, there was no hope for Tim Curry of *The Rocky Horror Picture Show*, but somehow the distributors managed to find a loophole that allowed the film to be screened for a few weeks while the banning was under appeal. I must have been fourteen or fifteen and under the age limit, but somehow I found a way of seeing it at least five times at the Protea Cinema on Oxford Road – Adam and I discussed the swimming-pool scene interminably – and then of procuring a bootleg video-cassette later.

Once I got too old to spend Sunday afternoons tucked into the back of the Mercedes with the *Holmden's* or the Map Studio *Street Guide*, I found another way to lose myself. During my last three years of high school I spent almost every Sunday afternoon working at the Children's Bookshop, which became my release from both the inevitable claustrophobia of family life and the nihilism of teenage suburbia.

Most Sundays, Adam would drop by in the torpid lag of the afternoon, long after we stopped being friends or even talking to each other. By this point our sexual interdependency and the furtive way we had to express it had made us come to dislike, or at the very best, mistrust each other. He dove for cover in suburban convention, tacking *Playboy* centrefolds above his bed and taking on what seemed to me to be the materialistic characteristics of a 'bagel-boy', which is the South African version of a 'Jewish American Prince'. Meanwhile I tried to find expression by being 'alternative' politically and socially, which in the end was really just another suburban convention in the end: choosing girlfriends who would pull me into a more bohemian, theatrical world and getting stoned listening to ska or reggae.

I had fallen properly in love for the first time, with a new best friend. He reciprocated with passionate but sexually noncommital devotion and so I remained sexually dependent on, and thus increasingly resentful of, Adam – whom I only saw, now, when he came to visit me at the bookshop. I would tell my manager, a woman named Janice, who was discreet enough never to raise an eyebrow, that I was going to take a break, and Adam would follow me down to the basement where the tea table was; we would tumble into an airless storeroom, one of us propped against the door as insurance, and have sex in less time than it took the kettle to boil.

When I came back from university and told Adam I was going to live openly, we split definitively: he was still in the closet and dating girls. Later, he came out too, and we always enjoy a chat, these days, on the frequent occasions we bump into each other; two middle-aged gay Jewish men from the northern suburbs with four decades of history behind them.

*

I started my studies at the University of Cape Town and – in those times of foment – I quickly become attracted to radical student politics, working on the student newspaper, *Varsity*. One of the most notoriously two-tongued apartheid cabinet ministers, Piet Koornhof, came to give a guest lecture in my Political Science course, and – playing to the liberal student gallery – made outlandish statements about the imminent death of apartheid. With all the righteousness an eighteen-year-old could muster, I rushed to my editors and gave them a story that would cause some embarrassment to the minister and the government. In retrospect, it seems to me that the fount of my indignation was a fury about lying and hypocrisy, a fury that touched at the core of my own life of lies: one of my most vivid memories of the time was attending a meeting where a Christian student leader was berating the editors for being supportive of the tiny gay students' group that had just been formed on campus; I had kept red-facedly quiet.

My Koornhof scoop was printed as a special issue, the minister hit the roof, and I was charged by the university with breaking the off-the-record rules that were, allegedly, at the very core of academic freedom. My colleagues and I became the *Varsity* Seven (or Six or Eight, or whatever it was; it was a time when *real* activists on trial were known as the 'Delmas Four' or the 'Upington Fourteen'). We got off with a sentence of 'suspended rustication' and it was, in relation to the terrible repression happening all around us, utterly insignificant. Still, despite the braggadocio among my comrades, it became the crisis of my early adult life, a fall from innocence and exposure of liberal hypocrisy. I had done what I believed I had been raised to do, which was to tell the truth, even if I couldn't do it with respect to my own identity, and 'the system' had come down on me like a ton of bricks: not just the supposedly liberal university I attended, but my parents, too, who were very anxious about my future, and convinced my sentence would jeopardise my ability to study abroad by causing my passport or my deferral from national service to be revoked. At that point all fit white South Africans were conscripted for two years, and in many cases to fight in the border wars the country was waging in Angola; this could be postponed only through university study.

I had gone to the University of Cape Town to begin work on a bachelor's degree while waiting to see if my applications to American colleges would be successful: the plan, agreed upon with my parents, had been that if I got into a good American university, I would leave UCT after six months to start the US academic year in August. When I received the acceptance letters from Yale and several other colleges it was in the thick of the *Varsity* crisis. I was thrown into crushing indecision, but my parents laid down the law: I was to go. They did not believe there was a future for their children in South Africa and, besides, my sometimes unbearably ambitious father wanted me to have the academic and intellectual life denied him. His successful career as an industrialist, coupled with my school results, meant that I could go to one of the world's best universities. Living abroad, too, would keep me out of jail.

And so I went to Yale. I chafed against it at the time. The world I had discovered upon leaving home seemed big enough, for the moment, to satisfy my dispatching desires, and suddenly those vapour trails disintegrating into the blue of distance at the edges of my sky did not seem so compelling: there were ideas, and people of all backgrounds, and struggles enough, at university in Cape Town. But over time my gratitude to my parents has grown: not just because of the education Yale provided me and the friendships I made and networks I became part of, but because of the space it gave me to find myself.

In retrospect, I understand my parents' response to my incipient activism as another book-burning moment, an action they took to ensure the stability of their family and to safeguard the future of the son they had raised. Like so many other well-meaning white South Africans, they were torn between their values on the one hand and the benefits of their privilege on the other, both of which they imparted to their children. The shortfall between these two can be measured in guilt, that basic unit of currency in liberal white South African identity. Even Bram Fischer and Ruth First – white South Africans who paid for their values with their lives – suffered from this shortfall for the privileges accorded them, privileges denied to their black comrades: his swimming pool, her sumptuous Citroën, their suburban comforts, their professional lives. On the other extreme were those white people who experienced no gap at all between their value systems and their privilege: their *herrenvolk* entitlement meant, of course, that they were entirely free of guilt.

We were somewhere in-between. It would be disingenuous to pretend that I had no sense of entitlement. I had my life ahead of me and I had dreams, and I was at best ambivalent about putting all that at risk because of what others were denied. When I finally returned to South Africa after 1990, after four years of study and three years of living and working in New York, I constructed a myth to explain how and why I had been absent during the turbulent preceding decade, which had defined all my new friends and colleagues. Although I was indeed coming home on the wave of optimism following the unbanning of the liberation movements and the release of Nelson Mandela and the other political prisoners, I refused on principle to claim for myself the identity of a 'returning exile': I had come back on holiday frequently during my seven American years, and I could have avoided conscription even if I had stayed in South Africa by continuing my university study, as many of my peers did. I had gone away, I said, because my parents had told me that they would not finance my education if I remained in South Africa. This was unfair to them: they exerted intense pressure on me, to be sure, but I was already an adult and the decision had been mine. When I think back to why I did not rebel, and stay, I find two reasons. The first is that I also feared the consequences of my activism. And the second is that I was gay, and I prayed that going away would make it easier.

At that time, I believed I would have a life in the theatre, and I chose Yale over the other contenders, on a miserable whirlwind trip with my parents, because of the billboards advertising productions of the college dramatic societies lined up outside Yale Station. They flashed theatricality, and thus openness about homosexuality, (or perhaps the artifice that might conceal it) from their hoardings at the corner of Chapel and Elm. Once I got there, I kept up the pretence for a while – I invented an Indian girlfriend – but let it slip very quickly, and diverted my anti-apartheid energy into the gay rights movement that was so prominent on American campuses, particularly at Yale, in the early 1980s.

I might not have wanted to leave South Africa, but once I was away I became giddy with new worldliness. I might have played on my exoticism to gain social capital, but I was far more interested in the Sandinista Revolution than the South African one; I wanted to read Virginia Woolf and Adrienne Rich rather than Nadine Gordimer and J.M. Coetzee, and I listened to Billy Bragg rather than Miriam Makeba. In my freshman year I walked out of my very distinguished

English professor's class because I found his reading of *Paradise Lost* to be patriarchal, and signed up with a young feminist lecturer instead. In my sophomore year, I joined the picket lines to support the university's striking clerical and technical workers. But it took me a while to connect such activism to what I had left behind in South Africa.

In the spring semester of my sophomore year I enrolled, on what seemed to be a whim, in a seminar on South African literature. The professor was a white South African, Stephen Clingman – who would later write Bram Fischer's biography – and he was particularly tough on me for what he diagnosed quickly as my mushy liberalism. I had written an essay called 'Athol Fugard and Consciousness', and Clingman said something to me along the lines of: '*What* "consciousness"? You need to understand what this word means in the South African context.'

And so I found myself, one wintry evening, weeping in my booth in the Cross Campus Library over Steve Biko's *I Write What I Like*, which was of course banned in South Africa. The tears were those of recognition: not just at the way the founder of the South African Black Consciousness Movement gave expression to something I had detected as a youngster but did not have words for, in his description of how apartheid collapsed black people from within, but at how his words resonated with the way I felt in a world that devalued me because of my sexuality. It would be overstating things to say that Steve Biko gave me my final push into self-acceptance, but he played his part. I found my way to Franz Fanon and then to Bayard Rustin and James Baldwin and back in time to Langston Hughes, and incorporated what I learned from these black gay American writers into my understanding of myself and my own native land.

Bachelors and Maidens

Somewhere toward the back of my parents' red-leather photo-album with the gold springbok embossed on the cover are some photographs, dated March 1968, of my toddler brother Antony and myself, aged three and a bit, with our parents on Clifton Fourth Beach in Cape Town. The South African parliament would just have extended the prohibitions on mixed marriage to citizens married outside of the country, and the United Nations would soon call on all member states to adhere to a cultural, educational and sports boycott of South Africa. In one of the photographs, my mother and I are both lying on the sand facing each other, our eyes locked and our mouths open in the kind of smiling engagement that so vividly animated my childhood.

In another, my father leans on his side, an arm around each of his sons, the obligatory bucket and beachball completing the tableau. I

find these images from Clifton deeply comforting. Perhaps because we are holidaying out of season, there appear to be no other people on the beach, and the sense I get from them, now, is not just one of containment but one of completeness, too, as if the whole world consisted of just the four of us.

At this point my parents had not yet made the shift to large-format Kodachrome, and the photos in the album are black and white, wallet-sized. When I scanned them and blew them up on my computer screen I was able to make out, in the background, just beyond the tableau of my father and his sons, a lone male figure walking toward the pile of smooth, massive boulders at the extreme western end of the beach. These rocks are known as Bachelors Cove and were the gathering point for 'queer society' in the city: men would gather on the rocks at the end of the day to swim, talk, cruise, and bathe naked beneath the dying sun, although we of course knew nothing of this. A man thus walks away from the containment of my early childhood, leading my adult eye and imagination toward another place, beyond the frame, and to another photograph, from another red-leather-bound album.

In the early 1990s, while I was writing a history of gay and lesbian life in South Africa, I came across a huge scrapbook, bound in red leather, with the title 'Special Projects' printed across its cover, in Johannesburg's small Gay Lending Library. The euphemistic title reflected beautifully what was within: a decade's worth of meticulous clipping and pasting of newspaper articles, from the mid 1950s to the mid 1960s, with nothing in common save that the maker of the scrapbook had collected them together. Some of the articles are explicitly about homosexuality – particularly those dealing with police raids on parks or 'cottages' – but a great many can only be identifiable as 'gay' because of their context in the scrapbook: society-page photos, articles about suicides, even a clip of a young man winning a prize at a local supermarket.

The scrapbook was an obsessive endeavour, its author's 'Special Project', a determined attempt to find the homosexual subtext in South Africa's mass media. I spent hours pouring over it, and eventually tracked down its creator: his name was Joe Garmeson, a great fulsome bear of a man, a banker and a toastmaster, given to grand proclamations and florid stories. He was a hoarder, an historian's dream, with cupboards full of photographs, notebooks and journals. Garmeson died in 2001 and these items became the foundation collection of the Gay and Lesbian Memory in Action (GALA) Archives at Wits University, where they constitute an extraordinarily detailed account of white male homosexual life in South Africa through the twentieth century.

In one of Joe Garmeson's albums is a series of photographs of young men on the rocks by the shore, some time in the 1950s, taken at Bachelors Cove. In the image from the series that compels me the most, Garmeson looks directly at the camera with his matinee-idol smile as he poses with four friends. Their bodies fold into each other as they sit on the rocks, as if they were sirens, or beached sylphs from a water ballet. Such is their intimacy that you would not need to find their photo in a big scrapbook labelled 'Special Projects' to know they were homosexuals.

In another photograph we see the matinee idol sitting on the rocks and looking, once more, straight at the camera. But this time he is posed in an almost classical triptych: his arm is around a blond friend, and both of them have a hand on the shoulder of a brown-skinned man who sits beneath them, caressing their legs. In the background, oblivious to this flagrant transgression of the laws forbidding both racial mixing and public indecency, two fishermen carry on their task of catching dinner.

Looking at the photograph now, I see that it is captioned 'Durban, 1951'. It would have been taken at Blue Lagoon at the mouth of the Umgeni River on the Indian Ocean coast of Natal, a favourite fishing spot for all races and clearly not yet declared a 'non-European' beach under the Separate Amenities Act in these still-early days of apartheid. But somehow I missed this caption when I first saw these photographs, a few years back, and I have developed, over the years, my own narrative around the image. I decided that it must have been taken on the rocky promontory between Bachelors Cove and Maidens Cove, one of the only coloured beaches on the entire Atlantic seaboard, as I had been told – perhaps by Joe Garmeson himself – that white and coloured or Malay men cruised and courted across the colour bar on these rocks. Here, between Bachelors and Maidens, in another of the few gaps in the stitching of apartheid, just beyond my childhood holiday idyll, these men from different races developed networks of desire, affection and even just friendship.

*

'350 IN MASS SEX ORGY!' This was the headline of the *Rand Daily Mail* that landed at our front door on 22 January 1966, when I was one year old. A 'queer' party had been raided in Wychwood Road, in the Johannesburg suburb of Forest Town; nine men had been arrested for 'masquerading as women' and one for 'indecent assault on a minor'. It was, of course, a garden party; it took place, of course, around a swimming pool. Although my parents do not recall the incident, they must have pored over the article, for they had several homosexual friends, and many names were printed.

'Masquerading' was on the books to prevent criminals from concealing their identities by dressing up as women, but it was occasionally used to intimidate drag queens and gay cross-dressers when nothing else was at hand to charge them with. One of those arrested on these charges was the hairdresser Michele Bruno, who was wearing

his showstopper ostrich-feather coat: 'There had been a few of these parties in the past,' he told me, 'but this was the biggest one yet. It was heavily advertised. No wonder the police found out about it. There was really nothing illegal going on. They were just looking for a way to intimidate us.'

Bruno remembers being at the party, in a grand old Forest Town house, and feeling 'a tap on my shoulder. I turned round, and there was this man dressed in a suit who said, "Excuse me lady, you're under arrest for masquerading." He said *lady!* I suddenly got cold and this very handsome policeman said, "Don't worry, dearie," and helped me into my coat. In the car one of these policemen put his hand up my skirt, I'm sure it was just to see. We were taken to The Grays, and then to Marshall Square. They call me into a room. They tell me to strip, until I am standing just in a black bra with a red suspender belt holding up the stockings, and the cottonwool sticking out of the bra. And men's underpants.'

'Why *men's* underpants' I asked, on cue.

'If you were ever caught wearing women's underpants, the charge would be more. It was somehow better to be caught wearing men's underpants; we knew this.' Bruno paid a ten-rand admission-of-guilt fee and was discharged; his camp, throwaway rendition of the experience masks the trauma that followed. The police released the names of the offenders along with their mugshots, which were published on the front page of the Afrikaans *Beeld* newspaper, faces barely concealed by an 'X' taped over the eyes. Michele was in his salon the next day, working on a client, when he heard his name announced over the radio news. The humiliation and distress of this public exposure was the worst moment of his life.

Three years before the riots following the police raid of a gay bar in Greenwich Village, South Africa underwent its own Stonewall moment. The raid provoked a massive public outcry, and a Parliamentary Commission of Inquiry was launched. According to the official police report, officers had found 'a party in progress, the like of which has never been seen in this country. Mr P.C. Pelser, the justice minister, proclaimed: 'we should not allow ourselves to be deceived into thinking that we may casually dispose of this viper in our midst by regarding it as innocent fun. It is a proven fact that sooner or later homosexual instincts make their effects felt on a community if they are permitted to run riot.'

'Queers' were as threatening to the white civilisation as communists or miscegenating heterosexuals, and the state proposed legislation that would make it illegal to be homosexual. A spirited defence by a 'Law Reform' movement developed within the gay community; one of its leaders was Joe Garmeson, and its meticulous submissions managed to temper the legislation. Nonetheless, three amendments were finally made in 1969 to the very Immorality Act under which Pam Beira and Joe Louw had been arrested in 1962: the first was to raise the age of consent for male homosexual acts from sixteen to nineteen; the second was to outlaw dildoes (which, police reported, were the primary tools of the trade of lesbianism); and the third was the infamous 'men at a party' clause, which criminalised any 'male person who commits with another male person at a party any act which is calculated to stimulate sexual passion or give sexual gratification'. Most absurd was the definition of a 'party': 'any occasion where more than two persons are present'.

*

By any definition, there was a 'party' going on, in roughly the same era as the Wychwood Road raid, in the 'boy's room' inhabited by a domestic worker named Peter, coincidentally also in Forest Town.

I heard about this scene from Phil, an older black gay man, who was explaining to me how he shuttled between his straight life in Soweto – he was married, with children – and his gay life in the city.

Phil was a married grandfather; he owned a home in a middle-class part of Soweto and drove a car, and had been retired for a few years from his clerical job at a commercial company in the city. Wiry and lightskinned with a neatly trimmed peppercorn beard and expressive crescent-shaped eyes, he had a stammer that might have been exacerbated by age, but was nonetheless full of gentle mischief and somewhat blunt lasciviousness; he was known as 'Mr Soweto', he told me, because of his popularity with the young men, a trail of whom were always in his wake.

We got to the stories about 'Peter's Place' in Forest Town in a rather roundabout way. I had asked him where, in the days of high apartheid, he had been able to hang out in the city – beyond, of course, the toilets at Park Station where he did most of his cottaging. He told me about the Non-European Dining Room at Park Station, established by the authorities to show the world that blacks really were 'separate but equal'. It might have been an apartheid PR exercise, but it was also, Phil said, 'the only place in town' where black people were afforded the dignity of being able to 'sit down and have a drink, and eat a meal'.

According to Phil, most of the waiters at the restaurant were gay and, very quickly, a subculture developed around them. Telling me this story, Phil slid into another, about female prostitutes, who also frequented the restaurant. They would be picked up by white johns outside the station, and when they went back to the johns' homes in the suburbs, they would make an arrangement with the servant in the back room: if the house was raided, the working girl would rush into the 'boy's room' and climb into bed with him, pretending she was his girlfriend. She might be charged with contravening pass regulations, but at least she (and her client) would evade the far more severe Immorality Act.

The reason why Phil was telling me this story became clear, as he continued. It was a story about curfew and what one did if one missed the last train. Instead of running to the station, where the police would be waiting to pile all the laggards into their vans and haul them off to the Fort, you would make your way down the hill to Forest

Town, and end up – like the prostitutes – in a 'boy's room': in this instance, Peter's place.

From the way Phil tells it, you might indeed *plan* to miss the last train back to Soweto: 'Oh brother,' he said, slapping his thigh, 'those were the days! His room would be full, so full of young men who are afraid to be roaming the streets at night.' As was often the custom, Peter raised his bed on sandbags and bricks to protect him from demons, 'and he would make a bedding all around him for everyone coming in. I remember one time it was so full that you couldn't open the door. I slept against the door, but in the morning, when I woke up, I was next to the bed, maybe even under the bed, because those were the days, if you have got someone gay next to you, you'd enjoy yourself for all the dry months that you never had a gay person with you!'

Forest Town was on page 17 of the *Holmden's*, between Jan Smuts Avenue and Oxford Road, on the route we would take into town when I was a little boy. As an adult, I have lived alongside the suburb for many years, first in Killarney just to its east, and then in Melville to its west. When I am in Johannesburg, I drive through the suburb once or twice a day. Each time I do, I get goosebumps thinking of the atomised geography of my home town; these two underground gatherings that happened contemporaneously in the same leafy old randlord suburb around the time of my first birthday, one in the main house and one in the boy's room, just across the yard and yet off-limits to each other.

*

It was not only the new 'men at a party' legislation that broke up the scene in Cape Town, on that rocky promontory point between Bachelors and Maidens. In the late 1960s, at around the time those photographs of my family were taken at Clifton, there were apparently complaints about housebreaking from white householders, and so the authorities erected a ten-foot-high fence right across the promontory. So determined were the authorities to prevent the coloureds from Maidens from crossing Bachelors into Clifton that the fence was actually extended, for about twenty feet, into the icy

Atlantic Ocean. The stated reason was to stop vagrancy and crime, but the net effect was to shut down one of Cape Town's last and most enduring spaces for cross-racial intimacy.

Whenever I am back in Cape Town, I make a point of going to the rocks between Bachelors and Maidens. Well beyond the end of apartheid, the fence had been left standing; when I visited one summer's evening a few years ago, I was mesmerised by the way its diamond mesh bisected the fiery and swaggering Atlantic sun as it set. In 2012, while I was writing these words, I returned once more. The fence was no longer there, although coloured working-class families were still huddled on one side, and well-oiled white tourists were splayed out on the other. Soldered into the rocks, the sturdy iron bars that once supported the fence still marched into the sea, a trace of the way old frontiers exert their force.

Spyglass Hill

It was only when I came back to South Africa in 1990 and began work-ing and living in Johannesburg that the *Street Guide to Witwatersrand* became a real navigational tool rather than simply a means of edifica-tion or meditation. I was in my mid twenties, and after my sequestered suburban childhood and my years studying and working abroad, I was distressed by how little I knew of the city of my birth. I lived in inner-city suburbs that I had only previously encountered through Dispatcher; of course, my years of study meant that I could direct someone effortlessly to Aberdeen Road Westdene or Hellier Street Troyeville, but now that I lived in these suburbs I was mesmerised by their vistas over the gritty city. This was not the undulating, wooded suburbia of my childhood; we lived in little Victorian houses on tiny plots, or in art-deco mansion blocks, and from our windows we could see the world.

Because I had studied and worked in the United States for seven years, I had missed the upheavals of the 1980s. My absence meant that, unlike so many of my peers, I had first encountered black town-ships neither as an army conscript nor as an anti-apartheid activist. I think I ruptured the boundaries of white South Africa and went into townships only twice, on trips home: once, with a friend who worked in squatter camps on the Cape Flats, and once researching a piece about 'culture as a weapon' in the anti-apartheid struggle. I came home, now, with an unfinished novel after the first year of a Masters of Fine Arts programme at Columbia. It was about a white South African curio collector named Miranda Charms who owned a bou-tique called Tristes Tropiques on Yeoville's trendy Rockey Street; her world falls apart when, on a buying trip, she crosses the boundary of the Tugela River into Zululand and a series of mishaps occurs, including the revelation that her assistant is in the ANC underground and on the run from the authorities. It owed more than I cared to admit at the time to Rian Malan's deeply anguished book, *My Traitor's Heart*, and had a bounded view of South Africa that was, when I looked at it after only a few weeks back home, so excruciatingly suburbanised and expatriated that I threw it away and devoted myself to exploring my home town and my country properly.

I worked mainly for the South African *Mail & Guardian*; with the *Street Guide to Witwatersrand* in the side-pocket of a succession of VW Golfs, I sought out assignments that took me to the furthest reaches of its pages, from the battlegrounds of the East Rand townships as political violence enveloped them, through to creepy intelligence sources on plots outside Boksburg; from brothels on the outer fringes of Randburg to gay shebeens in KwaThema. I spent days at hospitals in Tembisa; evenings at drag shows in Ennerdale. I actually went to Riverlea, that *Holmden's* island; I visited friends in Dobsonville and Eldorado Park, and attended funerals and political rallies in Soweto. Finally, I was able to send myself out across the city whose geography I had studied for so long, and my dispatching years meant that I always knew how to get there, even though I had no idea what I would find.

Along the way, I developed a journeyman's appreciation of the limits of cartography, particularly of the townships and the squatter camps mushrooming around them now that apartheid's 'influx control' regulations had broken down. In my absence, many of those numbered or blank streets had been humanised with names, but there were still many that remained unidentified. And if there were unnamed streets in the mapped world, then there were unmapped streets in the real world too: blank neverlands that revealed themselves to be throbbing with humanity, a problem that Map Studio tried to resolve by developing a striped shading in its legend for informal settlements. The stripes suggested danger and impenetrability, and did not do justice to the true porousness of these places.

The lack of detail was compounded by the fact that township

residents did not use street names at all, even if they were belatedly named in the *Street Guide*, but rather – perhaps by force of habit – the bureaucratic numbers originally assigned by the township planners: '1418 Zola' or '2520 Vosloorus'. The residents were also maddeningly – if understandably, and often endearingly – imprecise: 'You go to the robot, and then you via the garage ['via' being a verb in the South African vernacular] and once you have passed the church you must ask someone where Ma Khumalo's house is.' The dispatcher in me railed against this even as the romantic in me was attracted to the notion of community it implied. I, after all, had not grown up in a world where you could find me by saying 'Turn right at the Goldbergs' big white wall with the two rottweilers snarling at the gate and then ask someone where Ma Gevisser lives.'

My partner C and I bought our own first home together in 1994; we watched the South African transition from apartheid to democracy from our vantage point on Hellier Street, a tree-lined cul-de-sac that climbed up the back of Troyeville Ridge, in a house that was built in 1899, with a broad front *stoep* up a sweep of stairs under deep Cape Dutch gables. How thrilling to be, finally, in the single digits of the inner city. I knew, from my dispatching childhood, that pages 7 and 9 where I now lived had among the best street names to be found in the *Holmden's*; now, as I zigzagged up and down the ridge on streets called Arethusa and Benbow, Barossa and Boxer, I scored my own tracks into Johannesburg's landscape for what felt like the first time. We lived opposite the Marymount Maternity Home – where generations of Joburgers had been born – and 'the Gandhi House', a glorious belle-époque villa incorrectly identified as the Mahatma's Johannesburg residence (he had, in fact, lived a few houses higher, up the ridge, in the first years of the twentieth century). I had been raised in a world that I thought of as 'new': the homes of my childhood were new-builds in new suburbs with new gardens that settled around us as we grew up. In Troyeville, though, there seemed to be depth and density: we lived cheek-by-jowl with old working-class Portuguese families, young urban hipsters, and – as the decade progressed – black Mozambican migrants and coloured and Indian families too.

Suddenly, too, there was desperate poverty in the inner city as apartheid's gates opened and landless peasants moved to town, renting by the room or by the square metre from landlords who could no longer sell their properties due to 'red-lining' – the refusal of banks to grant mortgages on purchases in the inner-city suburbs. Just down the road from us, in Jeppe, were Zulu single-sex migrant hostels, and so the violence that engulfed the reef in the early 1990s was on our doorstep too.

Although apartheid was only formally ended when F.W. de Klerk announced the unbanning of the liberation movements in 1990, the system had in fact begun its inexorable collapse in the early 1980s, through what the political analyst John Kane-Berman astutely termed 'the Silent Revolution': black people defying the Group Areas Act (which prescribed certain areas for each race) by moving into the inner city, close to work. Hillbrow became the focus of this revolution because of its proximity to town, its profusion of cheap accommodation, and its porous and somewhat libertine reputation as a haven for migrants and misfits. The authorities tried, half-heartedly, to stem the tide, but when a court ruled that the city would have to find alternative housing for evicted black families, the system capitulated and Hillbrow was declared a 'grey area'.

By the time I moved back to Johannesburg, Granny Gertie had long forsaken the neighbourhood and moved into a Sandton retirement village; her residential hotel was now surrounded by buildings controlled by the Nigerian drug syndicates that battled for control over Hillbrow with the more established Balkan mafia. The Great Synagogue, where I had my bar mitzvah, with its incongruous Byzantine domes presiding over Wolmarans Street, became a fried-chicken outlet; the congregation gutted its interior and rebuilt a small-scale replica in the Northern Suburbs.

Some time later, in the early 2000s, when I was working on Constitution Hill, we sent a researcher to interview the residents of the apartment blocks on King George Street overlooking the Old Fort to ask them what they would like to see in the development. These flats were now rented by the square metre to economic refugees, mainly from Zimbabwe. The researcher came back with astonishing feedback: the new tenants had barely even noticed the frenetic construction happening within the ramparts just beneath them. This was not just because the stunning views north were now almost totally blocked by the perpetual laundry of too many people living in too small a space, but because they were illegal immigrants who feared xenophobic harassment and arrest. They kept their heads down, as blind to the view as the white people had once been, living in those same blocks when Bob Gosani took his *tausa* images, when Cecil Williams's friends threw their parties and couldn't see him, detained during the 1960 State of Emergency, in the courtyard of the Fort below.

Not Spyglass Hill.

*

When I returned to South Africa in mid 1990, I found a group of activists in the midst of preparations for the country's first ever Gay and Lesbian Pride March. They were led by Simon Nkoli, a high-profile anti-apartheid activist and former political trialist who was the movement's icon, and many of the organisers had backgrounds in the anti-apartheid struggle. I had been a willing foot soldier in the AIDS activist movement in New York in the late Eighties but now, for the first time, I felt I had found a political home. I was among fellow South Africans, black and white, who made the connections I had been grasping at somewhat unconsciously since my childhood, trying to find the links between my own sense of alienation because of an illicit sexuality and the subordinate position of the majority of my compatriots.

Despite the encroaching poverty and the way inequality became more visible once the barriers protecting the apartheid city had been lifted, there was still, in the interregnum, a wilful optimism to Johannesburg's vitality. Hillbrow's gay bars were as busy and as racially mixed as they would ever be, as were the cafes on Rockey Street and the cinemas around the Carlton Centre. When the annual Pride march squeezed through those Hillbrow canyons that had impressed me so much as a child, the effect was exhilarating: people of all colours waving and cheering as the carnival rolled down Pretoria Street. This seemed to be the spirit that enabled the drafters of South Africa's democratic constitution to forge a Bill of Rights that explicitly protected people from discrimination on the basis of sexual orientation.

I secured a statement of support for the Pride March from the just-unbanned African National Congress, through Albie Sachs, the former freedom-fighter who had lost an arm and an eye due to a letter bomb, and who would be partly responsible for the equality clause in the constitution. Later, as a judge on the Constitutional Court, Sachs would write the brilliant judgment enabling same-sex marriage. Such was the anxiety about disclosure at that first Pride march, however, that we agreed to provide paper bags for closeted marchers to wear. In the final event, the rains came down, pulping our decision and exposing those few who had chosen to be concealed; years later I met one of these, an Afrikaans woman, who described the Chicken Little experience of it. The only thing that fell on her head was rain, she told me, and she has marched ever since.

In 1996, just after South Africa's new constitution was passed, out-lawing discrimination on the basis of sexual orientation, I watched a particularly edgy transgendered woman howling at the crowds as she sashayed through Hillbrow, yelling 'I'm in the Constitution!' to the onlookers lining the streets. I approached her afterwards to ask her what, exactly, her new empowerment meant. She was reeking of cheap booze, but still astonishingly articulate: 'It means sweet motherfuck-ing nothing at all. You can rape me, rob me, what am I going to do when you attack me? Wave the constitution in your face? I'm just a nobody black queen.' She paused, and then her face lost its mask of bravado and bitterness. 'But you know what? Ever since I heard about that constitution, I feel free inside."

*

Thirteen years later, as I write these words, the Johannesburg Pride parade is in a state of some turmoil. By 2012 it had become so depoliticised – a commercial party, really – that a group of activists from a campaign called One-In-Nine took the decision to disrupt it. The group takes its name from the statistic that one woman out of nine in South Africa is a victim of sexual assault; the protest was against the number of black lesbians who had been killed or assaulted in 'corrective rape' attacks, and the lack of action the authorities were taking to deal with the crisis. The activists interrupted the parade with a 'die-in', calling on the Pride participants to join them for a thirty-second action, but the Pride organisers reacted with vehement aggression, kicking and dragging the protestors, and even threatening to drive their vehicles over them. Although, indeed, a large number of the Pride celebrants are black, the organisers were white, and looking at the footage of the incident, it is hard not to read it through the prism of race.

In the years prior to this, I had begun interviewing gay, lesbian, and transgender refugees in South Africa who were seeking asylum on the basis of having been persecuted back home because of their sexual orientation or gender identity. Despite South Africa's progressive constitution, however, many of them were too scared to reveal that they were gay to the overworked and surly officials of the Department of Home Affairs who governed their destiny. Emile, for example, was a somewhat delicate and shy Burundian man in his twenties who sought refugee status on the basis of political persecution. His father, indeed, had been hacked to death before his eyes because he was a member of the minority Tutsi tribe, but the reason Emile fled his native land, he told me, was that he had been caught in bed with his male lover and arrested. After bribing his way out of jail and passing through six countries in six weeks locked in the back of a trafficker's van, he arrived in Johannesburg and sought help from a gay organisation he had found online.

I met him about a year later, some time after he had been granted temporary status while his case was assessed. It was in mid 2008, shortly after an outburst of xenophobic violence that had started in Alexandra township, eventually causing the murders of sixty-two people and the displacement of an estimated 100,000 across the country. Black migrants and refugees in South Africa lived under constant fear of xenophobic harassment by locals who believed – in an environment of dire unemployment – that foreigners were taking their jobs, their homes, their women. And then there was the constant threat of crime on the streets of South Africa's cities: Emile had been mugged and stabbed in Pretoria and was so now so fearful that he did not have the courage to go job-seeking, despite the safety that his temporary refugee status allegedly gave him. He had found a middle-aged white boyfriend and lived with him in the suburb of Parktown North: 'I am happy that you have the constitution,' he said to me, 'but it means nothing to me, as I am a non-South African, and as far as I can tell it does not seem to protect me.'

In 2013, at a refugees' rights organisation in Cape Town called Passop – People Against Suffering, Oppression and Poverty – I spoke to gay and transgender refugees who told me that Emile's relationship had collapsed and that he had returned to Burundi. One of them was a young Congolese named Junior Mayema: he was slight and effeminate, like Emile – immediately identifiable as a gay – but fiercely assertive and articulate. He fled Kinshasa in 2010 during his second year at law school, he told me, because of the perpetual harassment, and death threats from members of his family. He had read online that same-sex marriage was legal in South Africa and so he had found his way to Cape Town and applied for asylum – unlike Emile, on the basis of his sexual orientation: 'I am gay,' he told the Home Affairs official, a black woman.

She was incredulous. 'But there are no gays in the rest of Africa,' she said. 'We only have them here in South Africa."

'Look at me,' Mayema responded, suggesting in the retelling that he might have been camping it up a bit. 'Tell me I am not gay.'

He was given the temporary asylum permit, but by the time I met him two years later he had decided to apply to the UN High Commission for Refugees for resettlement to a third country. He had come to see, he told me, that he was even less safe in South Africa than he had been in the Congo.

As far as Passop could tell, only four refugees had been granted asylum on the basis of sexual orientation or gender identity by 2014. Junior told me stories about the way he and others had been victimised by officials and by others in the queue at Home Affairs. He also showed me photographs of his swollen, bloody face after having been gay-bashed; when he reported it at the local police station, he was jeered at and told to go back to the Congo. 'In Kinshasa I experienced homophobia,' he told me. 'But here I experience homophobia, xenophobia, and racism.'

I have met other African gay and lesbian migrants in South Africa who have found enough economic security, through work, to hedge themselves against the constant threats of xenophobia and crime. I know two Nigerian men in their late twenties, for example – a microbiologist and an economist, both now working as traders – who are determined to stay in South Africa, where they earn well and where they could imagine living freely with their partners, away from the perpetual family pressure to get married. But talking to Junior and his comrades in Passop I found myself devastated by the bitterness and sense of grievance they harboured toward their current host country.

Listening to Junior and his fellow refugees, I have been thinking about how much the psychic trauma of displacement must be exacerbated by shattered expectations. This has led me back to consider my own family's migrations, and their comparatively easy landings. How much more difficult it must be when the imagined sanctuary turns out to be less secure than the home you were forced to leave behind.

Umtshotsho

In April 2009 I found myself in Town on an autumn evening, inching down rush-hour Jeppe Street in the swirling cacophony of hooting and hustling and hawking, dodging overstuffed minibus taxis and overburdened commuters, driving eastwards through the canyons of Little Ethiopia. The buildings where I used to visit doctors and buy my brandy-balls have been gutted, transformed into multi-level markets run by cartels of East African traders. Their smooth modernist skins of concrete and glass now provide protection to these immigrant traders, from the xenophobia and crime on the city's streets, as they sell cheap Chinese goods to the crowds of poor people coursing along Jeppe Street on their way to or from the taxi ranks.

Each of these vertical internal cities is organised around a coffee shop and restaurant, and this is where Johannesburg's Ethiopian community now gathers, in suites that still sometimes have plaques, outside, bearing the names of the Jewish doctors who once peered down my ears and into my eyes. 'Medical Arts' is now 'Majesty', 'Lancet Hall' now 'Johannesburg Wholesale Centre No. 2', and all services have been privatised, including the provision of water and electricity – and, of course, security – to the merchants inside. Every time I drive past these cities within cities, or enter them for a coffee or a meal, I think of their facades as the latest iteration, in my home town, of that space between page 75 and page 77 in the *Holmden's*, another frontier opening out into another borderland; another laager, too, certainly, and also another wall. You could drive down Jeppe Street every day of your life and have no clue about the new residents burrowing like hermit crabs into these sleek glass and concrete cubes.

I brought my car to a stop and parked, eventually, at the end of Jeppe Street, against a little square that I remember well from my teenage years because it was home to the nightclub Idols: I used to go there occasionally with my friends, pretending not only to be eighteen but gay, too, so we could get in. The guys in my group would pair up with each other and so would the girls; the first time we did this, the flames of shame and excitement licked against each other inside me with such intensity that I was convinced the old queen at the door, if she cared, would notice, and rumble my double-cover. Inside, amped up on the poppers we bought at the bar, I would try desperately to avert my gaze from the semi-naked men dancing in what I remember to be cages. No one, alas, ever called my bluff.

In those days, you'd find junkies and rent boys in the shard of park that slivered up to the railway lines at Noord Street; all white. Later, driving past it in the years following the collapse of the inner city, I noted that the park had become the preserve of homeless people and drunks and barely dressed teenage prostitutes, all black, gathered round bonfires in what felt like post-apocalyptic pods on cold winter evenings. Now, with brightly coloured low-cost housing developments all around and the city's redevelopment of the park, the scene I pulled up to could have been in Brooklyn or London's East End: an inner-city playground, mothers with shopping bags watching as a coach cajoled kids around a miniature football field; some men holding up a corner with their over-animated expostulation.

*

There is always a corner of optimism in Johannesburg, the promise of vitality, the prospector's dream, and I was here, that evening, for just such a glimmer, a visit to the artist Nicholas Hlobo, perhaps the most celebrated of South Africa's new generation of global art stars. Hlobo worked from a studio in an old factory here, on the eastern fringe of town, not far from the new Arts on Main development with its art galleries, restaurants, artists' lofts and trendy hotel, but in a neighbourhood that was, even if in the process of being rehabilitated, by no means gentrified. Hlobo, in his mid thirties when I met him, appropriates the (traditionally female) Xhosa art of needlework through sculpture and tapestry, stitching cut-up rubber tyre together with coloured ribbons into intense tableaux of his own relationship with Xhosa rites. He stitches himself, too, into these tableaux through edgy gender-disruptive performance that is severely at odds with his rather diffident personal manner and his slight, unassuming physicality.

I was visiting Hlobo to see his latest work, *Umtshotsho*. In traditional Xhosa society, the *umtshotsho* is a peer-regulated youth organisation that holds parties for adolescents: mock-fighting, dancing and dating take place, a dry run, as it were, for lives of war and procreation, to channel the libidos of adolescents before the boys go off to be initiated into adulthood by circumcision. He walked me through his work, a gathering of massive, multivalent, amoebic, hermaphroditic figures hanging from the ceiling or slumped into chairs, gathered in huddles as if at a party in a living-room. I told him that I thought my own *umtshotsho* parties were those painful Saturday nights I endured throughout my teenage years, where you'd look for a dark gap among all that rampant heterosexual activity from which you might ogle the male object of your desire, and fantasise about pulling him in for a quick and surreptitious encounter.

A couple of memories washed over me in Hlobo's loft, as I wandered through his *umtshotsho*. An afternoon school bus ride home, in the tenth grade; my best friend, Bradley – the school stud – decides that I have to break my virginity, not knowing, of course, that I have been fucking Adam for several years already. There is fevered discussion on the bus, and a weeping girl in a front seat. Her name is Gina, she is fat, the 'school slut', in love with Bradley. He has told her that he will fuck her only if she fucks me first. The entire bus seems to divide on the issue – should she do it or shouldn't she? – and one of my loyal girlfriends comes shuffling over to me shamefacedly (or mischievously) to reveal the plan: Bradley will invite me over to his house to help him with homework, and ask me to get some books out of the cottage in the back. When I get there, Gina will be lying on the bed, naked, covered in the American flag. So well developed is the plot that a soundtrack has even been chosen: my deflowering will take place to the swooping guitar of David Bowie's 'Ziggy Stardust', a deep irony, given that this ambisexual anthem provided me with some of the most powerful lyrics for my budding homosexuality. I storm off the bus, furious and humiliated – but nowhere near as humiliated, I imagine, as poor Gina; I find an affliction to keep me away from school for the next few days.

Another Northern Suburbs *umtshotsho*: an afternoon at the Killarney flat of one of the wilder mothers of our set of friends; let's call her Jeannie. Bradley arranges for six girls to come over – I think they were from posh Roedean School – for the six of us guys, and a pairing-off takes place. It is worse than being picked for teams at school: eventually there are just two of us left, myself and an equally miserable girl. Jeannie, stoned, frantically tries to convince us that even if we are not attracted to each other we should take the opportunity of experimenting with each other as this will stand us in good stead for later in our lives, and the poor girl eyes me with terror. I suggest we go for a walk and she readily agrees, in part, I imagine, to flee Jeannie. We wander around the suburb for a while, talking about school and our shared interest in drama, and agree that when we get back to the flat we will say we went to The Wilds and snogged. I don't even remember her name, and I never saw her again; she was the first person to whom I said the words, 'I'm gay.'

These memories came washing over me as I wandered through Nicholas Hlobo's studio, permeated by the acrid smell of the rubber he was working with. His own *umtshotsho*, I saw, might be humorous and playful, but the features on his characters' often ghoulish mask-like faces derived unmistakeably from traditional Xhosa practices of scarification. They brought blood to the surface in an expression of manifest pain and vulnerability. You might, like any kid at a party – like the way I felt on the school bus or in Jeannie's Killarney lounge – sometimes feel lost or panicky rather than welcomed and affirmed at this *umtshotsho*. The installation was bathed in red light emanating from a lamp on a side-table; the colour flashed danger as well as desire.

Up on Hlobo's pinboard, to the side of the burgeoning installation, there was a quick, but powerful, little sketch: two bodies under a blanket, the shapes suggesting one mounting the other, and the words 'the *soma*'. *UkuSoma* is the Xhosa word for the kind of regulated, non-penetrative thigh-sex that adolescents are encouraged to practise at an *umtshotsho*, where the passive party can be either a boy or a girl. Hlobo did not experience this himself: he was barred from participating in the *umtshotsho*, he

told me, because he came from a Christian family that eschewed the traditional Xhosa rituals. Was this *umtshotsho* artwork he had created, then, part of a fantasy – something he had imagined to compensate for the one he might have been denied as a teenager?

He responded, with a kind of light laughter, that although he had a lover while at school in the Transkei, it was only when he came to Johannesburg in 1994 to work that he had found his own *umtshotsho*.

Lodging with an aunt in Tembisa township and coming into town every day to work measuring cement bags, he became thoroughly bored and began wandering the city, creating his own coordinates by discovering and mapping the urban environment around him. It was in this way that he stumbled into the Artist Proof Studio in Newtown and eventually found his way to the fine arts programme at the Technikon. It was this way, too, that he found himself at the magazine rack in CNA on Commissioner Street, looking surreptitiously at an edition of *Exit*, the gay magazine, and – too nervous actually to buy it – scribbling down the address for the Skyline, Joburg's iconic gay bar at the Harrison Reef Hotel on the corner of Pretoria and Twist Streets in Hillbrow.

'It was very difficult to find, no signs, it was like you needed a password,' Hlobo remembered. 'There are these steps but you do not know where they lead to, so I walked up and down.' He asked, but no one seemed to know of the place. 'Then I came across these drag queens and I thought, "Aha! These are the people I should ask!" "Oh come with us darling, we going there," they said, and I followed them. I was so nervous I tripped on the stairs.' Thus did the Skyline Bar become Nicholas Hlobo's *umtshotsho*. He would be there every day, rushing to get the train back to Tembisa in time for dinner.

*

It is a source of wonder to me now that I did not know, during my frequent teenage scuttles down Hillbrow's Pretoria Street from the bus stop to Exclusive Books and Estoril, that I was walking along the 'high street' of one of the world's first 'gay villages' outside of North America; a mini-Castro all of three city blocks long that had been bustling since the Sixties. 'When I started living in Hillbrow [in the Seventies],' a gay man remembered nostalgically when I interviewed him in the early 1990s, 'I used to go to a gay butcher, a gay tailor, a gay greengrocer. There were gay or gay-friendly restaurants all the way up and down Pretoria Street. So you felt safe. You didn't really care. We'd often walk with linked arms or even kiss on the street.'

I had a sense of this, of course, from the number of gay men sitting at the pavement tables at the Three Sisters Café, crammed into Estoril Books, or just cruising up and down Pretoria Street, their sweet fragrance trailing their leather. But I did not know about the Skyline until 1984 or so, when, I too, saw an advert for it in the gay magazine of the time – it was still called the Butterfly Bar then – and went to the bar on one of my early visits back from Yale.

The Butterfly Bar

Meet friends, share jokes and enjoy the excellent service in an atmosphere that's made The Butterfly Bar a way of life.

Harrison Reef Hotel
Corner Twist & Pretoria Streets
Hillbrow - Johannesburg

The Butterfly had the feeling of a small-town community gathering point, with all sorts clustered along the long counter. There were glamorous fashion-world types, older men in leathers, gaunt junkies and, down at the end of the bar, the rough trade, Afrikaans boys from the working-class western or southern suburbs there to turn tricks; all presided over by the elderly, toothless, Granny Lee, a coloured transvestite who passed for white.

The gay pastor Paul Mokgethi has told me how he and a group of teenage friends from Soweto who called themselves the 'Ted Dynas Club', after the gay character who was killed in the TV series *Dynasty*, found out about the Skyline when they started coming into Johannesburg in the mid Eighties. Apart from Granny Lee there were no other black people in the bar at the time, even though Hillbrow was already very much a 'grey area': it was, in fact, illegal to have black people and white people together in a place where liquor was being served. Mokgethi remembers the explicit racism the Ted Dynas lads encountered from the patrons when they entered, and how they were protected by a barman named Norman who would give them Cokes but no alcohol and who carved a little space for them down at the end of the bar, by the rent boys. I remember the young black men from my visits to the bar in the mid Eighties: they were jumpy and preening and reminded me of chickens, given to staccato bouts of self-conscious campery. I am ashamed to admit that I assumed that they were working boys, rather than teenagers simply looking for their own *umtshotsho*, just as I had been a few years previously in Hillbrow and Nicholas Hlobo would be a few years later.

Michele Bruno, the cross-dresser who had been arrested at that Forest Town party in 1966, had been a regular at the bar since its inception in the late Sixties, and he recalled it, for me, at the same time that the Ted Dynas Club and I would have visited it: 'There were two doors. One going into the hotel was where the smart gays sat, and one opening onto the street was the "rough trade". My chair was on the border. I was working at a salon in Killarney, and I'd drive up through The Wilds every evening to Hillbrow to spend some time at the Butterfly. It was my local.' But in the mid Eighties 'it started getting a bit rough. One was hearing stories about people taking home black guys and being beaten up and even murdered.' When the scene started changing, Michele stopped wearing his jewellery to the bar – and then stopped going altogether.

Was it the pioneering presence of gay people living in Hillbrow that turned the area into a tolerant 'liberated zone' of sorts, laying the groundwork for it to become Johannesburg's first deracialised neighbourhood in the 1980s? If so, there is irony in the way most white gay people moved out as soon as it did deracialise; those few who remained were enveloped by the new multiracial and then immigrant culture. Still, the Skyline remained the heart of Johannesburg's black gay scene for many years to come until it, too, moved out to the suburbs. GLOW (Gay and Lesbian Organisation of the Witwatersrand), the multiracial gay organisation I joined, held its meetings there and, upstairs in the ballroom of the Harrison Reef Hotel, Paul Mokgethi and his fellow elders conducted the Sunday morning services of their Hope and Unity Metropolitan Community Church, a black gay institution in the city, after evangelising in the bar downstairs the previous night. When GLOW's founder, Simon Nkoli, died of an AIDS-related illness in 1998, the city of Johannesburg put up a street sign on the corner of Pretoria and Twist, outside the bar, proclaiming it 'Simon Nkoli Corner'.

*

The flashing red light at my *umtshotsho*, once I was confident enough to explore my sexuality above ground, was the AIDS epidemic. I remember sitting with a group of friends at The Bar on Second Avenue in the East Village, in 1988, listening to the older activist Douglas Crimp: 'The tragedy of your generation is that you will never know what it means to have unprotected sex. The tragedy of my generation is that we do know.' I was in my early twenties, living in New York, with a couple of failed college love affairs behind me and a trail, too, of unrequited crushes. I was beginning my adult sexual and romantic life, and people were dying all around me: because they were gay, because they had sex. Particularly in the face of the way the epidemic aroused stigma against gay people, it was difficult – sometimes impossible – to keep at bay the notion of homosexuality itself as a deadly pathogen. I became a victim of this myself, when a homophobic doctor misdiagnosed a chronic-fatigue condition as AIDS in 1988, despite a negative HIV test. She thought the test was inaccurate and that I was lying about my sex life, or perhaps she convinced herself that my sexuality alone was the pathology. It took repeated tests with a more sympathetic doctor, and six months of crisis, to convince me that I was not infected. Among my many reasons for coming back to South Africa in 1990 one was, certainly, flight from the culture of morbidity that enveloped gay identity in New York at that time. This was folly, of course. The epidemic was as severe in Johannesburg as it was in New York, particularly among gay men, whom it hit first; it was just that nobody talked about it yet.

Coming back to South Africa meant abandoning a rocky year-old relationship with a fellow student at Columbia, a fellow African, from Ghana. Back home, I was quickly set up with a Jewish man very similar to me. We became inseparable friends, in the end, but never lovers, and I joked that if the world was divided into 'selfists' and 'otherists' then I was the latter: I needed somebody very different to me, in the end, to make up the whole. My first boyfriend, upon returning to South Africa, was a coloured man I met through GLOW, while organising the 1990 Pride march. In those first months home, I found other sexual partners too and few of them were white. This was neither a choice nor a conscious decision, but as I write these words now, with the heightened awareness of my dispatching tendencies, it does not seem strange to me at all. In fact, given my generation and my consciousness, it seems like destiny. It was 1990: Nelson Mandela was free, apartheid was over, and I was back in the city of my birth, trying to find those routes, across the gap between pages 75 and 77 of the *Holmden's*, that I had previously only imagined. Given the nature of my street-guide-named-desire, of course these routes would be sexual and romantic too.

So much for my theory of selfism and otherism. Very soon after my return I was introduced to C by my housemate because he felt we had much in common: we were both intellectuals, we were both politically minded but iconoclasts rather than party men, we had both recently returned to South Africa after many years studying in the United States, and we could both laugh at ourselves and the world. I knew, from very early on, that we saw things the same way, and I felt an immense relief come over me. This, I think, is what love means; I had found my life partner. We were on the same side of the runnel, the same side of the Sandspruit. No, let me amend that: we were both in the borderland itself, between pages 75 and 77, even though we came from different sides of the Sandspruit, drawing the patterns of our own life, our own Treasure Valleys, in the white space, the *terra incognita*, of a new relationship. That he was of Indian background and I white had symbolic value, to be sure, particularly in the early years of our relationship, which were the early years of South Africa's freedom.

But it quickly became just another detail to be plotted onto the map of our lives together, like the fact that he is Hindu and I am Jewish, or that he is from Durban and I from Johannesburg, or that he works in public policy and I am a writer, or that he is considered and I am impetuous.

Edenvale

It took C and I more than eighteen years to tie the knot. South Africa legalised same-sex marriage in 2006; we might have done it before then, as many of our friends did in private commitment ceremonies, but we had little interest in the rites and symbolism of marriage, even after it had become one of our new rights. We decided to do it, three years later, solely because it would facilitate our move to France, where C had been offered a job. It was, we told each other, merely an administrative matter. We could have done it more easily — through a gay rabbi I know, for example, or a gay judge who is a friend – but we wanted to see the system work for us, and so we decided to go to one of the Home Affairs offices. Even though we lived in Melville, on the other side of town, we chose Edenvale, because friends had had a positive experience there. And so, on a January morning in 2009, I drove across Johannesburg to a satellite town that was not even in the *Holmden's*, to make the booking.

On arrival, I was not encouraged. The office was on a scrappy strip of motor repair shops and panel-beaters and, like all Home Affairs offices, it was grimy and arcane, contemptuous and chaotic; the last place on earth you would want to get married. In the old days, the Department of Home Affairs had been the processing room of apartheid: it told you who you were and where you could (and could not) be. It was still a place of profound alienation, of a thousand frustrations and rages a day.

And I was about to have one of them. I had been waiting in the queue since 2.30, and had only made it to the front just after 3.00. Although the office closed at 3.30, processing stopped half an hour before and I was just too late, I was told. I would have to go home and come back tomorrow. I was on the brink of a spirited lecture on the meaning of 'Batho Pele', the government's new slogan of 'People First', when one of the women behind the desk looked up at me, gold hoops in her ears to match her attitude, and barked: 'Same sex or opposite sex?'

It took me a moment to comprehend. 'Same sex,' I said, a little too loudly, looking around to see if any of the other clerks in the room would look up in shock, or perhaps just interest. They did not.

'The marriage officer likes to do the same-sexes early in the morning,' the woman said briskly, consulting her book. 'Too much paperwork, you people. You've made our lives much more difficult.'

Before I could protest, the woman shoved a form across to me, noting the time and date of our appointment. Pulling out a green highlighter, she underlined a reminder that at least two witnesses were required. 'We have room for twenty,' she said, 'so bring all your friends and family.'

'No, no.' I protested. 'It'll be just two. We don't want to make a fuss.'

'Why not?' When I shrugged and spluttered an answer ('purely an administrative matter'), she looked at me severely: 'A marriage is a big deal. Make a fuss. Don't forget the rings.'

We would not be doing rings.

'Why not?' she repeated, before answering her own question: 'Ah, you don't want to make a fuss!' And then, in counselling mode: 'Do you think you are a second-class citizen just because you are gay? You have full rights in this new South Africa. You have the right to make a fuss. I think you need to go home and have a very serious chat with your partner. We will see you on the 22 of February. With witnesses and rings. Goodbye.'

Here I was, an entirely empowered middle-class middle-aged white man, being lectured by a young black woman about my rights. And here we were, three weeks later, with rings but, alas, only two witnesses, our friends Philip and Sedica, being ushered up the stairs by a delightful security guard who told Sedica that she was a beautiful bride but who shifted the compliment effortlessly to me when corrected.

We found ourselves in 'Room 8: Marriages' at the back of the building, overlooking a scrapyard next door. It was a parallel universe: the room was draped in lace the same colour-palette as the orange-and-brown dried wildflowers set in vases between white porcelain swans. There were wedding photos of various couples tacked on the walls and, on every available surface, cascades of what turned out to be, on closer inspection, empty ring-boxes.

'You like it?' trilled a voice behind us. An older Afrikaans woman had entered. She introduced herself as Mrs Austin: she was actually in finance, but she loved marrying people so much that she had applied for a licence and now did it two mornings a week. 'This is all my work,' she said of Room 8, explaining that every couple she married was invited to leave its ring-boxes behind, and that among these boxes were 'same-sex' ones. She was proud of the fact that she had married more gay couples than anyone else in the province.

Mrs Austin made no secret of her disappointment at our lack of campery: where were the feathers, where the champagne? After some jocularity over whom would be the 'man' by signing the register first, she led us through an unmemorably bureaucratic script ending in 'I do' and a kiss before presiding over what was clearly, for her, the more significant part of the proceedings: the swopping of the rings. I slipped onto C's finger a delicate band of red gold fretted in the South Indian style of his ancestors, while he screwed onto mine a thick chunk of silver. Exhaling approval, Mrs Austin extracted a red heart-shaped ring-box from her installation and balanced it between our two hands, which she delicately arranged for a photograph. We spent more time on this ritual than we had on the actual ceremony, and as we posed, I admired the contrasting styles of our rings and what they said about our relationship.

It was, in the end, the lack of moment of it all – the unportentousness, if there is such a word – which finally moved me. Even though Mrs Austin kept on referring to us as 'same-sex' and heterosexuals as 'normal', we were swept out of Room 8 on a tide of hilarity and we giggled all the way to breakfast. Even the fact that she could not furnish us with a marriage certificate – the computers had been down for six weeks because someone had stolen the cables – did not defuse the good feelings. We were a white man and a black man, free to be together in the country of our birth, treated with dignity and humanity and much good-natured humour by a system which had denied both for so long.

Well worth the fuss.

The Ballad of Phil and Edgar

Although C never takes his wedding ring off his finger, mine sits in a bowl on my desk amid the flotsam of a work-at-home life: clips, coins and lozenges, bits and pieces of technology, a passport photo. I often fish the ring out and fiddle with it while I work, as I am doing right now. I screw it on and off, I flick it into goalposts made of books, I tap it against the teapot. I weigh it in my palm and am impressed, each time anew, with its heft. When I rub it, I conjure the empty rows of chairs at Mrs Austin's chapel on the day we were married and I fill them with family and friends, with characters fictional and historical, with all the people we might have invited to witness our union had we succumbed to one of the more conventional affairs that grace our families' respective photo-albums.

My parents are always there, at this imaginary Edenvale, as are C's parents, whom I never met. So too are two older men, Edgar and Phil, whom I have interviewed several times over the past decade. Phil was the man who told me about his curfew-busting evenings at 'Peter's place' in Forest Town; Edgar his oldest and closest friend. It would be presumptuous to call these men fathers, or mentors, or even friends: we did not, for example, invite them to the farewell party we held shortly after our marriage, at which we revealed to our astonished friends that we had eloped. But such is the pleasure of an empty chapel: you can fill it retrospectively, endlessly, variously, and I often find Edgar and Phil there, sitting on those grey office chairs amid the ring-boxes and the swans.

*

Their own wedding bands were the first things I noticed when I met Phil and his friend Edgar for the first time in 1998, at a Soweto tavern named Scotch's Place. Both rings were assertive and masculine, planed rather than curved, and spoke of the substance and solidity of their wearers. Edgar, like Phil, was a married grandfather; he owned a home in a middle-class part of Soweto and drove a car; he was approaching retirement from his own clerical job at a commercial company in town.

These were the days when a wedding ring still meant you were straight, or in the closet. And so Edgar and Phil's fingers flashed a particular code as the two men sat in the semi-obscurity of Scotch's interior, having chosen a table that put them directly in the flight path between the door to the yard and the bar. As patrons streamed in and out, Phil or Edgar would mutter something sotto voce, and a young man or two would linger for a moment, engage in conversation and maybe sit down. By the time I left, three hours later, chairs had been pulled up all around them and tables pulled together. All these kids had impossibly waspy waists, with button-down shirts neatly tucked into smartly pressed jeans, or tank tops riding well above the navel: 'Look at them,' Phil said, with desire and disapproval. 'We were not as free as they are today. Today they are very free. Very showy. You can see them miles away. I won't go around with a boy in a skinny top and a belly button outside, no. No, no, no, no.'

Edgar and Phil themselves dressed with conservative style – sharp shoes, crisply ironed slacks, Pringle shirts, fine watches. If Phil was diminutive and light-skinned, Edgar was tall, dark, and well built – 'a typical Zulu man', Phil riposted playfully, pinching him in the side. Edgar had the easy, straightforward confidence of a matinee idol or the lay preacher that he was: his shirt collar was opened to a gold chain, and he was given to exuberant laughter and emphatic stress.

The men bantered gently with each other, their intimacy suggesting that they might be old and comfortable lovers, which is how many saw them, although neither used this term to describe the other. Their friend Roger – a white man who introduced me to them, and them to each other – told me that he believed that in another life, a free life, Phil and Edgar would have been a couple. Over the course of our relationship both suggested to me, in one way or another, that this might have been so.

Both men moved to Johannesburg with their families during the war-time boom years when they were little boys: Edgar from Zululand and Phil from the farmlands of the Orange Free State province. Both families settled in Pimville, the black township that was the germ of Soweto, although Edgar and Phil would meet only as adults. Their fathers found jobs and their mothers took in washing. And so Edgar and Phil, like so many sons of Soweto, would be sent into town to fetch and drop the laundry at white people's homes.

As happens with boys all over the world when they discover trains and cities, their lives changed. Having delivered the goods for his mother, Edgar told me, he would go 'fishing' – as he liked to put it – in Joubert Park or at Park Station on his way back to the township: 'I was sixteen, a Zulu boy. Hefty! Plumpy! I wore shorts, very tight shorts! I was a fit young boy; men of all races would be attracted to me.'

Delivering washing for his mother provided Phil, too, with access to the city: he was seduced by one of her clients, and realised the possibilities of the world beyond Soweto. He dropped out of school, much to the fury of his ambitious parents. 'I was too streetwise,' Phil explained to me. 'I liked the money. It was my chance of meeting men.' One of Phil's favourite haunts was Union Grounds, in Joubert Park, where white soldiers were barracked after the war. 'He is on one side of the fence and you are on the other. He pulls down his pants, and puts his whatsisname through the fence, and you put your hands through the fence and get hold of him, and you do your thing. There and then. And he gives you two and sixpence.'

When I asked if he was worried about being seen, he deadpanned back: 'The lights in those days were not as bright as the lights today.'

*

Phil married for love. He met Mo on a train and fell for 'her beautiful country smile.' She was on the way to the city to finish her teacher training. He carried her luggage for her from the station to the student residence and kept an eye on her once she was there. Their courtship was urban and sophisticated, even in apartheid Johannesburg: on their first date he took her to the movies at Sophiatown's famous Odin Cinema. This must have been in 1955, just months – or even weeks – before the bustling cosmopolitan district was demolished almost brick by brick to be replaced by the white suburb of Triomf ('Triumph') and its 65,000 inhabitants forcibly removed to Meadowlands, outside Soweto.

Such was Edgar's love of men, on the other hand, that he paid no attention to the possibility of marriage until his parents died in 1957. By that point he had fished his way through vocational school in Soweto, where he had studied carpentry, and his Pimville church, where he had become a lay preacher. Now, after his father's death, he discovered that he would only be able to keep his meagre inheritance if he married. So he accepted the woman chosen for him by his family, and they quickly had a family; he gave up carpentry, too, and found the clerical job he would keep until retirement.

Now that Phil was married, a neighbour found him a job as a messenger in town. Such were his wits that he was soon promoted to a desk job. He quickly came to understand, as he put it to me, that 'you have to be rich to be gay,' not least because one had to support two parallel lives. 'I think in married life', he told me, 'you should be a responsible and trustworthy man, and that's why, up to this date, I'm still in the closet.'

Phil and Edgar put much stock in being exemplary family men: to provide, to be home for dinner, to be sober. Gay men, Edgar had it, were particularly good at this: 'the wife knows that you are responsible. She knows, at least, that you like to *improve the house!*' This cut them the slack to lead their complicated lives.

They also experienced, alongside the pleasures of fatherhood, the often unutterable pain of raising children in South Africa in the latter half of the twentieth century. Neither of the men could bring themselves talk about the loss of their sons: Edgar's to AIDS and Phil's to the struggle. The latter disappeared during the township uprisings of the mid 1980s; his parents assumed he had gone into exile to join the liberation army of the African National Congress, but he was not among those who returned after 1990.

Neither man ever discussed his sexuality with his wife, but Phil still cringes with humiliation as he recalls how he was once caught out by his wife. He had borrowed a book on homosexuality from a friend, and she had come upon him reading it. He spluttered an excuse, and when the book went missing he assumed she must have thrown it away. Unbeknownst to Phil, she had actually read the book herself, and loaned it to several of her girlfriends so that they might better understand their own marital circumstances. I know this from the book's owner, a younger black gay man, whom Mo once told: 'I know what he is. I can deal with it. He's a good man. And at least he is not running with other women. I'm not going to lose him.' Such are the tragic silences in marriages that she was not, ever, able to say this to Phil himself.

Phil was torn, he told me, between the love of his wife and the love of his male partners. 'Gay life and straight life are different things. The comfort you get from a partner is different from the comfort you get from your wife. A partner is more intimate than a straight wife.' When I asked him to elaborate, his response was startlingly concrete: 'In the African tradition, sucking is taboo. Licking one's body, for a married woman, no. But with a gay boy, he can do whatever. He kisses you, he licks you, he sucks you, he does all the wonderful things. Once you have tasted a man, it's not easy to forget.'

The last time Phil and I met it was shortly after the polygamous South African president Jacob Zuma had been forced to concede that he had had a baby – his twentieth child – through an extramarital affair with a young Soweto woman. Phil disapproved strongly of Zuma, but had some sympathy with his situation: older men needed younger partners, male or female, to keep the lifeblood – the blood-lines – coursing. Like their fathers, Phil and Edgar had more than one spouse; unlike their fathers, though, their second wives – their second lives – were secret. They were, as the township expression goes, 'After Nines': gay only 'after nine', once the wife was in bed and the kids asleep.

Looking back on his life, Edgar told me: 'I would advise anybody to honour their relationship and be honest, because otherwise it kills you, spiritually and otherwise. Even at work your concentration is divided. In the life I have lived, you should have a room for disappointment.'

In my middle-class life, my suburban childhood and my urban adulthood, I have always had a room: for sex, for love, for rest, for reading and writing, and – of course – for disappointment. Phil and Edgar had to make their rooms where they could find them.

*

Phil once said to me, about his life: 'To be black and gay, uh, uh, uh! It was double trouble.' He explained: 'Gay life in Johannesburg, it was very tough, especially amongst blacks because of the curfew, and your freedom and your privacy was the most important thing. With whites, I would say, it was much easier.'

Once Edgar and Phil came to the city – first on the washerwoman pretext, and then because of their jobs – they found a new level of freedom. Or perhaps, more accurately, they learned how to play a new game of cunning and courage, taking advantage of the opportunities now available to them while avoiding the double-jeopardy of being black and being gay.

You might meet another black man in a desperate tussle in a locked toilet stall at Park Station or through a furtive grope on the crowded train home, but if you wanted a bit of space and a bit of time – if you actually wanted to undress and caress – you needed to find a white man. This was not so easy. A whole raft of laws prevented black people and white people from doing anything other than working together – and even then, only if blacks were in menial positions; and in this time of intense political repression (Nelson Mandela was arrested in 1962 and sentenced to life imprisonment in the Rivonia Trial in 1964), any interaction across the colour bar could be interpreted as subversive activity and land you in jail.

All through the 1950s and early 1960s, there were periodic crackdowns on homosexual activity around Joubert Park, particularly at those edges of the park where black men and white men met, such as the post office steps on Wolmarans Street. Both Edgar and Phil managed to avoid arrest, but they know many men who did not. Phil recalls the humiliation visited upon two friends who were arrested in a sting at the post office – and were forced into shuffling along the pavement to the police van, past commuters who could well have been their neighbours, with their pants around their ankles.

Once he was working in the city, Edgar found his way, during lunch hour, to the post office; here he and other black men would linger on the steps, waiting for a white man in a car to pick them up. This is how he met his first white lover. For five years, the man would collect him at lunchtime, take him to his flat in Malvern and get him back to work in time for the afternoon shift. 'I accepted it. If it's love, it's love at its best. If it's not, it's not. I've always lived that way.'

Sometimes, the white men would invite you back on the weekend, for a party; here you would meet other black men – also married, also from the township. 'You'd have to go through the tradesman's entrance,' Phil told me, 'or you'd be introduced to the watchman as someone bringing the washing. Or you'd pretend to be helping your friend by carrying a heavy thing into his flat, or delivering a loaf of bread.'

*

In this way Phil and Edgar found themselves frequently, over the years, at the home of their friend Roger. Roger's home was high up on one of the dramatic ridges east of the city, where he had transformed a rather ordinary 1930s bungalow into an Edwardian folly, with conservatories, statuary and gazebos. When I visited him, I thought immediately of the suburban boundaries that had both contained and confined me as a child; I thought, too, of the washing lines obstructing the views of the city on those blocks of flats over Constitution Hill, and about how, and why, we turn away from the horizon rather than embracing it. Roger had planted borders of soaring cypresses, entirely obstructing the house's magnificent view over Johannesburg. This was quite deliberate, he told me: he needed to make a refuge for himself and his own black partner, and for their black friends, by preventing the possibility of people peering in.

Roger's intention was 'to make a place where our black friends could meet us and each other safely – something they could not do in the townships – and feel secure in the white part of town, particularly if it was after curfew'. There were certain rules, particularly in Roger's previous residence, which had been in a small block of flats: the bath was always full, for example, so that you could wash off someone else's bodily fluids if there was a raid, and the music and chatter was always kept low, so as not to attract attention.

Edgar became uncharacteristically dreamy when he talked about Roger's garden: it seemed to him, as a younger man, nothing less than Eden itself. One can imagine how he felt, arriving there after having escaped his family-filled matchbox home, the incessant township noise, the sharp-elbowed train, the Eloff Street crush, the crime-filled streets, the curfew gauntlets: 'Sometimes I would just go there by myself, even if I did not have a boy, just to sit in that Garden of Eden and chat to Roger.'

The reference to not having a boy stems from the usual nature of the gatherings at Roger's home or other white friends: they were about sex, and they were somewhat transactive. The white men would provide the space for their black friends and their partners to have sex freely and without shame or fear of disclosure; their black friends – Edgar and Phil, in particular – would bring along a wake of young men to share with their hosts. It was never, however, explicitly about money, and neither side felt exploited.

In fact, Phil is emphatic, and characteristically straightforward, about the way he has benefited from his lifelong friendship with Roger. As I sat with him, in March 2010, in his home – a solid facebrick suburban ranch-house with a red-tiled roof that would not be out of place in a 'white' suburb like Randburg or Centurion – I asked him if being gay had opened up a broader world for him.

'Oh yes,' he replied. 'Yes, yes, yes, yes. I got in touch and I got wiser. If I wasn't gay I wouldn't be staying in a house like this.'

Was he suggesting that his white friends had paid for it? Not at all:

his employer had been an early facilitator of mortgages for black people, and he had been one of the first homeowners in Soweto, over fifty years ago. He explained, with a sweep of his hand that took in the leather couches, the flokati rugs, the books on the bookshelf, the babbling Italianate water-feature and fishpond, the modish patio furniture around it: 'This, all of this, I copied from the white friends I used to visit. Roger taught me a lot.' Phil and his wife were also, frequently, Roger's guests at business functions; Roger's liberal younger colleagues would invite them home to their families, as a mark of their worldliness, 'so I would go to their homes, see all these beautiful things, and I would say, "One day, I'll have those things to myself. I'll have a house like this."'

One of the things that Phil and Edgar shared, in contrast to their other black gay friends, was that neither was particularly interested in white men as sexual partners. Phil has had four lovers in his life, he says; all black men from Soweto. The first three broke his heart. The fourth had been with him for the past four years. His name was JB, he was twenty-three years old, he lived with his family in one of the squatter camps surrounding the township, and he worked as a security foreman.

*

In the 1970s Phil befriended Charles, a man from Zululand who had come to the city to work and left his wife and children back home. Like thousands of other migrant labourers, Charles rented a room in one of Johannesburg's single-sex hostels at Mzimhlophe, on the northern fringes of Soweto. But when he met a white man and moved into his house in the suburbs, his room became available. He sublet it to Phil.

For the first time, Phil and Edgar had their own space, in the township. It was tiny, not more than two metres square, with a single bed, a tiny table and a wardrobe, but 'it was a special place for us,' Edgar told me. 'We called it "our flat". We would pay rent every month. It was exciting to have our own place. We knew very well that we are at home here.' The keys would be left in a safe place at the hostel, and the men would make their way to the 'flat' individually, for an hour or a night, if they had a partner. On weekends when they could both find a way to be away from their families, they would be in the 'flat' together. The tone in Edgar's voice as he described this suggests nothing less than marital bliss, experienced in an environment of cosmopolitan sophistication.

Most of Mzimhlope hostel consisted – like all single-sex migrant hostels – of communal dormitories, where workers were housed in subhuman conditions. But because Charles held a good job and had connections (the hostels were tightly controlled by *indunas*, overseers, from Chief Mangosuthu Buthelezi's Inkatha Zulu nationalist movement) he had managed to secure a single room along a lane reserved for foremen and other senior workers. This lane, just to your left as you entered the sprawling compound, had been commandeered by gay men. Here Edgar and Phil could go about their business protected not only by a single-sex environment where many men took 'wives', but by the extreme alienation of the place. 'We were left alone,' Edgar told me. 'People in the hostel, they just drink for themselves. At the hostel you just live your own life. You are not curious about other people's lives. It was cool.'

Anti-apartheid social scientists and activists have conventionally viewed the single-sex hostels as carceral institutions akin to prisons, where the 'involuntary homosexuality' that developed was a pathological symptom of the economic system that produced the hostel in the first place: men had been forced off the land and away from their families to work as the 'black gold' of the South African economy. Certainly, conditions in the hostels were degrading and often violent. And certainly, as in prisons, many of the younger, more vulnerable men were – and still are, on the mines – forced to become 'wives'. More recently, historians have begun to understand the homosexual relationships among migrant labourers as a form of resistance rather than oppression, but this reading, too, is limited by instrumentalism. Some men – like Charles, like Phil and Edgar – simply were homosexual, and found their space at places like Mzimhlophe.

When Phil and I spoke about the confounding legacy of the hostels, he told me the story of his sole visit to a mine-hostel, where life was far more regulated than it was in township hostels like Mzimhlophe. He had been invited by a friend, George, whom he had met at Mzimhlophe, to attend a dance. When he got to the hostel with a group of friends, however, the *induna* at the door did not know of a George and would not admit him. Eventually, Phil managed to explain who George was, and the *induna* exclaimed, 'Oh, you mean Margaret! James Bond's wife!' Phil was surprised to discover that George had transformed into a glamorous and buxom hostess; James Bond was the chief *induna*, and so Phil and his friends were made especially welcome. During the dance, Phil was particularly entranced by a beautiful young girl who could not have been more than eighteen, and who danced with seductive shyness. Phil wanted her immediately, but she was not available, as she was mourning her husband, who had died in a mine accident six weeks previously. At four o'clock, those on the evening shift had to change and go back to work, and the girl – now dressed for work – came back to say goodbye before going underground. 'I couldn't believe it,' Phil said. 'It was a man in gumboots and a helmet and overalls. He was a man, now, going underground, to work, maybe to his death, in that furnace, with the heat and the noise. But he was just a little boy; that's what I knew from having seen the dance. How can you send a child like that into the earth?'

*

Edgar and Phil lost their room in the mid 1980s, during the township uprisings that eventually shook apartheid off South Africa even as they also denied Phil his firstborn son. Mzimhlophe, like all hostels, was a stronghold of the anti-ANC Inkatha movement; the Zulu migrants who lived there would go on the rampage in Soweto against the township residents, generating much antipathy against the hostel, which became a fortified bastion. It was no longer safe to go there, so Edgar and Phil stopped; when Charles tried to get the room back for them once things settled down, he was told that it had been commandeered by another man, who had paid the *indunas* protection money to keep it.

At roughly the same time, the parties in town, at places like Roger's, stopped abruptly. Phil blames politics for this too: 'In 1986 there was a lot of hatred instilled in black boys. We would try to get them to come to town, but they were not interested in being with whites any more. And police were also suspicious when they saw a group of blacks in town: they would stop you and harass you.' Roger remembers being stopped, during one of the States of Emergency, taking Phil and Edgar back to Soweto: he had to pretend that they were waiters at a function of his, and that he was giving them a lift back home. All the same, he was forced to drop them on the boundaries of the township and leave them to find their own way home late at night.

As apartheid collapsed and the new society began to form itself through the violent years around 1990, Edgar and Phil found their places in the new mixed gay bars of Hillbrow. Edgar loved the Skyline, while Phil preferred the more sedate Champions, opposite Park Station, where he kept his own bottle of gin behind the bar and was feted as a village elder. You no longer needed to go to the Park Station toilets – or Roger's house – for sex: if you could pay the entry fee, you could go to sex clubs like Gotham City, or later, the Factory; or – once the censorship laws started crumbling – to sex shops with film booths like Adult World.

Meanwhile, in Soweto itself, places like Scotch's opened, and a younger generation started to reject the 'After Nines' identity. For one thing, the youth uprisings from 1976 onwards had constituted a generational revolution: they were no longer bound to their families, or tradition, in the same way. As a black middle class began to grow, young black professionals got their own places, in Soweto or in formerly white suburbs, making the space that people like Roger had once provided.

After he lost Mzimhlophe, Phil found a lover who had not married and who had his own place in Soweto. Perhaps because of the space, Phil feels that he experienced real love – and heartache – for the first time: 'A friend once said to me, "Never love a man. Don't give a man your whole heart 'cos he'll break it." Really, loving someone, it's terrible. When I love a person, I love that person to be with me whenever or wherever. If I've got a free weekend, I would love to be with that person. But if I know my children are coming, I have to stop that person from coming. Ja, that friend was right: "Never love a man."'

*

Phil told me this story in March 2010. We were sitting together in the living room of his house, a tray of tea and biscuits between us, the sliding door closed against the prying ears of the housekeeper bustling about the kitchen. I had been unable to see him for a few years because his wife had been severely ill and he was nursing her. That we were able to meet in his home at all was due to the fact that he was now a widower: Mo had been dead nearly a year.

He told me about her suffering with great empathy and sadness. Clearly her death had given him more space – his young lover JB stayed over once or twice a month, for example – but he did not view this as a new freedom. Since Mo's death, 'a lot of whites who I have met have asked me, "Phil, why don't you come out into the open?" I say, "I've lived a lie for so long, I would hate to bust this balloon. I don't know what would happen. So I would rather take this with me, to the grave."'

JB had been with him 'thick and thin' through Mo's illness and then the bereavement period, and his family had accepted the young man's presence. Still, as always, he had needed to concoct a story: he told his children that JB's father had been a work colleague, and that when the man had died young, he had become a father-figure and a mentor to the young man. 'You have to lead the life of a lie,' he told me. 'You have to tell lies and be careful you are not caught. That has been my life.'

As if to make this point, Phil's sister arrived unexpectedly while we were talking. As she made her way across the lawn, Phil and I hurriedly agreed on a story to explain the unusual presence of a white visitor: I had come from England with a gift from my father, who had been Phil's boss many years previously. I received the sister's warm greetings – 'Welcome to Soweto! You are at home here!' – as I scurried off to the Maponya Mall to await a phone call telling me it was safe to return.

*

The last time I had seen Edgar was two years previously, in 2008. I had asked him to participate in the exhibition I was curating about gay, lesbian and transgender life in Johannesburg. Although Edgar was ill and lame – he had much trouble walking and needed a chair – he agreed to take part as long as we used a pseudonym and did not identify him in any way. For this reason, we used as his signature portrait a close-up photograph of his left hand, blown up into a four-metre-high banner; his wedding ring a flash of gold on the ashen parchment of his wrinkled hand.

We arranged for a wheelchair and a van to transport him to the opening, at the Apartheid Museum, between Johannesburg and Soweto, and I wheeled him into the auditorium for the opening event. I had not seen him for a few years and I was startled by how much he

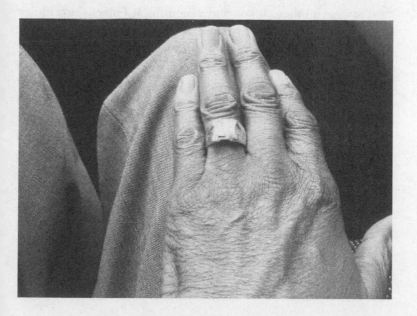

had changed: the only memory of his former heft was to be found in the folds of skin hanging off his gangly frame. Still, he was sexy, an outrageous flirt, his handsome face igniting every time a younger man paid him any attention.

I had watched him intently as the South African Chief Justice, Pius Langa – a black man of his age – gave a keynote address underscoring the constitutional equality that gay people now had in South Africa: 'This is *wonderful!*' he had said to me afterwards, gesturing expansively at the crowd: 'Just seeing these young people makes me feel free even if it is too late for me.'

Edgar had told me at the time that he hardly ever saw Phil any more. In recent years, they had been getting together once a month, when Edgar went to Baragwanath to collect his medication: Phil, who lived near the hospital, would drive over to collect him, bring him back to his house for tea, then take him home. Now, Phil told me, when I went to visit him in Soweto, Edgar was too ill to get to the hospital, and Phil did not like to drive the distance, all the way across the sprawling township, to Edgar's home in Dobsonville. So the two men saw each other only very occasionally, at funerals, usually, or when Phil did make the drive from time to time.

I tried to get hold of Edgar in 2010, and failed: he was not answering his cellphone, and I could not, of course, call him on his landline. I mentioned this to Phil, who told me that Edgar had become very ill with prostate cancer. Shortly after my visit to Phil, he decided to drive over to Zondi, to check up on his old friend. When he arrived at the house, he learned that Edgar had died a few days previously, after a night in the hospital. The funeral had not yet taken place, however, and he was able to attend.

I called Roger. Yes, he said, Phil had called to tell him about Edgar's death, but when he tried to get information about the funeral, Phil seemed vague and confused. Roger worried that Phil might be developing memory problems, but it seemed to me, from my short phone conversation with Phil, that something else was going on. Phil must have understood, from his own deeply distressing experience of having been excluded from the bereavement – he would not have even known about the funeral had he not arrived unexpectedly at Edgar's home – that his friend was being reclaimed in death by family and clan and church, from the world of the 'After Nines'.

*

Edgar once told me that he had two 'wedding rings'. He wore one on the third finger of his left hand and the other around his neck. If the former, his solid gold signet, conjured up the respectability of a Soweto patriarch, the latter, a lush red silk tie, reminded him of his second life. It had been given to him by a male lover, since deceased. His family might have seen it as just another item in his snappy wardrobe, but he wore it with purpose: 'to remember him and his closeness. He worked for Liberty Life and he treated me so well. He was amazing! We would *go places*. It's still there, the tie. It's red, beautiful. *I love that tie!*'

I stroke and bother my own wedding band. I roll its generous barrel between my thumb and forefinger and then flick it on its side to press against its edges until I fear it might cut me. What has happened to Edgar's wedding rings? Perhaps one of his grandsons will use the signet at his own marriage. Perhaps another will inherit the tie, oblivious to its significance to his grandfather but reminded of his own particular love and longing every time he knots it.

Ultimate Dispatcher

My own father was diagnosed with cancer in 2008, and on the day C and I got married he was in hospital, recuperating from a second round of surgery. We went straight from Edenvale to the Sunninghill Clinic, to show him and my mother the rings, before going off for the night to a country hotel. Despite his condition and over our protestations, he insisted on throwing us a party, just as he had for my brothers when they married. A few weeks later, on the night before C left for Paris to begin his job, we invited a few people around to my parents' home. Although he was very ill, my father played the host with his trademark bonhomie and gave a characteristically well-wrought speech, brimming with love and cut with emotion. It would be his last public act; he was back in hospital shortly afterwards, and he died on 23 April, the day after the 2009 elections that would bring Jacob Zuma to power.

I went to see my father in hospital on the eve of the elections, as I did every day. The nurses had told him that the Independent Electoral Commission (IEC) was arranging for ill voters to cast their ballots from their hospital beds, and in what would be our last conversation, we chatted about this. Unusually for a man of his race, class and generation, my father had become a member of the ANC after it was unbanned in the early 1990s. Although I had chosen not to, being 'ANC' had been central to my identity since my university years: I subscribed to the liberation movement's values and had felt the need to cross the racial line and merge my aspirations with those of the majority; to bridge the impenetrable political boundary as it were, between pages 75 and 77 of the *Holmden's*.

Despite his pain and discomfort, the thought of voting animated my father. 'Who will you vote for, Dad?' I asked him.

'Certainly *not* the ANC!'

I agreed with him, and showed him an article I had published in that day's *Star* newspaper. In it, I had written about how I had lost my political home in these elections because of the way the ANC had became fat and arrogant, too seduced by its own liberation mythologies, and with an undue proprietary sense of ownership over the state and South Africa's destiny. I had written that even though the party still articulated a vision of social democracy closest to my own, my democratic duty now lay elsewhere: to do what I could to put a check on the arrogance and abuse of the ruling party.

I would probably not have made the effort to leave my father's bedside and drive across town to vote if he had not felt so strongly about it himself: I might have convinced myself that my abstention would register as a protest vote. I had learned politics from my father and developed my passion for political journalism at his side, learning to read newspapers over his shoulder. My earliest memories of political activism were from about the age of thirteen, when he was a campaign manager for the 'Progs'. By the time I left school, I could no longer square the values I had learned from my father with the all-white system in which he still participated, and we started disagreeing with each other quite fervently. Later, he too would be somewhat radicalised by the turbulent Eighties: he fell out with many of his political contemporaries when he began espousing the belief that armed struggle in South Africa was justified, according to the doctrine of a 'just war'.

But now, he told me as I sat by his bedside, he would vote for the Democratic Alliance, the successor to the 'Progs', the opposition party that was made up largely of white, coloured and Indian voters. The night before election day, however, he would become too ill to put up any further resistance to a transfer into the dreaded intensive care unit: he would not be able to vote, even if the IEC had managed to send a mobile ballot box round to the hospital. And so, as I left the hospital for a couple of hours to drive across town to my polling station, I told myself that I was doing it for father as much as for fatherland. The worst part of my decision was the distance I now felt from the others in the queue; from the majority of South Africans for whom the ANC remained 'home'. For the first time in my life, I voted with the minority – albeit not for the Democratic Alliance. I chose a new party of ANC dissidents, the Congress of the People (COPE), as a hedge. As I drove back to the hospital I took comfort, at least, in the fact that this minority was now less racially defined than it had been in 1994: most of the black people I loved or trusted were also, for the first time, not voting for the ANC.

Upon my return to the hospital I discovered a commotion: Jacob Zuma had dropped in to visit the survivors of a terrible bus crash that had injured several ANC activists. The hospital lobby was ululating with excited nurses and bristling with security men in black sunglasses. Inside the intensive care ward, my father's soul still seemed to be transmitting to us through impassive, sad eyes, even though some form of stroke seemed to have robbed him of any ability to move or communicate. I told him what I had done: who knows if he heard me. We left after a while, but were called back at midnight to sit with him, and I wept as he died.

We sat with the body, as is the Jewish tradition, until the men of the Chevra Kadisha had been aroused from their sleep to collect it. Sitting there was not at all as ghoulish as I had imagined it might be. On the contrary, it was unexpectedly comforting in the way it asserted the boundaries between the spirit and the flesh, a border so clear, a line drawn by death, a line I had not previously understood.

*

My father had been an aggressive atheist, but in a letter to me before his death he had requested an orthodox Jewish funeral, appending a photocopied page from an essay on the philosopher Isaiah Berlin to explain himself. Berlin's own choice of a traditional funeral, his biographer, Michael Ignatieff, wrote, reflected 'a choice of allegiance and belonging, rather than a commitment of faith. He could subscribe to the rituals of Judaism without subscribing to their content. He did so serenely, refusing to see any contradiction. The faith of his fathers had disposed of these matters and burial and mourning very well for centuries. Why should he quarrel with any of it?'

I did not share my father's serenely reconciled views, perhaps because I, unlike him, was not raised in a traditional Jewish home; perhaps because my homosexuality was forbidden by this faith; perhaps because I long for some kind of faith in a way that he did not. Still, I was grateful for his views, refracted through Isaiah Berlin, in the way they prescribed a path for us two days later, up the steep slope of the Jewish section of West Park Cemetery, behind the coffin and toward the gravesite. Being a 'principal mourner' for the first time in my life, I appreciated all the more the sombre rituals of Jewish burial as I had witnessed them so often here at West Park: the eloquently silent trudge behind the coffin punctuated only by the calling out of the names of pallbearers; the plaintive and incomprehensible prayer; the release of a plain pine coffin into hard red earth; the scrape of spade against sand; the mumbled mourners' Kaddish. I stood interlocked with my mother and my brothers, our spouses a half-pace behind us. I felt nothing, nothing at all, during the ceremony, except the physical press of my family's bodies against mine – a hand in a hand, an arm around a back, a head against a shoulder, a hand holding a neck. But it came to me, later, that I was not just burying the twentieth century through which my father had lived – apartheid, communism, the struggle, Mandela, the flush of democracy – but my own long life as a child. I was forty-five years old.

So many times have I trudged in the silent and sombre train behind a coffin covered in black cloth as it is trundled up the hill through West Park Cemetery that this city of the dead feels as much a part of my internal geography as the city of the living that surrounds it. There is, I always feel when in one of these processions, an unresolvable paradox to the route. On the one hand, we have very clear directions: we are headed to plot 113 in block W of the Orthodox section; death is as certain, and as bounded, as the rectangular hole into which the coffin will be dropped. On the other, we do not have the faintest idea of the destination: death, by definition, is *terra incognita*.

'The Venice of the South'

There are some nice old trees in the more established sections of West Park but the newer reaches of the Jewish cemetery approximate the grasslands that existed before the Witwatersrand was settled. Around my father's grave, right up against the koppie at the top of the cemetery and with excavations all around us for other new burials, the landscape seemed especially harsh and brittle. Burying the dead here scours you and dries you out, and you are grateful for the Jewish ritual at the end of it that requires you to wash your hands with a two-handled jug – one that you hold with your death-soiled hand and the other with your now-clean one. But West Park also, quite appropriately, makes you think about the earth: the red earth you shovel onto the pine casket, the red earth into which your loved one is dropped, the earth you wash from your hands, the earth you traverse so carelessly in a day and in a life. Often, I have left a funeral here discomforted by our denial of this earth, and I have been wondering, recently, if this is a condition specific to Johannesburg.

*

In *Portrait with Keys*, Ivan Vladislavic describes Johannesburg drily as 'the Venice of the South', because 'the backdrop is always a man-made one. We have planted a forest the birds endorse. For hills, we have mine dumps covered with grass. We do not wait for time and the elements to weather us, we change the scenery ourselves, to suit our moods. Nature is for other people, in other places.'

'Nature' was actually imported into the Highveld. There were almost no trees on the grasslands of the Witwatersrand, and Johannesburg's developers realised that if their upper-end real estate was going to be attractive to foreign investors, it needed to be shaded. And so, when they planted the Sachsenwald Forest on the northern slopes of Parktown Ridge to provide pit-props for the mines, they decided to multipurpose the trees to provide shade for the settlers and to reduce the dust of the veld and of the mining activities. The project succeeded. Look at Johannesburg's northern suburbs from the top of one of the ridges, or from my bedroom window up in the Melville Koppies, or from the sky or the Google Earth view, and you will see a vast forest that the birds have indeed endorsed; the largest man-made urban woodland in the world, according to the city's publicity shtick: plane and oaks, blue gums and jacarandas, immigrants all.

Like the people who flooded into the city at the same time, these trees are exotics and have rooted well – even though they have been threatened by democracy. In an echo of the nativism that flickered across the country in the first decade of freedom, the new government declared shortly after coming to power in 1991 – not without reason – that South Africa's exotic trees were severely depleting its water table, and needed to be uprooted. In Cape Town, shock teams took to Table Mountain to clear it of Port Jackson pine. The jacarandas that drizzle Johannesburg with their surreal purple haze every spring looked like they might be targeted too before they were granted a reprieve on the grounds of age: nearly a century old, they will die their natural deaths soon enough anyway.

Trees were needed on the Highveld not only to prop up the mines and provide shade from the harsh sun, but to stake a sense of place into the seeming emptiness of the landscape, writes the urbanist Jeremy Foster; to stake a sense of temporality, too, into the 'time-lessness' of these seemingly featureless folds of high-lying land. Foster writes that when you plant trees you mediate a sense of history, because trees have lifespans and change 'seasonally at a pace synchronised with the unfolding of human society'. The greening of Johannesburg, he says, was also an attempt by the city's new European settler population 'to isolate itself from a regional environment they perceived as hostile ... In this treeless region, most white settlers saw the park or forest as a metonymic fragment of an imaginary "home", a triumph of civilisation over nature.'

If the veld lurking on the edge of my childhood was the place of black people and Boers, of poisonous puff adders and ticks and bilharzia snails in stagnant pools, then nature itself was conscripted to encamp a suburban laager against such threats: a canopy of oak trees and jacarandas and blue gums, a European screen of green, a fragrant curtain against this wilderness of cracked red earth and yellow grass and thorny silver scrub.

*

Rising above Johannesburg's man-made forests are piles of white-and-yellow sand extracted from the mines and dumped, in *mesa*-like formations, along the southern perimeter of the city. Slimes dams, tailings dumps: the names given to these man-made hills are wonderfully onomatopoeic. They were the mountains of our childhood, covered in grass and planted with trees and, in one case, with the Top Star drive-in cinema, long an iconic image of – and view-site over – the city. There are 270 of these mine dumps spread over 400 square kilometres, fashioned from more than 400 million tons of earth removed from the mines. They provide the negative image, above ground, for what is going on below, and you can trace the route of the ore-bearing reef from above by following their line from east to west just south of the ridges of the Witwatersrand. It is no coincidence that – with the exception of a couple of anomalies, such as Alexandra – the green canopy of the Johannesburg urban forest spreads northward from this, while the tightly packed, treeless, zinc-roofed mass of township housing, glinting silver in the sun, is to the south of it. The mining lands formed an obvious buffer between the white parts of the city and the black ones; an urban vacuum, in effect, that reminded me conceptually, when I visited Berlin for the first time in the mid 1990s, of the empty space left by the destruction of the Wall.

Once the mines were depleted and shut down, the mining lands became even more desolate, with rusting infrastructure strewn between the slimes dams as if by a capricious giant who had come out to play in his sandpit and then got bored and stomped off. The open shafts began to decant toxic water into the biosphere, and the abandoned miners' houses and hostels became squatted by the poorest of the new migrants seeking refuge amid the discards of the modern city, the car wrecks and the scrapheaps.

Much of this empty land cannot be developed because it is, literally, undermined. The water filling the dolomitic rock cavities to the south and west of Johannesburg destabilises the landscape to such an extent that the earth's crust often collapses into sinkholes. I first heard about sinkholes from Granny Gertie, who had traded her grand piano – her only asset of any value – for some land that had turned out to be riddled with them and thus useless. I remember some terrible nightmares about our secure suburban redoubt collapsing into the earth, and needing to be reassured that we were far enough away from the mines not to have to worry about this.

All children, I imagine, express their unconscious terrors through the metaphors provided by their environments: if I were Californian I'd have been waking up with the house shaking; if I were Sicilian, covered in molten lava. We know how humanity's tampering with the environment has exacerbated the risk of natural disaster, but Johannesburg is different, for its vulnerability is entirely man-made; a paradoxical consequence of the city's very conception.

*

I think I have always known this, but I only really understood it when, in early 2012, I took a tour of the mining lands with Johannesburg's own Erin Brockovich, a woman named Mariette Liefferink. Liefferink is a glamorous Afrikaner, then in her early sixties, a former housewife and Jehovah's Witness missionary, who found new meaning by exposing the way mining waste was contaminating the environment. With her always reddened lips, her wardrobe of dramatic Chinese silk coats and her coronet of peroxided hair, she had become a familiar sight in the mining towns west of Johannesburg as she has picked her way tenaciously across the ghoulish landscape of mine dumps and run-off dams in stiletto heels, gathering research on and showing the effects of what has become known as Acid Mine Drainage.

One of the major challenges that faced mining the Witwatersrand, she explained to me, was its very high water table: the name itself means 'Ridge of White Waters'. And so the mining companies set up extensive pumping systems to drain their underground caverns, thus creating a huge 'void' – the scientists actually use this word – beneath the city. For as long as they mined, they pumped, but as the older mines became worked-out and shut down, the pumping stopped. The mines began filling with water which became contaminated with salts, sulphuric acid and heavy metals – including uranium – as it interacted both with exposed rock and abandoned infrastructure. In 2002, this water began decanting through open disused shafts out of the Western Witwatersrand Basin, releasing water of a foul rust-red colour (the result of the oxygenation of iron pyrite) into the region's water supply and leaving a thick crust of solidified heavy metals known as 'yellow boy' along the sides and beds of rivers and dams.

As we watched a sulphourous rust-red cascade of water gushing out of a shaft outside of Randfontein on the West Rand, Liefferink cited studies demonstrating that this decanted toxic water was unfit for human or animal consumption or for agricultural use, and that it would eventually kill all aquatic life. Due largely to her activism, the state had recognised the severity of the problem, and had begun an ambitious programme to neutralise the water. Scientists in the field believe this will make a difference in the long run, but no one can say how long it will take, and Liefferink believes the matter requires urgent intervention. The only solution, said told me, was to begin pumping out the water from the mining cavities again – and to commit to keeping these pumps going ad infinitum.

Liefferink took me to Tudor Shaft, an abject informal settlement literally on top of a mine dump outside the township of Kagiso, where we met an elderly man covered in lesions: these, she said, could well be the result of exposure to radioactive uranium. Tudor Shaft was one of thirty-six areas in the province of Gauteng that had just been declared radioactive hot spots by the National Nuclear Regulator. All mine dumps contained tracings of radioactive uranium and cyanide, Liefferink told me, and the regulator had ascertained that more than one and a half million people lived on top of them or too close to them, and would need to be moved. As at Tudor Shaft, most of these people at risk lived in informal settlements: a toxic wasteland is an easy fit for surplus people.

Upon arrival at Tudor Shaft, Liefferink pulled several bags of Woolworths groceries out of the back of her hefty four-wheel-drive *bakkie* and began to distribute them. In that listless, unfocused way of very poor and hungry people in the mid-afternoon heat, children were corralled into a line by an elder, each to be handed an Easter Egg and a polished red apple. This ritual, she told me, symbolised her good intentions and ensured her continued access to the community. Still, when she stopped on the way out to caution a group gathered around a rough kiln making bricks out of the toxic sand, a woman came rushing up to the *bakkie* screaming bloody murder, accusing her – presumably because of her white skin – of being an agent of the Democratic Alliance.

Liefferink had found her own voice, she told me, fighting for her own rights: resisting the construction of a Shell super-service station in her backyard in bucolic Bryanston, close to where I grew up in the Northern Suburbs. In the process, she had come up against a corporate system that tried both to bribe and extort her. She had understood the enemy and vowed to fight it. 'We have mined our gold,' she said to me as we drove back to Johannesburg. 'We have benefitted from it. It defines us. We are eGoli [place of gold]. We are Gauteng [the province of gold]. But gold has become our curse. If we had done a cost benefit analysis in 1886, gold mining would never have been sustainable ...'

She is right, of course, to hold both the mining houses and the state accountable. Still, as I tried to internalise the landscape of blood-coloured water against the neon crust of 'yellow boy', this topography of my home town, this dystopia just a few kilometres away from my birdsong-endorsed eyrie on Melville koppie, it seemed to express a deeper dilemma. None of us would exist – the city itself would not exist – were it not for these violations against nature. There is no reason for Johannesburg before or beyond them, but now it exists, despite them. This is our inheritance.

*

And a part of this inheritance is being smuggled away before our very eyes.

In recent years, as the gold price has risen, the city's mountains have begun fading away. The mining companies have begun resifting the mine dumps for gold deposits and they are disappearing, taking the Top Star drive-in with them. In this second-brewing of the mines, the original attempts to secure the dumps with grasses and trees have been disrupted: now, more than ever, the heavy mineral and sulphite deposits are blowing across Johannesburg and running off into its rivers.

The disappearance of our man-made mountains has become a favoured trope for our labile city. Here is Lauren Beukes on the topic in her celebrated sci-fi novel *Zoo City*, and if you didn't know Johannesburg you might think that the description was part of her own dystopian vision of the city: 'I drive out south,' says the novel's spunky narrator, Zanele, 'to where the last of the mine dumps are – sulphur-coloured artificial hills, laid waste by the ravages of weather and reprocessing, shored up with scrubby grass and eucalyptus trees. Ugly valleys have been gouged out and trucked away by the ton to sift out the last scraps of gold the mining companies missed the first time round. Maybe it's appropriate that *eGoli*, place of gold, should be self-cannibalising.'

I have always admired the way William Kentridge depicts Johannesburg's mutability by rendering the city in charcoal, making animated films which show its landscape being perpetually sketched and erased, built and modified. Once the mine dumps began disappearing life seemed to be imitating Kentridge's art, and he found a perfect new job for his eraser: in his 2011 film, *Other Faces*, we watch the Village Deep mine dump being rubbed out before our very eyes,

and the big screen of the Top Star drive-in comes tumbling down. 'A mountain is a fact,' said Kentridge in his acceptance speech for the Kyoto Prize in 2010. 'You can turn around, you can come back in ten years, the mountain will not have moved. The mountain itself, the idea of a mountain, of a piece of heavy earth, stands as a metaphor for understanding eternity. The opposite is true of our mine dumps, which in my childhood I had assumed were my hills.'

As a child, Kentridge said, he felt 'cheated of landscape. I wanted a landscape of forests, of trees, of brooks – but I had this dry veld, beyond the green gardens of the city.' He resolved this for himself by starting to draw 'the terrain itself – partly as a way of taking revenge against its barrenness, it's dryness'. And he describes the congruence between his medium – charcoal – and this barren, mutable landscape: 'There is a way in which the dryness of the winter veld, when the sun is very harsh and the grass is bleached very white, or else is very black from the veld fires, corresponds to the tonal range of a white sheet of paper and charcoal ... There was a way in which the winter veld fires, in which the grass is burned to black stubble, made drawings of themselves.' You could rub a sheet of paper across the Johannesburg landscape itself, Kentridge said, and you would come up with a charcoal drawing.

About water in Johannesburg, Kentridge spoke of its danger – how it floods the cavities made by mining, thus causing geological instability – but also of its function as a 'utopian blessing' in his drawings: 'You can draw a very dry landscape; then with a single line of blue, you transform it, you bless it with water'.

There were no such blessings in the *Holmden's*, which was not only insouciant of topography, but bound by its two-colour-print limitation: once the red had been allocated to boundaries and the green to main roads, there was nothing left in the palette for Mother Nature. Those rivers that were plotted in the road atlas were done so in black, rendering them invisible in the urban grid, and many of them were omitted entirely. The natural world was restored by Map Studio with its full-colour printing – although often, in my teens, when dispatching actually turned to discovery, I found myself disappointed by the way the blue turned out to be a dry riverbed, or the green swathe of parkland revealed itself to be a monochrome patch of veld.

As a child, I felt not so much cheated of landscape as oblivious to it. Beyond my vivid childhood memories of the Sandspruit, I had no knowledge at all of the profusion of streams which flowed down the continental watershed of the Witwatersrand and fed into these two substantial rivers, the Jukskei to the north and the Klip to the south, that drained into the Indian and Atlantic Oceans respectively. You need know only one thing about these two rivers to get a sense of their marginality to the development of Johannesburg: the township of Alexandra is sited along the Jukskei and the township of Soweto along the Klip.

To the extent that I thought about nature at all, it was elsewhere. Given my father's job, we spent many weekends and holidays in the forests on the Eastern Transvaal escarpment: that was where wilderness resided, and even there, it was bounded by the battalions of pine trees marching relentlessly over the mountains. Nature was what we got when we arrived in Sabie after a few hours in the car, suffocating in the fug of my father's Peter Stuyvesant cigarettes. What we drove through to get there was known as 'the veld': it was a transit-zone, rather than nature itself.

Or nature was the beach, and the sea, where we went for summer holidays. As a boy, I had read in a children's compendium of Norse myths of Canute's defiance of the tides, and I turned this into a solitary game I played along the shore: I would walk up and down the beach endlessly, controlling each wave by beckoning it in, commanding its arrest, and then dispatching it out again. Every young child I have taught this game to has been enthralled by it, for the same reason that I was: the illusion of mastery it gives you over the elements. Nature bent to our will.

*

The Central Witwatersrand Basin, which lies directly beneath downtown Johannesburg, was expected to begin decanting toxic water in 2016. Initially, when the predictions were that this would happen in

2012, a wave of apocalyptic anxiety was triggered in Johannesburg's newspapers, with some prophesies reading like something Lauren Beukes might write: a bubbling-up of foul rust-red liquid which would, finally, envelop Frenchfontein, this city of sin. Reading one of these in a 2010 newspaper article, I was struck by the prediction that about 60 million litres of water a day would decant onto the surface, 'equivalent to water from 24 Olympic pools hitting the city's streets daily ...'

The swimming pool as measuring unit for a volume of water to be unleashed upon the city seems apt for Johannesburg – well, for my Johannesburg at least. Despite the fact that we went, occasionally, to the Zoo Lake (there was an annual holiday children's show of *Treasure Island* performed there, on a pontoon stage set up in the skanky water), the only blue in my internal Johannesburg map was that which filled swimming pools. Like William Kentridge and Ivan Vladislavic, I, too, imagined my world as flat, thrown into relief by some mine-dumps. Given the natural topography of the Witwatersrand as represented so beautifully in those conical scratches made by Tompkins, such obliviousness is inexplicable. It strikes the adult in me as precisely the consequence of the type of blinkering we endured as white suburban children in apartheid South Africa. We lived in an artificial world, our own void of sorts, dug out of the earth by the hunger for gold.

The Ecstasy of Immersion

Walk, on a Sunday, along any of the rocky koppies that punch holes through Johannesburg's urban fabric, and you will see members of the syncretic black Zion Christian Church standing in circles in their blue-and-white robes, or their militaristic khaki uniforms, beating their drums with long curved sticks, jumping high and singing their hymns. Now go down to one of Johannesburg's rivers or streams and you will see full-throttled baptisms, *sangomas* communing with their ancestors and officiating at ritual cleansing ceremonies, *inyangas* foraging for the medicinal plants they will take back to their township or backyard consulting rooms, the faithful of all denominations collecting water in two-litre plastic Coke bottles for rituals to take place back home. Because they assert the natural world within the urban environment, Johannesburg's rivers – like its koppies – are places where modernist reason must give way to the spiritual and metaphysical, where people can escape the materialism of the city and enter the territory of their ancestors, or their guiding spirits.

The Klip River has its headwaters beneath the concrete of central Johannesburg. It runs down the Witwatersrand toward Soweto through industrial and mining lands before spooling through the wetlands around which Soweto is built, flowing just a hundred metres past Vilakazi Street in Orlando West, where both Nelson Mandela and Bishop Tutu lived, and just beneath Freedom Square in Kliptown, and through squatter camps before leaving the township through Avalon Cemetery. Along some of its banks there is now newly landscaped parkland, part of the huge post-apartheid investment in the township and the first real attempt to create a riverside Johannesburg. Still, it is one of South Africa's foulest rivers – because of acid mine run-off, and because of the seepage of overflowing sewers into it. A 2012 report indicated that it had a hundred times the acceptable level of E.coli bacteria in its waters.

One Sunday in early 2012 I went to Soweto to visit Nkunzi Nkabinde, a *sangoma*, who had promised to take me to his 'sacred spot', as he called it, along the river. Nkunzi was one of the founders of an organisation of gay and lesbian *sangomas*; he was also part of a project at the GALA archives demonstrating how traditional African cultures have long found space for homosexual and transgendered people by understanding them to be possessed by the ancestors and assigning to them the roles of healers or doctors in their communities.

Nkunzi published a book in 2008 entitled *Black Bull, Ancestors and Me: My Life as a Lesbian Sangoma*. Since then he had begun the process of gender reassignment, finally conforming his outer female body to his internal male spirit with the medical assistance of hormones and surgery. In *Black Bull* he explains the roots of this: he was born female but claimed by a male ancestor. This accounts for his gender-non-conformity and also gave him the space, in his past female life, to live openly as a lesbian. As a woman, Nkunzi's sexual and romantic impulses for other women were understood to be those of this male ancestor, and because Nkunzi 'belonged' to the ancestor, he was released from the pressure facing other women: of needing to marry and have children. 'Nkunzi' is, in fact, the name of the male ancestor who possessed him; his female birth-name was Zandile.

In *Black Bull*, Nkunzi describes the initiation by which this ancestor entered him, through a cut in the skin made by an all-powerful *inyoka* – or snake-spirit with green eyes – when he was forced to plunge, terrified, on a moonless night into Soweto's foul Klipspruit Dam. 'The most difficult stage of the initiation happens in water – a river or a dam – in the darkest hours of night,' Nkunzi writes. 'My two sisters and a few of the elders were present. Family members must accompany the initiate on this part of the journey in case of drowning. Many don't survive.'

To be fearful is a crucial part of the initiation, Nkunzi explained to me as we sat in his small, neat home in Protea Glen, a new middle-class development on the outskirts of Soweto: 'You need to be scared of the spirits, so that your ancestor can come and protect you from them, and this is how he enters you. With your ancestor present, you conquer that fear.' Hence, even in some of the deeper pools of the urban Klip, there is the presence of an *inyoka* spirit, and we headed off to one of these now, a spot where Nkunzi goes to meditate, to perform his rituals and to commune with his ancestors.

I was expecting, I think, to be taken somewhere on the edge of human settlement, deep in the reed beds, shielded from civilisation. But no, Nkunzi's *inyoka* lives in the very middle of the township: right under the Old Potch Road bridge, down a rutted track behind the Sasol Garage, just metres from the Regina Mundi Church, home to so many apartheid-era funerals and protests.

There is a waxen landscape of burned-out candles on a ledge under the bridge; an archaeology of previous *sangoma* rituals. The Sunday buzz of the township was all around us, but here is where Nkunzi finds his peace, never mind the litter or the fag-ends of fires, the music pumping and the roar of cars on Soweto's busiest road overhead. 'It's beautiful,' he told me. 'I will come on a clear night, when I feel I don't have power, and I will be guided to a certain star in the sky. I will follow that star's light down into the water, and dive in to follow it. I'll take a deep swim, until I can no longer see the star. Then, after coming out, I'll feel I have my ancestors with me again, and I know that wherever I go, it's on the right path.'

*

The celebrated Soweto-born photographer Santu Mofokeng has produced a series called 'Radiant Landscapes', that documents humanity's desecration of the natural world. Mofokeng, now in his fifties, is a former struggle photojournalist who inhabits the borderlands between the physical and the paranormal himself; he has done his best work documenting spiritual ecstasy, using the camera to paint such rituals in black and white, with eloquent shadow and perspective-shattering blur. But his 'Radiant Landscapes' could not be more different, particularly the images he took of devotional activity along the Klip River in 2011, where he deploys a sharp-edged hyper-realistic colour to bring out the lurid palette of the rocks stained rust-red by the acid in the water and the deposits of 'yellow boy' left on them.

In one image we see a baptismal priest in his green-and-white robes submerged in a narrow channel of water flowing over radio-active rocks; there is something biblical, apocalyptic, in the colour palette. In another, his shutter arrests the water of the river, in mid-air, as it is thrown from a yellow bucket borne by a *sangoma* onto two large men sitting on the rocks, their Soweto-sized beer-bellies hanging over their shorts. It is a composition that balances rank earthiness with clear ecstasy; balances, too, the invigorating shock of the cleansing spray of water with our knowledge, just by looking at the discoloration of the rocks, that the men are being showered with a solution of salt and acid and uranium that cannot be doing them much good.

I first saw these images at a retrospective of Mofokeng's work at the Jeu de Paume gallery in Paris in 2011. According to Mofokeng, healers would not traditionally use the Klip River for ritual cleansing, because the river was considered sewage. But, he writes in his exhibition text, he had been disturbed recently by the sight of people wallowing 'in ecstasy and in abandon in the "sewer" ... oblivious to the danger of contamination'.

Could it be, the photographer wondered, that these devotees 'consider themselves immune to any afflictions and disease'?

Nkunzi Nkabinde answered this, for me, when we visited his sacred pool. Certainly, most healers prefer to travel up to the Magaliesberg to conduct their rituals in its uncontaminated mountain waters, but what is to be done if you have a client who needs cleansing – or if you need congress with your ancestors – and you both need to be home to put your baby to bed or to get work the following morning? Anyway, he concluded, 'before you even jump inside the water, you are praying, asking the ancestors for guidance, asking them to clean the water'. He laughed, somewhat scornfully, at my preoccupation with the water's contamination as if to say, what is a little radioactive uranium, some stray E.coli bacteria, up against the power of the ancestors? He had nothing to worry about.

'Nothing?'

Well, almost nothing. Every time he submerges himself in the pool, he has to overcome his mortal fear of one thing: 'sharks'.

Sharks?

'I'm terrified of sharks.'

'But Nkunzi, surely you know it is not possible for there to be sharks in the Klip River. And even if there were, then surely the Acid Mine Drainage would have killed them by now.'

'Still, I fear them. They are a *terror* for me.'

'Because you need to have fear of something, so that the ancestors will protect you?'

He nodded.

'Why not fear something real? Why not fear the polluted water you're swimming in?'

He looked at me, gentle scorn pulling his eyebrows up and creasing his forehead.

'*Umlungu*', the eyebrows said. 'White boy'. Yellow boy.

*

Nkunzi has always favoured male attire: men's slacks, an argyle sweater, a leather jacket, a cloth cap. Stockily built, he walks with an assertive butch swagger but does not deny his femininity: 'Nkunzi dances like a woman and slaughters like a man,' reads the blurb on the back of *Black Bull*, and this strikes me as just right, even after his gender transition. In the decade I have known him, he has always claimed his space comfortably, even when living as a woman. He met his wife, Johanna, when they were both ill in hospital; she had never been with another woman before. They were married in her family's charismatic evangelical church, where the congregation considered Nkunzi to be a man even before he went through the transition process. Desperate to be a parent, he adopted the abandoned baby of a relative; he and Johanna now raise the child. If in contemporary South Africa, working-class black lesbians were vulnerable to 'corrective rape' attacks then Nkunzi did not fear this himself when he was still in a woman's body: no man would mess with a *sangoma*, he told me.

Still, growing up dirt-poor and in the wrong body was difficult, and the river has always been something of a refuge for Nkunzi. It was a place he could seek retreat – alone, with other *sangomas*, or with his ancestors – from the troubles of his earthly, urban life: an abusive, often absent father; a struggling family that was often not able to put food on the table; the difficulties he faced, when younger, because he did not conform to gender stereotypes. It was a place, too, during his *sangoma* training and initiation, where he first experienced a world that did not include, or need to account to, men.

Unlike the fast-flowing Jukskei, which churns its way over rapids in Alexandra, the Klip winds through massive reed beds, and many Sowetans consider the river to be unsafe because of the way the reeds can shield criminal activity. They give cover, for better or for worse, and for Nkunzi they became not only an important borderland between this world and the next, but a liminal space at the edge of society where he did not need to be bound by its rules, rules about how he should look and behave.

As I stood with him at his pool, I remembered the stories of Edgar, who grew up in Pimville, alongside the Klip River, in the 1940s. Edgar, like Nkunzi, was Zulu, and knew and loved the landscape of rural Zululand. He had first discovered his 'love of men' while herding livestock with his age-mates along the banks of the Mvothi River, he had told me, and it was while swimming with them that he first practised *hlobongo*, the isiZulu word for thigh-sex, which in Zulu culture, as in Xhosa, is acceptable among boys as well as between boys and girls. Edgar loved to recount how King Shaka had encouraged *hlobongo* among his male soldiers. As he put it to me: 'Men would just be on their own for a decade, in battlefields and what have you, and they would do this, and I tell you, it's a beautiful experience to have a man with you. Zulus do it *professionally*!'

It did not take Edgar long, when his family moved to Pimville, to find the Klip, and to join other boys in recreating their traditional age-mate groups after school. It was not the Mvothi but still, they made do. They prodded the few scrawny goats and cows about; they swam; they did their stickfighting; and they found each other's thighs.

*

Recently, I looked again at an unforgettable image of a mass baptism in the late 1950s taken by the great black South African photographer Ernest Cole, whose portraits of black life were a sensation when they were published as *House of Bondage* in New York in 1967. There is an epic quality, an infernal energy, to Cole's vision: the water churned into a maelstrom by the mass of bodies draped in drenched clothing; the scream of the woman at the focal point of the image as she is pulled into the water, contorted into that narrow range between agony and ecstasy; the way the photographer looks down on the scene from above, letting the water fill his frame, decapitating three figures so that their expressions are visible only in their beseeching, clapping hands. House of Bondage: you look at this image and you think of the

Nile and the Jordan, of the Mississippi and the Middle Passage. You think: these people are not free.

There is another image of Cole's that has stayed in my mind, exhibited alongside his 'Baptism' at a retrospective of his work at the Johannesburg Art Gallery in 2010. It portrays a less formal kind of baptism: a group of boys have stripped naked and are running through the municipal sprinklers irrigating a sun-scorched park in Cole's native Mamelodi township. The boys are arrested in motion as if they were Greek athletes – here a discus-thrower, here a wrestler, here a sprinter – and the image is all the more striking because Cole's other images of naked people, his signature images, are of undressed black men lining up, at a mines recruitment office, to be examined as chattel or cattle before being contracted to work. These images have become emblematic of the dehumanisation of the South African migrant-labour system and, in their proximity, there is redemption to the sprinkler image: even in the house of bondage that was Cole's South Africa, these joyous children are free, abandoned to the waters.

*

I was thinking of both Cole and Mofokeng's images when I came across a series of slides documenting the Hope and Unity Metropolitan Community Church (HUMCC), the black gay charismatic church set up by a visionary pastor, the Reverend Tsietsi

Thandekiso, in 1994. The HUMCC used to meet in a ballroom at the Harrison Reef Hotel in Hillbrow, just above the Skyline bar, and in among the images of prayer, of ceremony and celebration amid the tatty old velvet, threadbare carpeting and net curtains of the Harrison Reef, were a series of startling photographs of a 1996 baptism in a suburban swimming pool, taken by my friend, the anthropologist Graeme Reid.

The landscape of these photographs could not be more banal: highveld-yellow lawn, a big old pool filled with familiar suburban milky-blue water; a boxy post-war bungalow in the background. The images capture Thandekiso, middle-aged and robed in white cloth, performing the baptism on a younger man. Standing around the pool observing the ceremony are four other men in bathing suits. Three of them have their heads bowed and are praying; the fourth, draped in a towel like a toga and leading the prayer with his palms outstretched, gives the composition the note of a Greek chorus. Look back to the left, across the lawn, and you'll see, sitting on a chair on the patio under an umbrella, a slumped white man.

The fact that there is a baptism taking place in so banal a suburban setting is only marginally more startling than the fact that there are a group of semi-naked young black men around this swimming pool, just after the death of apartheid, overlooked by a white seigneur. I took the images to show to Paul Mokgethi, who replaced Thandekiso as head of the church, and whom I recognised in the photos. The pool did indeed belong to the white man, Mokgethi told me, a Dutch psychologist who lived on Barry Herzog Avenue in Greenside and whose boyfriend, an SAA air steward, was an elder in the church. These ceremonies were 'rebaptisms', a staple of the charismatic practice: you renounce your old church – in the case of Mokgethi and his coreligionists, more often than not the homophobic institutions you had fled and sought sanctuary from in the HUMCC – and you embrace your new faith. It was one of the most memorable experiences of his life, Mokgethi told me, although he conceded it was unusual to use a pool rather than a river: 'It just seemed safer. In a river, the current can sweep you out, and several of us were worried because we do not know how to swim.'

Mokgethi went through the photographs with me and identified the participants. Of the five, two (including Thandekiso) would die of AIDS-related illness; a third would be shot in the head when he was walking home from the Skyline Bar in 2005. 'He was originally from Zimbabwe,' Mokgethi told me. 'We took his body back there, to bury him, because no one would come and collect it.'

*

Like the Klip River, the Jukskei also rises in the city. It flows north along its eastern perimeter, churning down rapids as it enters Alexandra, flooding its banks every rainy season and leaving squatters homeless. Until the relatively recent laying-down of sewers, the township's human effluent streamed down open dongas into the river, especially during the rains. Even after the sewers were laid, there were problems, I was told by Sizakele Nkosi, an Alexandra ANC politician, because the township's pipes were so much narrower than Sandton's, even though all of Sandton's sewage needed to flow through Alexandra to get down to the sewage-treatment plant on the Jukskei: 'It was the *shhhit!* from Sandton that was causing the trouble in Alex,' she said, hissing the word out and bringing it to a sharp plosive resolution for effect. The effect was good enough to bear repetition: 'The rich man's *shhhit!* must trouble the poor man.'

Later, I sat in an Alexandra room with two elderly residents: Ntate Frans Molefe, a retired office clerk, and a feisty old woman named Ma Thoko Buthelezi, who had lived in her two rooms off a yard on Seventeenth Street for sixty years, and raised her family here. Ma Buthelezi had an environmentalist's understanding of the dangers of the Jukskei: 'Before,' she said, 'there was no trouble with the river. All the children were playing there. I did my washing and bathing there. But now everyone throws their rubbish in, and the town council doesn't keep it so clean any more ...'

Ntate Molefe's approach to the dangers of the river was more meta-physical: 'They say there is a big snake in there that is killing people. Sometimes the snake comes like a football on the water. You swim over to it to get the ball, then it takes you. Four kids were killed this way, they've never been found.'

'It's the waters that take you,' Ma Buthelezi corrected him. 'The currents. Then they will find your body all the way at Fourways.'

But Ntate Molefe stood his ground, and in a way the two old people – both long-time residents of Alexandra – agreed: the river somehow portended the illness of modern times. 'People hang themselves off the bridge every week, off the London Road bridge,' Molefe said. 'Recently they found *four people.*'

As he spoke, I thought of H.I.E. Dhlomo's epic poem, *Valley of a Thousand Hills*, written in the 1940s, which tracks the dispossession of black people through the perversion of nature: 'a flooded stream all dark and fierce with Wrong' running through a landscape where hills are replaced with 'mountains of strife', where trees are replaced by 'the swelling song of woe' and where 'a fog of tribulation spreads' as 'erosion sweeps men's souls out to sea.

*

I have been collecting images of the ecstasy of immersion; counter-moments to the kind of erosion suggested by H.I.E. Dhlomo. I've tacked several up onto my wall, alongside the photographs of Ernest Cole and Santu Mofokeng. There is that young couple, the white woman and the black man, locked in an embrace that can only be imagined beneath the coruscations of the water in Bram Fischer's swimming pool; there are my parents held in transparent embrace in the translucent waters of Xai-Xai. There is a still from the swimming-pool scene of *The Rocky Horror Picture Show*, that triggered my own adolescent fantasies of boundlessness: 'Don't dream it, be it.'

And there are photographs from Durban's annual sardine run, when people of all races would flock down to the beach to gather up the silver fish. 'Race doesn't count as waves of humanity leap into the water to meet the thick shoals of fish,' reads a typical caption to one of these images, in a 1963 issue of *Drum* magazine. 'Apartheid in the water falls by the board, and people become – well, just people! And they have a hell of a good time!'

One of my favourite images in the genre was taken by one of *Drum's* star photographers, Ranjith Kally. Kally had the eye of a social critic, and his image works against the utopian 'race doesn't count' narrative in the way it presents a metaphor for whom, in South

African society, holds its slippery, silvery wealth – and, perhaps, how Mammon is a force great enough to overcome social convention. Still, there is something undeniably joyous in the scramble, as people forget their differences and flout the laws of the land in their pursuit of the fish. The sardine run, always covered in the newspapers, attained a carnivalesque status in the South African calendar.

But beneath the conventional images of ecstatic immersion there is always an undertow of darkness. The authors of *Anatomy of South Africa*, a 1966 study of white racial attitudes from a supposedly liberal and scientific perspective, used one of the sardine run images to canvass attitudes in what they claimed was the first public opinion poll in South African history, taken in 1964, the year of my birth. The photograph, an uncredited newspaper image, shows a fully dressed white woman in the shallows, her plastic basket of fish at her side, and her mouth roundly open in some kind of expression of disquiet or disapproval as a brown-skinned youth seems to be barging in front of her bearing a large wooden oar. A white man looks on in concern.

The authors showed this image to their respondents as part of a 'social values study' and asked them to tell a story to explain it. 'They were on the seashore,' said one respondent, 'the mixed groups of Whites and non-Whites. She must have said or done something – what she herself doesn't know, because she doesn't yet know the likes and dislikes of non-Whites ... The next minute he had grabbed an oar and hit her viciously ... If her White friends had not come to her and rescued her ... – she screams when she thinks what could have happened. Never again will she advocate social integration.'

The published response of another participant is more extreme: 'I notice that the Native in the picture pushes his way in between the White people in an unruly and unmannerly way. One woman clearly disapproves ... The picture tells me one thing only. This is the odium and offensive of multiracialism ... This picture upsets me. I don't like it. I don't like White women being pushed around by Natives ... The more I look at it the more I work myself up against the Native. I think my feelings are the same as the Whites in the picture. They don't like what they see.'

Of the thousand white South Africans canvassed, 73 per cent agreed that the 'colour issue' was the greatest problem facing the country, and 56 per cent believed that the best solution to this problem was some form of apartheid. Only 9 per cent saw the solution to be 'economic development of the Native', and an even smaller number – 4 per cent – believed that integration was the answer. Nearly 16 per cent did not have an answer.

*

Two decades later, in 1987, the Reverend Allan Hendrickse marched into the sea. He was at a white beach in Port Elizabeth, accompanied by two fellow politicians, to protest at the continued segregation imposed by 'petty apartheid'. Hendrickse was the head of the House of Representatives – the 'parliament' representing coloured voters – and even though he later shamefully apologised to President P.W. Botha for his defiance, the moment was a turning point: the laws of petty apartheid began to be ignored, or revoked. The photograph of the protest, which has become one of the iconic images of the collapse of apartheid, holds me now because of the way it captures the moment

before immersion, the moment before liberation; because of the way it – quite literally – performs the breaking of a border, a boundary between shore and sea, between what is permissible and what is illicit, between what is clothed and what is naked.

South Africa is a land of bellies, and I sit the image next to Santu Mofokeng's 'radiant landscape', where one of these bellies is being doused by a *sangoma's* holy, toxic water. Looking at the Hendrickse photograph today, it seems just as shocking that two big fat men, two politicians, have taken their clothes off in front of the cameras, as it is that they are doing so on a whites-only beach.

The Wilds

When I am working in Johannesburg I end most days, if I can, with the dog-owners walking circuits around the dams of the Braamfontein Spruit – another tributary of the Jukskei – in the Johannesburg Botanical Gardens at Emmarentia. I usually walk with either one of my friends Philip or Carol: they have a pair of poodles apiece and their own dark frizzy Jewish hair to match, and we set off southward from the car park, through the copse of pines along a steep embankment before crossing the spruit at the lip of the park and following the course of the stream as it pools in a series of little dams. The walk is through landscaped parkland rather than veld, and we will sometimes break the rules to stray into the dog-free zone: the terraced stone rose garden laid out in art deco style, or the aloe garden, alight in mid-winter, or the swathe of picnicking lawn dipping down to the Emmarentia Dam across which rowers scull in the twilight. The park is glorious in all seasons: the wetland irises in springtime bloom, the summer birds razzling the reed beds, the palette of blonde grass and oxide-red earth against an intense, thin-aired winter sky.

On a nice evening you will trip over almost every Johannesburg dog you know, and some you wish you didn't, whose owners have crowded into these few-square fenced hectares of nature as the security situation has rendered wilder places inaccessible. When I first came back to Johannesburg in the 1990s I would tramp, sometimes alone, over those conical hills, those rocky koppies, sketched by Tompkins on his map. The Wilds was already too dangerous by then, but I would walk across Langerman's Kop to the east or the Melville Koppies to the west, with views across Johannesburg that belied my childhood experience of the city as flat and featureless.

Later, when I moved to Melville myself, the koppies were directly across from me, almost as close as The Wilds had been when I lived in Killarney and equally as inaccessible. As I looked out over them, I often thought of the infamous gang leader Nongoloza, who initiated the highly codified organized-crime gang culture that exists to this day. Johannesburg's hills belonged to his band again, it seemed, and the rest of us were left the valleys.

Even so, there are notices at the entrance to the Botanical Gardens' valleys warning walkers to beware of muggers and to use the park only when others are around: hence the busyness between four and six, contrasted with the park's virtual emptiness on weekdays, save for the neighbourhood's domestic workers threading across the grassy slopes. Even during the dog-walking rush hour you learn to be alert; to stay away from dark-green glades where attackers might lurk; to remain on open, high ground where you can be seen as dusk approaches; to walk in silently selected little clumps of people, even as you keep to yourself. '*Entre chien et loup*,' is the evocative French expression for dusk: 'between dog and wolf'. In 2010, Carol and her husband, Neil, lingered just into wolf-time with their poodles: Neil was kneed to the ground with a gun at his head while they were robbed; the couple were set free only after intense and urgent supplication.

Two years later, I would be held hostage, at gunpoint, with my friends Katie and Bea at my old flat at Wildsview, by three men who had crossed the palisade fencing from The Wilds just beneath. It has come to me since that the reason I have recently become so preoccupied with nature in Johannesburg is precisely because of the way it has been landscaped into frontiers: the blue gums and pines patrolling the perimeters of the suburban gardens of my childhood, carving a parkland with shade and birdsong out of the harsh Highveld; the toxic white mountains and the band of undermined veld dividing Johannesburg and Soweto; the Sandspruit forming the uncrossable boundary at the edge of page 77 in the *Holmden's*; The Wilds separating the mean streets of Hillbrow and Yeoville from the bounty of the Northern Suburbs.

*

The Wilds was established in 1937 on land donated to the city by Johannesburg Consolidated Investments, one of the big mining houses, because it was too steep to be developed into residential property. The grant stipulated that it was to remain open land for public use, and the decision to landscape it into an indigenous garden was made when a new home had to be found for the plants propagated for the massive rockery at the 1937 Empire Exhibition to commemorate Johannesburg's silver jubilee and the coronation of King George VI.

The park was developed as a showpiece for indigenous vegetation from all over South Africa: there are slopes of Cape fynbos and glades of subtropical milkwood or coastal yellowwood, banks of proteas and pockets of aloes, all landscaped into European-style botanical gardens that are not 'wild' at all, and certainly not anything like what would be found on an indigenous highveld koppie. In effect The Wilds is an artificial settler-fantasy of wilderness rather than wilderness itself; in the tradition of the national botanical garden, it practises a sort of vegetal nationalism, celebrating the nation through its floral diversity. But in recent years it has grown into its name with tragic irony.

'What a world!' exclaimed Enos Mhlanga, the chief horticulturalist of The Wilds when I went to visit him in 2011. 'Not even the plants are safe.' He was showing me his particular pride, a ten-foot-high giant cycad twice the age of the city it overlooks from its eyrie, a hothouse not a hundred metres from the kitchen window through which the three armed intruders would enter the flat at Wildsview a few months later. Literally under lock and key, the cycad was splashed with red paint across its base to identify it. It was also implanted with a microchip to enable it to be tracked, and compared with a DNA sample of its bark deposited in a 'barcode library' at the University of Johannesburg.

Mhlanga would retire a few months later; he had been running The Wilds since 1989. He had come to Johannesburg as a migrant in the Seventies from Bushbuckridge in the lowveld bordering the Kruger National Park to take a job with City Parks. He had worked his way up from a gardener at Joubert Park ('we made the park lovely but we were not even allowed to sit on the benches') to his current position, picking up a string of qualifications along the way. Once the pretty stone restaurant just off Houghton Drive closed down, the Parks Department converted it into offices and lodgings for him, and so he lived in the place I used to go, as a little boy, to have tea and scones with one or another Killarney aunty.

The things Mhlanga loved most about his urban home were those that reminded him of his native bushveld, like the flock of guineafowl on the Eastern Ridge or his beloved cycads. There are about 150 specimens of these rare and valuable trees in The Wilds, ancient and primordial, one of the world's oldest species, with lifetimes up to eight hundred years scored into their thick knotted trunks, the cycle of each year recorded by another circle of exuberant fronds.

Mhlanga tended his turf meticulously for the quarter century of his tenure, although budget cuts stripped seventy men down to ten and no one came to visit any more. In 1939, 45,000 people entered the park on weekends; that number remained stable until the late 1980s, when the footfall plummeted dramatically following the changing complexion of the inner city and a soaring crime rate on the koppies. Now, Mhlanga and his team kept the beautiful stone contour paths tended for the odd *inyanga* doing some foraging or ritual (one of the major causes of the fires which have devastated The Wilds), the homeless people who squat in the caves on the eastern ridge (the other cause of fires), a few smooching teenagers and bridal photo parties on weekends, the kids who come with their schools to do rock climbing, the 'Friends of The Wilds' Sunday morning dog-walking group – and Vincent, my erstwhile neighbour from Wildsview, who used the park as his garden and his retreat, in a way that I often longed to in the five years I lived at Wildsview, but never did.

'It's a hundred per cent safe here, on the western ridge, in the daytime,' Mhlanga assured me. 'If you come this side, I can guarantee your safety.' He swept his arm eastward, beyond Houghton Drive. 'But that side, it's different. We have a mugging there almost every weekend. Just don't cross the bridge, and you'll be fine.'

We talked about how sad it was that so few people now used The Wilds, given its proximity to the very poor people who now populated the inner-city flatlands of Hillbrow and Berea just beyond Louis Botha Avenue. So many of the inhabitants of these urban ghettoes came from rural areas themselves, and had so little access in their dense inner-city lives to nature and public open space – although I sensed there was more than a little relief, for Mhlanga, that most of them did not know about The Wilds. He had enough of a headache, as it was, keeping his cycads safe.

Cycad poaching has become a major problem in South Africa. They are a protected species risking extinction, and sell on the black market for astronomical prices: The Wilds alone has had at least thirty wrenched from its soil, each one a personal wound for Mhlanga. The Cycad Society maintains a database of media coverage of the problem. Here are some of the entries over the past six years: 'Three Suspected Cycad Thieves Arrested'; 'Four in dock for theft of rare cycads'; 'Plant "dinosaurs" dying out in South Africa'; 'Poachers are targeting rare cycads.' And my favourite, from 2006: '"Cycad raider in drag" nabbed again: The alleged cross-dressing garden-raider has been arrested again and accused of stealing rare and expensive cycads – only hours after he appeared in court on similar charges.'

I went back to the files of Independent Newspapers, but I couldn't find a photo.

*

As I walked The Wilds with Enos Mhlanga, a turn around a stone path would reveal an unexpected angle of Houghton Ridge, or the back end of the Johannesburg General Hospital, or the familiar vista of Hillbrow's tower-blocks poking through the aloes, or an aspect of the woodlands of the Northern Suburbs opening out beyond the lip of a rocky kloof. None of these views were new; just subtly and unexpectedly different. It made me think of how, lying on the couch watching television with C or reading together in bed, we wriggle into comfort around each other's bodies in a way that unexpectedly affords me a glancing aspect over him that I habitually missed, such as the gentle arc in the crease-lines that pull his eyes into a smile, or the hair that nestles like a copse in the hollow of his lower back. Such subtle changes of perspective over the familiar can renew love with such unexpected intensity that they leave you gasping for breath. That is how I felt about Johannesburg, walking The Wilds, in my forty-seventh year of life, for the first time since my childhood.

*

Later, in 2012, a few months after the attack, I forced myself to take a walk alone through The Wilds, up towards Wildsview. It was not as difficult as I thought it might be. I followed the route our assailants would have taken, making my way up the steep embankment from the grassed parkland around the dams in the valley through the glades of stinkwood and yellowwood to the path that runs along the upper perimeter of the park's western portion. It was early spring and the route was studded with clivias; when I had lived at Wildsview myself, I would often get up from my desk and walk through to the back-room window and lose myself for a while, looking down on these deep-shade plants upholstered with plump orange blossoms. Now I walked right beneath that window, on the path along the palisade fence on which the police had found a sock used by the three men to cover the spike of the fence as they vaulted over it.

As I looked up at Bea and Katie's flat and tried to recreate the path of our assailants, I heard the familiar booming voice of Aaron, the Wildsview caretaker, and the familiar whine of the elevator rising. I heard the familiar judder of the electronic garage door opening; I watched Katie's familiar gold Mercedes swoop out and around the familiar cambers of 10th Avenue. I felt a strange, almost echoing, sense of disorientation, as if I were inside-out, on the wrong side of my own experience or perhaps inside my own brain, on the inner side of that thin membrane separating my experience from my interpretation of it. I looked up at the back window and saw myself looking down at me. I thought about the frontier of fear: how hard-nailed it is into the landscape and how it defines us beyond reason. How easy it is to cross it. As easy as throwing a sock over a palisade fence.

PART TWO

ATTACK

Bea was sitting on one couch, and Katie and I on another.

On the television, a tightly coiled suburban Melbourne community was unravelling into a dystopia, revealing the violence of their everyday lives. There was a lot of shouting and swearing on the screen, and the angry interruption into our evening seemed, at first, to float above reality, as if it had materialised out of the television set.

There was a crash, from somewhere off to the left, that sounded perhaps as if the wind blowing in a summer night's thunderstorm was sweeping bottles off a windowsill. Katie rose to investigate. As she did, three men emerged slowly out of the obscurity, from the direction of the kitchen, wielding guns and shouting at us. One of them whacked Katie, shoving her back down onto the couch. Before I even knew what I was doing, words were leaving my mouth, rising above their own words telling us to stand up, to sit down, to shut up, to talk ('Where's the safe? Talk! Talk!'), to cooperate, to behave, promising to kill us if we did not.

'Our stuff is over there,' I said, 'in those bags.' I heard my voice as if it was not mine, and I noted that it was both too confident and too fearful: it boomed and faltered. 'That black bag is mine. There's a computer in it, and my wallet, and my car keys.'

One of the men responded by rushing towards me and, from the side, whacking me across the head. My glasses went flying, leaving me blind and disoriented. I heard Katie stifle a cry, next to me; he had hit her too – across her temple with his pistol. I watched, blurrily, as one of the men started upending the television and the sound system, making a terrific crash that plunged the room into obscurity – a lamp must have fallen and its bulb smashed – and brought an end to

247

The Slap. I could hear myself breathing heavily, and each breath seemed to bring me closer to the present. The shock that plunged us into silence and darkness seemed to galvanise those senses left to me, senses rent from my body by that slap to the head, and I found myself becoming acutely aware and calm, listening intently to the silence, now, a silence broken by mutterings in what seemed to be isiZulu as the three men whispered to each other.

It became clear why they had caused the electrical crash: they intended using the cords to tie us up. I followed my breath, in, out, in, out, and heard Bea's voice, calm and clear: 'Excuse me,' she said, as if she was talking to someone at a book-club meeting, 'but we've just made tea, I think the cup's still hot, you'll see, and I was wondering if you'd give me a sip before you gag me, because my throat is feeling very dry.'

From the motion I could sense to the extreme left of my peripheral vision and the sounds I could hear, I realised they had complied. I understood immediately what Bea had done, and what I needed to do, too. It was as clear as anything I have ever thought, and I will never forget it. We needed to communicate with them. We needed to make them look after us. We needed to get them to acknowledge that we were human beings and not animals, not disposable, and then they might spare us. And then the revelation: this meant we needed to see them as human beings, and not animals, too, if we were going to survive.

I have thought, in retrospect, that I afforded myself far too much agency by according myself this task. The men had alcohol on their breath and the behaviour of one of them – the gangly pop-eyed man who had smacked me – seemed high beyond reason, adrenalised by fear or something else. So fraught was the situation, so chaotic, so dependent on the rational behaviour of six individuals – three edgy assailants and three terrified victims, unevenly matched – that even the most careful, cooperative behaviour imaginable might not have saved us. Still, I had given myself a job to do, an objective, and it focused my mind.

*

The men pushed us roughly to our feet. As they did so, my body brushed Katie's. 'You like her,' one of them said to me, with a sneer.

I nodded.

'You two are cosy.'

I nodded again, and heard Katie say, 'Yes.'

They thought we were a couple and that we were visiting Bea. In the African way, they called Bea 'Grandmother' and Katie 'Sister'. Every time I heard them address the women like this, I thought to myself: These men are well brought up. They have grandmothers and sisters. They have become monsters. But they were not always monsters.

There were three of them and three of us.

Katie and I were in our late forties; Bea, a grandmother in fact, was in her early sixties. Katie and Bea are a couple: they have been together for many years. Katie is Irish: although she has lived almost all her adult life in Johannesburg and considers herself South African, she speaks with a soft brogue. She has a startlingly original intellect, and the enviable ability to see the world askance, an ability that sometimes makes her feel askance too; she is diffident and self-conscious and very funny and immensely well-read. Bea was born and bred in Port Elizabeth, and she has something of the Eastern Cape frontierswoman in her. She is always busy, always upbeat, always in charge: Katie, who collects, among many other things, valedictory school badges, once found Bea one which read 'Deputy Head Girl'. We all laughed, because of the way it brought her down a peg.

There were three of them and three of us. We could not control them, and we might not even be able to control ourselves. Would Bea try to do something? Would Katie melt? Could I conquer the rising, acrid terror in my gorge?

Could I sit still?

*

As my arms were being pulled behind my back and tied with cord, the short one was in front of me. I am of average height, but he strained to reach eye level with me. He was well-spoken. 'No heroes,' he said. 'We don't want no heroes.'

I nodded and verbalised assent. 'I won't be a hero. I will do what ever you say.'

'Yes, you will,' he shot back. 'You know why?'

I shook my head.

'Because we are the heroes.'

A beat.

'Why are we the heroes?'

I shook my head again.

'Because we are the ones with the guns.'

I heard Bea to my side: 'Yes, that's right. You are the heroes.'

'You must respect us,' the dark one said. He spoke with the heavily accented but fluent English of a Zimbabwean migrant. He was square-jawed and muscular, with the military air of a colonel about him: I figured he must be ex-army. He certainly seemed to be the most professional of the three, with a button-down shirt neatly tucked into smart pants unlike the baggy streetwear of the other two. He was, I laughed darkly to myself at one point, a typical migrant, so much better-spoken and polite than the rude South Africans; trying hard to impress. It was his gun that seemed most often trained upon us, heavy and steady, so much deeper in the barrel than I had imagined pistols to be, having never looked at one closely before.

'You must respect us,' The Colonel said. 'This is our job. This is how we do our work. You go to your work and we go to our work.'

Shorty took up the cry, with more edge: 'You must respect us or we will kill you.'

Poppy-Eyes upped the ante: 'We will kill you.'

'We respect you,' I said.

'Yes, we respect you,' I heard Bea say. 'We respect your work.'

Respecting them meant, most of all, telling them where the safe was, but they would not believe us when we told them there wasn't one. I felt the cords biting into the skin of my wrists and a tingle spread through my hands and fingers as the blood flow was impeded. The angle at which my arms had been pulled back behind my back was not comfortable, and I wondered if I should say something, as Bea had about the tea, but I thought better of it.

'Do you live here?' Shorty asked me. He would always be the one to engage with me, and I assumed he was the leader. He had a small, round face with a button of a nose, and wore a beanie. He would widen his little eyes when he spoke to me to make them angrier, but somehow I knew he would not be the one to hurt me. I was much more worried about The Colonel and his gun, or jumpy Poppy-Eyes whose irrationality was matched with an anger that seemed real rather than performed.

'No, I don't live here,' I responded, truthfully, terrified that by doing so I might be making the situation more difficult for myself or, worse, more difficult for Katie and particularly Bea, as the intruders' attentions were rounding inexorably on her, the presumed house-holder. In retrospect, the trauma that emanated from pressure to make a quick decision – a decision that held life in the balance – was greater, even, than that of helplessness.

'How did you come here?' Shorty asked me.

'In my car. It's parked outside.'

'Which one is it?'

'It's the green BMW with the black roof.'

'Where are the keys?'

I described them, and where I thought they were; one of them went to find them, and brought them back to be identified by me. I could not see them, though. 'I am sorry, I am blind without my glasses. Can you bring them closer?' They were waved right in front of my eyes, and I recognised the soft leather case. 'Yes, those are them.'

I noticed that, while they had bound Katie and Bea's legs, they had left mine free. My heart beat fast and I found myself drenched in sweat as my mind raced around this conundrum. Did this mean they were sloppy and unprofessional, stoned kids, loose cannons on a joyride? Or were they intending to march me, the man and the visitor, out somewhere – perhaps to my car, to kidnap me with it, or perhaps to my execution? Which was worse? The thought caused me to panic as I was gagged with what seemed to be a stocking. I suffer from blocked sinuses, and it took a few terrified gasps before my breath could establish a path through my nostrils and down my throat, down through the rising bile of my terror. I retched, and was admonished. I thought, consciously, of the breathing techniques I had learned in yoga class and I told myself that I needed to apply them here. I made my breath audible and listened to it. I followed it. I let it become me. I thought about how at any moment it might be arrested by a gunshot; that it would be no longer. I wondered if I would hear the gunshot before dying; if I would feel pain. I tried to remember the Serenity Prayer but when it wouldn't come to me I abandoned it while trying to hold on to its sentiment. I could not move. I could not talk. I could do nothing about my situation. I became calm.

*

The search for the safe became our assailants' *idée fixe*. In the process, they trashed the flat, turning everything upside down. There was always one man with a gun on us – The Colonel, it seemed – while the others prowled, looking behind artworks, sweeping books off shelves, emptying cupboards and bags, moving into and out of the kitchen. Sometimes one of them would come into the lounge eating something and, after taking a bite or two, would throw it across the room. The microwave seemed to be going a lot in the kitchen: my senses hyper alert, I heard its churn and its ping, and at one point I thought I smelled burning. I decided that this meant they were doing drugs, and I became more intensely focused on monitoring their actions to see if there was any change in them.

They found our wallets, and began interrogating Katie and me, but not Bea, about our pin codes. They wanted a pen and paper to write them down, and Bea – who, it seemed, had not been gagged – directed them to the study adjoining the living room. What followed restoked my terror. I had to remember which codes belonged to which cards in my wallet and then find a way of enunciating them clearly with a stocking stuffed in my mouth. I was certain I would remember the numbers but I had no confidence that they would hear them correctly through the gag, or that, in their chaotic confusion, they would take them down correctly.

Shorty came right up to me. 'You must give us the right numbers. I will send these boys to see if you are right, and I will stay here with the gun, and then they will phone me to tell me if you are lying. And if you are lying I will shoot you dead. Or I will leave you here tied up and when they come in three days to find you they will find you dead.' This last was his preferred threat, he used it often, always with the three days.

The men could not seem to attach the right numbers to the cards, or perhaps they were testing us. And so, over and over, they asked Katie and I to identify cards and repeat numbers, which they scribbled onto disparate scraps of paper which would then seem to get lost in the darkness and the gathering chaos of the room. At one point, after being forced to repeat a number several times, and retching every time I did so with the attempt to talk wedging the gag deeper into my gullet, I lost my patience. 'If you take this out of my mouth,' I mumbled, 'you'll be able to hear me better.'

Poppy-Eyes exploded, rounding on me, 'Shut up! Shut up! Shut up or I'll kill you *now!*'

*

While interrogating Katie and me about the cards, the men kept the pressure on Bea about the safe. One of them approached her angrily: 'What's this? Which of these keys is the key to the safe? Which one?'

I heard her voice falter, for the first time, as she tried to find the words to explain, clearly, how even though the long key looked like it might be the key to a safe it was actually the front door key for one of her properties in Cape Town. 'No, man,' one of the men responded. 'You are lying. You are lying. I am going to get the iron. Where's the iron? I'm going to get the iron and we will *torturer* you. You will tell us where the safe is and you will give us the key.'

'*Torturer*' was the verb; it was said often, and its additional syllable, its elision of actor and act, did its job. Katie and I, seated on the couch, were just touching, and I felt her body stiffen as she attempted to stifle a gasp. Bea's voice found its measure, again, as she attempted reason.

'This is not our flat,' she said. 'I am just a tenant. I rent the flat. Look, you can see, I don't have many things. I am not rich.'

Still, they continued hammering Bea with threats: 'Go to the kitchen and get a knife,' one of them said. When another came back into the room brandishing what looked like a big kitchen knife, I heard words coming out of my mouth, once more before I knew I had said them. 'Please come here,' I mumbled, 'I've got something to tell you.'

Shorty came striding over to me. I motioned for him to take the gag out of my mouth, and he did. 'Look me in the eye,' I said, mustering all the authority I could, 'Look me in the eye,' although as I was saying it I remembered that the last thing you were supposed to do when being attacked was look your assailant in the eye. Shorty obeyed, however, rounding his eyes once more to mime aggression and raising his brows in silent interrogation. 'We don't have a safe. Please believe me, we don't have one. Look at me. Look at us. You can see what kind of people we are. We are not the kind of people who would give up our lives just to save some things in a safe. We want to help you. We want to help you finish your job and we want to stay alive.'

He shoved the sock back into my mouth and walked away from me. It seemed to work for a while. The mood calmed down. I began listening to my breath again. I heard Katie's breath next to me. I tried to pair my breath with hers, so that we would breathe together and so that we would both breathe regularly. I broke into another sweat. My shorts felt so wet that I wondered if I had pissed without realising it.

That morning, I had been to visit C's niece in hospital: she had just given birth, and I had looked in wonder at the little brown nut of life in the crib. He had opened his eyes briefly, and for the fraction of a second I had seen a day-old soul. My friend Esther had recently given birth and my friend Ira was expecting twins any day. I thought of my god-daughters and nieces and nephews, the children I cared most about in the world. I worked hard to convince myself that it would be okay if I died, because I was nearly fifty, because there was young life, not just any young life, but young life that mattered to me. I thought about Katie and Bea next to me, and I hoped that they were thinking the same things about their grandchildren. I breathed, and I concentrated my mind on the image of one-day-old Callem in his crib.

*

All three men were back in the room.

'Come, Grandmother,' one of them said, and pulled Bea off the couch.

She cried, 'My knee! Careful, my knee! I have a problem in my knee, I can't walk!' But they disregarded her and she fell, screaming.

Katie and I lost the rhythm of our breath, both gasping. I remembered the lesson of Bea and the tea: 'Please,' I managed to gasp through my gag, 'you can see that she's an old woman. She has a very bad knee. Please be gentle with her. She's an old woman.'

Shorty and Poppy-Eyes must have unbound her legs, for they led her, limping, out of the room. The Colonel sat on the arm of a chair facing Katie and me, his gun trained on us. I felt relief that Bea, rather than I, was being led away, and then I felt terrible shame and guilt for having felt that, a shame and a guilt compounded by helplessness. After a while, we heard Bea's screams coming from the bedroom. Katie and I both started crying, attempting unsuccessfully to stifle our sobs. For the first and only time, The Colonel lost his cool, clearly discomforted: 'Shut up! Shut up! Stop being cry-babies! I don't want to hear any nyaah-nyaah-nyaaah'.

Bea's cries became increasingly urgent, and I heard a switch go off inside me. Later, the trauma therapist would explain to me that our primal brains, at the back of our heads, are reptilian, and that over the course of evolution, our mammal brains were added, then our primate brains, and then, finally, our human ones. When we are under deep threat, she said, we revert to our reptile brains: all sense and instinct, no intellect or emotion.

I became a reptile.

I heard Bea screaming, and then I heard her stop. I did not think about why she was screaming, and I did not think about why she had stopped or what she might be feeling, or not feeling. My only thought was that her screams would raise the alarm, and that this would make our situation worse, rather than better. I did not think about the newborn baby, Callem, or what was happening to Bea, or what would happen to us. I did not think about whether we would live or die. I breathed. I heard Katie breathe. I tried to regulate Katie's breathing by breathing alongside her. We were one organism: she was one lung and I was the other. I heard some noise in the passage. I saw Bea being led in. I could see that her blouse was undone.

*

We sat in silence, bound and gagged while the three men paced about, randomly looking behind pictures, returning repeatedly to a fireplace that had been converted into an electric heater, sweeping CDs or books onto the floor, emptying bags onto the floor, packing and repacking bags, going to and from the kitchen, turning on the microwave, conferring among themselves in what seemed to be isiZulu. They began interrogating us about our cars. Which were our cars, and where were they parked? Which were the keys to which cars? How did you get the cars out of the garage? Where was the garage? There was lightning and thunder outside. 'It seems like rain,' Shorty said to us with affable familiarity, as if talking to old friends after a satisfying dinner.

I was no longer a reptile. I focused on the contents of my bag. I had brought all my technology with me, for Katie to help me with a problem: my laptop, my iPad, my Blackberry were in my bag, as was a printout of a draft manuscript of my book – this book – with extensive handwritten edits I had made on it during the summer seaside holiday from which I had just returned. I had spent the previous week working off these notes on my computer, and had done, I felt, my best work yet. In fact, I had had a major breakthrough with a particularly sticky problem that day.

I knew the men would take all my technology, but would they take the manuscript? I debated asking them to leave it behind, but thought the better of it.

I preoccupied myself by running through the options. If they killed us and left the manuscript, someone would find it and publish it. If they did not kill us and took the manuscript, I would have lost my book but I would be alive. If they killed us and took the manuscript, all would be lost. I had backed up my hard-drive before going on holiday, and I had sent the manuscript to my agent, so in truth I had no reason to fear for the death of three years' work alongside my own, but I forgot this, and my entire being became focused on the manuscript. I suppose, in the end, it is easier to contemplate losing your work than your life.

At one point Shorty sidled up to me and asked me, in a conspiratorial way, as if we were now on the same side, 'How do we get out of here without the guard seeing us?' I told him, through the stocking in my mouth, that he could avoid Jonah by taking the lift down to the basement and leaving, with a remote, through the garage door. All three of them came up to me, at different times, verifying which one my car was, outside, and asking me if it had a Tracker device. I was just borrowing the car, I said honestly, it was my mother's and I did not know if it was fitted with a Tracker. Poppy-Eyes must have thought I was being recalcitrant, for he kicked me in the side, not hard, but with enough intent to raise the fear in me again.

The men came and pushed us off the couches and onto the floor, but then seemed to lapse back into aimless prowling, punctuated by staccato bursts of whispering. What was going on? Were they in disagreement about what to do next? Were they waiting for someone or something? Why had they pushed us to the floor? Was it because they were preparing to execute us?

The story needed to end one way or the other, either with their departure or our deaths, and I became desperately impatient. When they pushed me to the floor, they had shifted my body in such a way that I was lying on my shoulders, my head against the couch and the full weight of my upper body on my bound arms. The strain on my arms, together with the electrical cable cutting into my wrist, now became unendurable. I lost all sensation in my hands, and I began to panic. I am a terrible fidgeter, and I now became convinced I would not be able to keep still, and this would cause all of us to be killed.

This made me panic even further. My legs were unbound and I had the physical freedom to move, but I didn't want to attract attention to myself, or give the men any cause to think I might be a threat to them.

Katie sensed my discomfort and my disquiet, and tried to calm me by pulling my breath back into the rhythm of her own, and by edging her own body infinitesimally closer to mine. It helped for a while, but the pain and the need to move became unbearable again, and I knew I needed to do something. I remembered Bea and the tea again, and I decided to ask the men to help me. 'Excuse me?' I whispered through my gag. 'Excuse me?'

The men showed no sign of having heard me, and I was coming close to dangerous panic when Shorty came over to me: 'What do you want?'

'I am feeling very uncomfortable,' I said. 'I am not in a comfortable position. Could you help me move into a more comfortable position, please.'

He patted me down, and I immediately knew what he was doing: 'I don't have any weapons,' I said, 'I promise you.'

In a gesture that was shocking for its gentleness, he eased me into a seated position with my legs crossed, as if caring for a child, or someone disabled, and gave me a pat, as if to check that I was okay. I registered that he felt responsible for me, or that we were in some way collaborators. I registered, too, that when he moved me and folded my legs, he would have seen that my ankles were not bound, and yet he did nothing about it. This, together with the fact that he had helped me, reassured me: they were going to leave soon, I told myself, and they were not going to hurt us. In fact, I reasoned that they had deliberately left my legs unbound because they wanted to give me, the man, the opportunity to seek help once they had gone.

Still, my wrists were in terrible pain, and the numbness in my hands made them feel that they were going to explode. I considered asking Shorty to loosen the binds, but decided against it: I did not want to wreck the mood of collaboration that had been established, and to give him the sense that I might be playing a trick.

When he got up from helping me, his baggy cargo shorts slipped off his slight frame, and I occupied myself, for a while, by watching the way he kept on pulling his pants up, even allowed myself to smile at the Buster Keaton comedy of it: what kind of gangster goes on a heist with pants that won't stay up?

Indeed, he came back to me a little later and said, 'I want your belt.' My first thought was that he was going to use it to bind my feet, at last, or to whack me, and I flinched. With my own hands bound, I could not help him remove the belt, and in the manoeuvres that ensued there was an unexpected physical intimacy: I felt his body against mine and his breath, sour with beer and nicotine, against my neck as he struggled to unbuckle it and pull it out of its loops. The woollen fabric of his beanie rubbed against my face. It smelled of sweat and fear. It was repulsive and increased my impulse to retch from the gag, an impulse I stifled by attempting some forced jocularity. 'I'm a *mafuta*,' I said, a big fat man. 'You are going to have to wind it round you twice to make it fit.'

'Don't worry,' he reassured me, 'I will make a hole for it with a knife.' And he went off to the kitchen.

*

We were left in silence, again, a gun always trained on us. Then they came with duvets and covered us: Katie and I under one, and Bea under another. My eyes had grown accustomed to being without glasses, but now that limited sense was deprived me. One of the men said that the other two were going to check that we had given the right pin codes while he would remain behind. He said he would kill us if the codes were wrong, and that he might kill us anyway.

Then there was silence. Stark, white silence. It was an extraordinary relief after the mayhem, but then it was confusing, and unbearable. What was happening? Were they still there?

Were we dead?

As if in answer to this last question, the pain in my wrists and hands became unbearable again, and the duvet over me was making me feel claustrophobic too. I would rather die than sit still for another moment.

I managed to spit out the gag. 'Do you think they have gone?' I whispered to my friends.

There was no angry male voice to reprimand me, and so I gathered courage, and spoke a little louder, and a little more urgently: 'Do you think they've gone?'

'Not yet,' Katie whispered back. It sounded as if she was no longer gagged too. 'Maybe they're still here.'

'My legs are not bound,' I whispered. 'Should I get up to see?'

'No, wait a while, Marky,' Bea cautioned. 'Just another little while . . .'

I knew Bea and Katie were right, but I could not control my body any longer. The pain in my wrists was too great to bear. With my body, I twitched the duvet off us, and saw Bea next to us, under a blanket. The men had turned the lights on, and I took in the chaos around us. 'There's no one. They've gone,' I said.

I started crying from the pain in my wrists. 'Just wait, darling,' I heard Katie say, 'just give me a moment.' She had been working her hands out of the bounds, and had succeeded in freeing them, and in removing her gag. She had her hands and I had my feet. I stumbled up on my legs and careened around the flat, crying in a pain that was only exacerbated by my unguided movement, trying to use my chin to unlock the catch on the front door so I could call for help, and then stumbling into the kitchen to look for a knife to give to Katie to help her cut us loose. All the drawers were open, and I picked one up in my teeth, taking it back to Katie, who tried to comfort me and calm me as she undid my bounds.

Katie untied her legs, and then calmly released Bea. We helped her up and the three of us embraced, weeping. Bea told us she had been sexually assaulted. 'We're alive,' Katie kept on saying. 'We're alive. We're alive. We're alive. We're alive. We're alive, we're alive. We're alive.'

*

We freed ourselves just after midnight on the morning of 12 January 2012, about two and a half hours after the three men had entered the flat. Unlike my memory of the terror itself, which has the blow-by-blow hyper reality of a slow-moving and intensely vivid nightmare, the following hours flicker in and out of focus, in and out of sequence, in what feels like a form of cognitive pointillism. But no matter how far back I step, I cannot quite see the whole picture. I remember noise, insufferable noise and confusion, and the crowding of people into the flat, and the deep yet elusive thirst for quiet, and for clarity, and for my own bed, which was unavailable to me because the thieves had left with my keys and my car.

Bea led us down the staircase, ringing every bell and banging on every door. We found ourselves in a neighbour's flat two floors down. Most of the tenants in the small block came to help; I knew many of them from my own years at Wildsview. I remember being hugged by Paula; I remember being given Scotch by her husband, Jim, and then thinking the better of it and turning instead to the strong sweet tea Paula had prepared; I remember noticing, even through my blindness, the purple rage overwhelming Bea's battered eye as she and Katie held onto each other on a couch while I sat with Paula at the phone to cancel our credit cards. In this age of the outsourcing of memory to technology I found myself – without my phone or computer – with no way of contacting anyone, and this added to my disorientation.

Soon the police arrived in their inept yet empathetic groups of two and three and four, taking statements, and then taking them again, and then taking them again and again. Sometime before then I had found my way back up to the flat, with the help of a neighbour, to search for my glasses and my manuscript. I remember being confronted by the mayhem in the flat, mess such as I had never seen, and thinking, as I picked blindly through it, is this how it feels after a bombing raid? Is this how it was in Berlin or Sarajevo, how it is in Gaza or Baghdad? My glasses would only appear in the morning, but in the mess of papers on the floor, in those first minutes back in the flat, I found my sunglasses in their case and then my manuscript, and even through the shaded lenses things seemed clearer, brighter. My black shoulder bag was in the mess strewn across the floor too: I put my manuscript inside it, and put it on my shoulder, and did not take it off even when I passed into a brief medicated sleep on a neighbour's couch several hours later.

My friend Sedica came with her daughter Aliya and with C's number: as I recounted the story to her, the memory of my helplessness when Bea was led away caused me to weep in her arms and then over the phone to C too. The flat seemed suddenly filled with people. Jonah the doorman had been away from his post and had not seen anything; he was now responding to an interrogation from the landlord with such indignant volubility that I felt myself back in the terror. I went over to try and quieten him down, or to ask the group to move out into the hall, but they could not hear me, and so I had to scream. There was a bustle of concern around us – did Bea need the hospital? Did I need a tranquiliser? Unlike Katie and Bea, who were now slumped on chairs giving statements to illiterate policemen, I could not sit still. I wandered up and down in my sunglasses, in and out of all the upturned rooms of the flat, muttering the only word that seemed to do justice to the mess I encountered through my darkened sunglasses: '*bordel*'. It seemed, to me, that I finally understood the meaning of the French word. I felt like an alien, a survivor, a refugee. I did not feel like myself.

The first two waves of police officers that arrived were patrolmen; bobbies on the beat. Once they discovered the stolen car had belonged to me, they became as fixated as the attackers on extracting from me whether it had a Tracker device. The only way of knowing this and to get the details that would allow the private security device to track the car with a helicopter would be to call my mother. I was not willing to awaken her with the news of my assault, and so I became subject to a vigorous intimidatory interrogation that only ceased when I snapped: 'Look! I have spent the last three hours being terrorised by men telling me what to do. I am not going to be told what to do any more, by anyone. I cannot find out if the car has a Tracker till morning and that is the end of that!'

The man leading the charge, large and lugubrious with full, almost feminine features, retreated immediately and apologised: 'I am only trying to do my job.' I was conscious that this policeman, a trainee constable, and his partner were black men in their late twenties, the exact demographic as our assailants, although by the measure of their ability to speak English, they were far less educated, or worldly. I decided that I would not allow the evil that had been in the room just an hour earlier to rob me of my own humanity, and I made a conscious decision to see the good in them. They were trying hard to help us, with their limited training and means, and the sheer load of their case-work – they came from Hillbrow, the busiest and most violent precinct in the country – meant that we could not be anything other than sta-tistics, in the end.

Soon other policemen joined them, detectives in plain clothes, who seemed to be led by an amiable man with an unpleasant skin condition around his nose and whose languid manner extended to finding him-self without pen and paper to take notes. In fact, none of the many officers who presented themselves in those hours and whose sole func-tion seemed to be to take statements, seemed to have either, and there was a repeated call for 'foolscap'. I remember shuttling several times into Bea and Katie's ravaged study to find some.

Each of us had to give statements at least twice, once to the uni-formed men and once to the plain-clothes detectives; I had to do another one, too, about the stolen car. Even after we seemed to be done, the officers – plied with tea and biscuits – seemed to be in no hurry to get back out into the night. I had sought retreat from the noise on the balcony, but I had been followed out by one of the most well-meaning neighbours, a man who had twice been held up, very traumatically, at gunpoint, and who was reliving his own terrible expe-riences. I fled back inside, where I found Bea lying shell-shocked on the couch while Sedica and Aliya were listening to the detective's account of how, given the terrible state of the South African criminal justice system, he had once taken the law into his own hands by kid-napping a neighbour's son in the boot of his car and administering a bleach enema to him after he had been suspected of stealing. I told the men, who were still struggling over Katie's statement, that they had to finish up and leave.

I occupied much of the time observing Aliya, one week short of sixteen. At first I was troubled by her presence, and with Sedica's response when I had asked why she was here: 'She must see, she must understand, she must be prepared. And how could I have left her alone in our flat, hearing this?' Aliya is a young woman of extraordinary containment and prepossession; when she helped Bea into bed in Nigel's spare room downstairs, she held her – something of a stranger – with such calm empathy that my friend was able to weep, fully, for the first time since her assault. For hours, Aliya sat silently and bore witness in a way that fills me both with hope and despair: at the compassion of children and at the horror we subject them to.

Bea wanted me in the bed with them, and the three of us lay huddled together for a time, Katie and I enfolding Bea. Then I left them and went to stand, for nearly half an hour, under the scalding water of Nigel's shower. I finally fell asleep to the sound of birdsong, to be woken a short ninety minutes later by a ring on the doorbell: another set of police officers had been sent to take statements, because the men who had taken the first lot had done so incorrectly.

*

At one point during the night, Katie and I were telling the policemen about our attackers' wrong-headed obsession with finding a safe. 'But there *is* a safe,' the detective with the skin condition said.

'No, there isn't,' we responded.

'Yes, there is,' he insisted, and led us through to the main bedroom, also ravaged, to show us a compartment concealed beneath the floor of the built-in wardrobe.

I had lived in the flat for five years, Katie and Bea for four. I had stored my shoes over that very compartment, and yet none of us had known about the safe. The intruders, of course, had eventually found it, and using some form of improvised levering tools, had attempted to prise it from the floor into which it had been set. I felt a chill run through me: 'Our lives depended on there not being a safe,' Katie said to the policeman.

Later the following day, as we sat in a consulting room with the trauma therapist, Bea told us what had happened when she was led out of the living room. Once Shorty and Poppy-Eyes had found the safe, they had taken her into the bedroom to show it to her, and to demand, with a final display of force, that she cooperate. The men pushed her to the floor, and Bea remembered Shorty's shoes – flawless white Reebok trainers – in her face. They pulled her onto the bed and told her they were going to rape her if she did not give them the keys. Poppy-Eyes punched her hard in the face, and they undid her trousers and unbuttoned her blouse. Shorty pushed his index and middle fingers so hard into her abdomen that two livid round bruises were now blooming beneath her navel. One of the men grabbed her breasts, and another put his fingers inside her, but she knew, she told us, that they had no appetite for violating her. They were torturing her to get her to give up the keys, and it was for this reason that she had screamed so loud: she was performing, she said to us, conveying to them the impression that she had reached the limits of her endurance so that they would believe that she knew nothing about the safe.

Bea knew that we would hear her screams in the living room and that this would distress us, but she felt she had no choice. She believes her strategy worked, in part, because she swore 'on my God' that she was telling the truth. She asked the men for something to drink, and one of them – it must have been Shorty – asked her what she would like. She said she did not mind, but he returned anyway from the kitchen with a choice, fruit juice and milk, and asked her once more which she would prefer. He then helped her quite gently to dress. 'You can't go out there with no trousers on, Grandmother,' he said.

Later, back in the living room, as she was being bound up again, The Colonel had buttoned her shirt. 'It was gentle too,' she told us. 'It was done with respect for an old lady.'

*

In the trauma-debriefing session, Katie explained what had gone through her mind when Bea had been pulled out of the living room.

She had not become a reptile.

When Bea screamed, she experienced her beloved being raped.

When Bea stopped screaming, she experienced her beloved's death.

She decided that she could no longer live, having heard Bea's violent death, and so she resolved to make a noise, in order to get herself killed and, perhaps, to raise the alarm.

But this was her moment of deepest crisis. She felt my body breathing next to hers and she reckoned that by eliciting her own death, she could well be eliciting mine too.

After a few moments of terrible indecision, she fell back into breathing alongside me, her other lung.

*

The policemen who awoke me on the morning of Thursday 12 January at 7.30 a.m. to take my statement again introduced themselves as Dlamini and Nkomo. Dlamini seemed fresh out of Police School, lanky and smooth and eager to impress with designer eyewear and sharply creased trousers; Nkomo, somewhat older, was brooding and rumpled, taciturn to the point of sullenness. Like all the policemen we had encountered the previous evening, they called us by our first names rather than addressing us as 'Sir' and 'Madam' or 'Mister' and 'Missus'. This instantly democratising familiarity was interesting in what it said about changing power relationships in South Africa: they were younger and black and we were older and white. It also suggested an informality that was both comforting and disconcerting: the former because of the empathy and even friendship that came with it, the latter because it suggested a lack of professionalism.

Dlamini led things, but Nkomo, it turned out, was the senior of the two, and at one point when we were all getting ahead of ourselves around Bea and Katie's kitchen table, he calmly called for order – 'Order, order,' he said – and reminded us (including Dlamini, it seemed) that he was the investigating officer. It did not surprise me to hear, later, that it had been Nkomo who had put the screws on Gugu, Katie and Bea's domestic worker, and brought her to tears: he could be menacing, although the three of us would come to appreciate his stolid charm.

Dlamini and Nkomo felt strongly that Gugu was the prime suspect, as did their boss, Captain Appelraju (known universally as 'Apples'), a gruffly amiable Indian man who had also, apparently, been at the crime scene the previous night, although I had not registered his presence.

Gugu is a lively, sassy woman in her mid forties who had briefly worked for us before Katie and Bea moved in. She had become their good friend, and they adored her. For the police officers, her tears seemed to indicate her guilt – or, at the very least, complicity, even if unwitting. 'Maybe she was drunk one night and boasted that she worked for two rich women who had a safe,' Dlamini said. 'Maybe she was careless with the key. Maybe one of her sons was in trouble. Maybe she owed money. It's January. Believe me. I come from the township. I know those streets. Everyone owes money in January. It's a bad time.'

Nkomo summarised things, in his trademark laconic style. 'Why would she cry', he asked, 'if she had nothing to hide?'

'Sergeant Nkomo!' Bea shot back. 'I am sure you are an excellent policeman, but I don't find you to be a very good judge of women. Let me tell you something about women that you might not know. We cry. We cry for all sorts of reasons. If my employer's home had just been ransacked and I was being accused, I might also cry.'

All evidence seemed to point to the robbery having been an inside job. The three intruders had been so certain about a safe. They had clearly targeted Bea and Katie's flat, actually bypassing a flat downstairs where the keys had accidentally been left in the door. They had left just after midnight, when Jimmy went off duty. They had not harmed us physically, beyond the initial blows and the targeted aggression at Bea in an attempt to extract the safe key. And most important, there had been no forced entry: they seem to have entered with a key.

We were, at first, adamant that Gugu could have had nothing to do with it: if it was an inside job, I thought, it would have to be the cleaner, Alfred, whom I had once caught stealing a couple of hundred rand out of my wallet, and banished from the flat. But there were other clues pointing at Gugu, as a conduit even if not as a collaborator: she had recently lost her keys; she had a no-good son living with her. The policemen peppered us with stories of trusty servants who had caused – wittingly or unwittingly – not only the dispossession but the demise of their ingenuous employers. In mounting their arguments, they seemed to relish playing their trump card: they were black, and we were white, and they knew, better than we ever could, what their people were capable of.

And so, on top of the trauma of the break-in and the sense of vulnerability it provoked, there was the additional trauma – more so for Katie and Bea than for me – of allowing that someone whom you trust, someone whom you permit into the inner reaches of your existence, might have betrayed you; might have put your very life at risk. If you live in a country like South Africa, and if you have any conscience, this cannot but lead you to thinking about the intense inequality in your society, and about how a Petri dish of that inequality ferments in your very own home. You would also be forced to think about the deal you have made: to compromise your personal security so as to be able to live a life of comfort and ease dependent on cheap domestic labour.

*

Constantly, in those first days, Katie and Bea and I were exhorted to let our anger out, or to express our rage at these three men. But it wouldn't come for me, except when I found it rising, somewhat unhelpfully, against someone whose response to my ordeal disappointed me.

I became so worried about this that I checked in with the trauma therapist: If I was going to heal, did I not need to go through an anger phase? Was something blocking me from feeling the primal emotion? The therapist took a day or two to think about it, and came back to me: 'The primary emotion in a traumatic experience like this is fear, not anger,' she said. 'Anger is the response to this fear. It is common, and understandable, and even logical, but it is not the only reaction, and if you are not feeling it, that's fine.'

I found myself rereading Primo Levi, who wrote, of his memoir of Auschwitz, that he had 'deliberately assumed the calm, sober language of the witness, neither the lamenting tones of the victim nor the irate voice of someone who seeks revenge'. I cannot, of course, even begin to compare my few hours of hell to Levi's three years at Auschwitz, but the attack confirmed, for me that I, like Levi, have a personal temperament 'not inclined to hatred'. For Levi, hatred is 'bestial, crude'; he preferred, 'on the contrary that my actions and thoughts, as far as possible, should be the product of reason; therefore I have never cultivated within myself hatred as a desire for revenge, or as a desire to inflict suffering on my real or assumed enemy, or as a private vendetta'. Even less, he continued, 'do I accept hatred as directed collectively at an ethnic group, for example all Germans; if I accepted it, I would feel that I was following the precepts of Nazism, which was founded precisely on national and racial hatred'.

Hearing the story of our attack and the theory of the inside job, one of Bea's relatives exclaimed, 'Yes! That's exactly why I don't let black people into my house.' Similar iterations were in the air everywhere, even among more enlightened and empathetic white listeners. The violation of one's home and hearth is the primal settler anxiety, deeply embedded in white South African consciousness, epitomised by the image of the ox-wagon laager corralled against the savages beyond. It was at the foundation of Mau Mau anxiety; it is what happened in Kenya, it is what happened in Zimbabwe, and now, look, it's happening to *us*. How could these thoughts not be somewhere in the deep recesses of our own subconscious minds, too – well, Bea's and mine, at least – given that we had been raised white in apartheid South Africa? How could we not subject each passer-by on the street – each desperate panhandler at each traffic light – to our own form of racial profiling? In South Africa, young black men commit crimes. Their mothers protect them. Their fathers fence for them. Their families live off them. Even if you were a bleeding heart liberal like myself, and you believed that most crime was economically motivated and a consequence of our deeply unequal society, and that its violence was a consequence of our bloody, brutal history, you would still be doing the profiling: That is a young black man. He looks like the men who terrorised me. He walks like them and dresses like them. He lives in the same kind of place that they do. He has the same pressures on his life that they do. On the basis of my personal experience, he is a threat. I must avoid him.

It seemed to me that it was a slippery slope from that kind of reasoning to the precepts of 'national and racial hatred' that Levi describes: I must hate him. No: I would not fall victim to it. More than that: our own personal experience, during the attack, had actually proven the virtues of humanism. We had insisted that our assailants recognise our humanity, and in turn, we had to recognise theirs. This alone did not save us, but I have to believe that it helped. Certainly, it gave me the insights which have meant that I have learned from the attack, not just about myself but about my society, and this has added to rather than subtracted from my life's experience. Along with the exhilaration I felt in those first days – an exhilaration at being alive, at having survived – an immense sadness came over me. 'What have we done?' I found myself asking, repeating the plaint of the hymn '*Senzenina?*', which became something of a struggle anthem during the anti-apartheid years. What have we done to deserve this, of course, but also: what have we done to our society, our world? What have we done to enrage you, O Lord?

The way Shorty moved me tenderly when asked; the way he offered Bea milk or juice and helped her to put her trousers on. The way The Colonel buttoned her blouse. The way they called Bea 'Grandmother' and Katie 'Sister'. Perhaps, too, the decision to leave my legs unbound so that I could get help once they had left. These were well-brought-up boys, once, before they became monsters, emasculated by poverty, by unemployment, by the culture of entitlement, by the AIDS epidemic, by the degradation of traditional life and the failure of urbanism to provide any sane alternative.

Senzenina?

*

My friend Hugh calls Johannesburg a humanist city.

After the attack, I better understand what he means. People care for each other here: in the face of such immanent, omnipresent horror, we have to. The looks of empathy in most people's eyes as they heard about our ordeal betrayed that they had been through something similar themselves, or knew someone who had, or had thought about it.

On the one-week anniversary of the attack, Bea and Katie crumbled. They could not bear to spend the night in the flat, and so they checked themselves into a hotel. At reception, Bea kept on asking, somewhat maniacally, for a 'room on an upper floor', failing to register that the hotel only had two storeys. Once she realised what she was doing, she felt she needed to explain, and as she told the check-in staff what had happened she burst into tears. Within seconds she was surrounded by hotel staff who held her in a collective embrace until she was calm again. All evening, hotel employees kept on knocking on their door to apologise, in the remarkable African sense of the words, not 'I am sorry for what I did', but 'I am sorry for what has happened to you.' When I went to visit Katie and Bea in the hotel later in the evening, they told me the story, and we wondered if the apology did not have embedded in it some shame too: some collective guilt for the actions of these three sons of Africa.

I felt the collective responsibility, and the consequent care, in many encounters over the course of those days. Sometimes, it was laced with the edge of shame, but more often it seemed activated by a lived understanding of what it meant to be victimised in this way. It was deeply healing, and it helped knit me back into my home community, into the city and the country of my birth.

But alongside this empathy, I also felt its inevitable corollary: the fear and anxiety in others, that our experience raised. To live your life with ease in a city like Johannesburg, you have to live in denial at some level, otherwise you would never be able to leave your house, or go into the garden, or sleep at night. These attacks happen all the time, but you build around yourself a battlement of false security: I live in a flat; I live in a secure complex; I don't have a safe; I do have a safe; I don't have a gun; I do have a gun; I have dogs; I have electrical fencing; I am extra vigilant.

But the attack on three modestly well-off people in the fifth-floor flat of an apartment block in Killarney shatters such strategies of denial. As one of my friends wrote to me, with commendable frankness: 'What happened to you is terrible for you and Bea and Katie primarily, of course. But it is terrible for all of us, for our whole community, because it brings home how vulnerable we all are. I've been living in a state of denial, I think, that the statistics are getting better, that one hears less and less about such things. I've become less vigilant. Now I have to re-evaluate all of that.'

Others were not capable of such reflection. And so it happened, at times, that someone would rush up to me and, even before consoling me, blurt out, 'What happened? Do you think it was an inside job? Was it related to your journalism, do you think? The crime situation's getting worse and worse!'

Or, in one particularly unpleasant encounter: 'Those people really wanted to hurt you guys. They really must have something against you.'

'Actually,' I responded, 'they didn't seem to want to hurt us. They robbed us and terrorised us and threatened to kill us, but they didn't hurt us much.'

'But they were with you for three hours! Why would they be there for three hours if they didn't have something against you or if they weren't looking for something in particular?'

'They *were* looking for something in particular. Money. Jewels. *Valuables*. What all thieves look for. And according to the police, three hours is the bog-standard average for a home invasion of this nature. It was just another day in Joburg. Nothing special.'

Much as my interlocutor was annoying me, I felt terrible sharing this with her: she is a single woman, and she lives, like Katie and Bea, in a flat, no doubt because she believes it brings her security. She did not mean to be so blunt and insensitive, she just needed to still her own anxieties, to reassure herself that our attack was not random and therefore that it was less likely to happen to her. In most instances, I was not so harsh: as is so often the case when one is traumatised by violence or grief, I spent much of my time reassuring others, not just that I was okay, but that things were okay. That life was okay. That we survived, and that, therefore, there was hope. I made a virtue of this, most of the time, even when I felt hopeless myself, or desperate.

My most devastating encounter was with a thoughtful and empathetic man who has helped me through many a crisis. A week or so after the attack, in my own deepest trough, I called him and told him what had happened. 'It's very important to express your anger,' he said to me. 'Are you letting your anger out?'

I gave him my line: the empathy I had established with my assailants in an attempt to save our lives made it hard for me to be angry with them. Even as he commended the writer in me for being able to see things in so analytic a way, he seemed to take exception to it: 'How can you not feel anger? Even if you are not angry with them personally, how can you not be angry at the way these *fucking fucks have fucked up your life*?'

In the two decades I had known him, I had never once heard him raise his voice. I tried to ratchet things down: 'I don't think this is the subject for a phone call. Let's discuss this when I next see you. All I need right now is a good night's sleep . . .'

'Mark,' he said now, with what sounded like cold rage, 'listen to me. Are you listening to me? I need to be sure you are listening very carefully when I say this to you: You. Will. Not. Have. A. Good. Night's. Sleep. For. At. Least. A. Year.'

I remembered something with a shudder that brought home to me how the collective trauma of my home town sometimes obscures its collective humanity. The man had been the victim of a similar attack, a year or two previously.

*

For two weeks after the attack, I suffered from intense 'hypervigilance', a feeling distressing to me in its unfamiliarity, as I usually am what my friend Charlotte calls 'Joburg Man': briskly, almost unconsciously vigilant (if such a paradox is possible) without being neurotic. In my hypervigilant state, I could barely negotiate the few kilometres of familiar night-time road between Killarney and Melville. If I was out for dinner, my heart would begin beating fast at around 8.30, and if I was not home, barricaded in my bedroom by 9.30, the panic would overwhelm me. Thus did I spend several evenings behind the security gate in my bedroom redoubt, behind the security gate and with the alarm set, surrounded by my laptop, my books, my music, and enough food and drink so that I would not have to go downstairs before the pills kicked in and pulled me into oblivion.

C came over from Paris as soon as he could, about a week after the attack. On his first night back, I had the idea that we should be in the countryside, and so we drove off to the Magaliesberg mountains, to stay in self-catering accommodation adjoining a pretty country hotel. It was a bad idea, for all sorts of reasons: as night fell, the panic in me grew, and as soon as we finished dinner we had to drive the two hours home through the night to keep the demons at bay. C is a South African too, but he is not 'Joburg Man': he is intensely bothered by the security situation in the city, and would be hypervigilant even in Reykjavik. The attack traumatised him too: he was not able to talk about it to his colleagues in Paris, he told me, because of his own shame at how the attack confirmed preconceptions about the violence and brutality of South African life. We did not speak much during the few days he was able to take off work as compassionate leave, but he was gentle and comforting and deeply nurturing, and I spent much of our time entwined with him. Through his touch I seemed to re-enter my own body.

*

In the days following the attack, Bea and Katie and I were very frustrated with the police. I started using that new slogan of the South African public service, *Batho Pele* – 'People First' – as my own assault weapon. When, for example, I had to go to the police pound to collect my mother's car (it did, indeed, have a Tracker, and it was found the day after the attack in Berea, a couple of kilometres away), I was treated with the surly contempt I have come to expect in any interaction with civil servants. I was told I could not be helped because my investigating officer was away on study leave and his superior had gone shopping at Southgate. Having imparted this information, the receptionist proceeded to ignore me and continue her loud conversation with the colleagues clustered around her desk.

'*Batho Pele*,' I said, but not loud enough to penetrate the hullaballoo. '*Batho Pele!*' I now shouted. As if by programming, she snapped into action. 'Yes, you are right,' she said, and got to work trying to dig up someone to help me.

On the night of the attack, the fingerprints team had come and dusted the place down, but when we met with Dlamini and Nkomo the following day, they told us that it would take at least six weeks to get results, and more likely two months, because the labs were so overworked. When we said we had clear images of our assailants and would be able to identify them, Dlamini called the Identikit department to set up an appointment: he reported back that we could be seen in ten days.

'Ten days?' I protested. 'I can see Shorty and Poppy-Eyes and The Colonel vividly now. But in ten days my brain will be filled with so much other stuff. Why can't we do it now?'

Dlamini explained that there was only one Identikit office for the whole of Gauteng province, and it was heavily overworked. And so, ten days later, on a Tuesday morning, Katie and Bea and I drove into town for our 11 a.m. appointment at the Johannesburg Central Police Station, the old John Vorster Square, notorious as the home of the Special Branch, and the place where thousands of activists were detained and from which some – such as Ahmed Timol – 'fell' to their deaths out of ninth-story windows. When we arrived at the entrance to which we had been directed, we were told by a petulant security guard that we were in the wrong place; she pointed vaguely elsewhere in the huge complex that is jammed up against the elevated M1 freeway, leering over Chinatown and the elegant colonial sandstone Magistrates' Court.

Thus began our descent – or ascent, if I am to be literal – into one of the few experiences I have had that actually warrants the label 'Kafkaesque'. Grubby and decrepit, the buildings looked as if they had not been touched, let alone cleaned, since the Old Guard left nearly two decades previously, taking the name John Vorster Square with them. Most of the lifts did not work, and those that did, we discovered upon enquiry, seemed not be accessible from the ground level and could only be reached via dark stairwells and long, circuitous passageways (ill-lit because fluorescent bulbs had not been replaced) along which the occasional lost soul could be found who would more than likely ask you the way to the nearest exit before you had the chance to ask him the same question. If you walked into an office to ask directions, you would be met with a blank stare, or ignored, and so you just carried on walking.

'John Vorster still lives here,' Katie began muttering repeatedly, referring to the infamous former prime minister who had begun his career as the justice and police minister in the high-apartheid era of the 1960s. Every now and then, a white official would briskly brush past us, and Bea became enraged at the conspiratorial – or perhaps sympathetic – glances these men would give us, as if to say, 'We're in this African basket-case together; oh well, what can we do about it?'

Eventually, we found our way to the eighth floor. There was a printed sheet of A4 paper sticky-taped onto the wall reading 'Identikit Department', but no one in evidence save an elderly cleaner who blankly led us into an anteroom and left us there. The room was so filthy that Bea decided she could not stay there, and so we wandered out again into the hallway, where one of those white officials came brushing briskly past us, and asked us if we were being helped. We decided to accept his race solidarity and explained our predicament – it was now half an hour after our allotted time. He bustled off, and a few minutes later we heard a heavy tread raising, literally, a dust storm down the corridor, and a thickset black man with a moon face came striding toward us, taking huge steps, gasping for breath, holding out his hand and apologising profusely as he swept us into his office. He had just been transferred from Limpopo Province, he told us; it was only his third day at the head of the Gauteng Identikit unit, and he had no staff.

Why?

'They're all on stress,' he said. 'On stress', we discovered during our preliminary conversation, meant 'on stress leave'. The man – I will call him Captain Phaahla – itemised the complaints of each individual member (I do not remember all the details, although one involved domestic violence) and he seemed perilously close to having to book himself off too. His wife was also a police officer, but in its wisdom, the South African Police Services had decided to transfer him at short notice from Limpopo to Gauteng, but refused to move his wife with him, and so he was also acting as a single parent to three young children, all of whom he had just deposited for their first day at their new school.

Captain Phaahla prepared to ready his technology for the Identikit session, talking all the while in a staccato voice punctuated by increasingly shallow breaths. Objects were flying – or at least they seemed to be – off his desk, and the appointment seemed to be spiralling into chaos until Bea decided to take control. 'Captain Phaahla!' she said, in her deepest and most authoritative voice. 'I am going to tell you something which will save your life.'

He stopped and looked at her in what seemed to be horror, or fear, and Katie and I were similarly nonplussed. 'You need to breathe, Captain Phaahla. You need to breathe. And I am now going to show you how.'

In silent acquiescence, he nodded slowly, as Bea told him to put everything down, sit up straight, and close his eyes. She then led him through a simple breathing exercise she had learned from her Buddhist meditation practise, before asking Katie and I to join in too. Thus was order and calm restored, in this filthy little corner of the eighth floor of what used to be John Vorster Square, the traffic tearing along the double-decker highway just metres beyond the window and the fearful grime of decades accumulating around us, as the four of us closed our eyes and breathed together before beginning our Identikit session.

We sat there transfixed, as this gentle, talented and deeply committed man led us through the reconstruction of our assailants' faces on his laptop computer. He had joined the police, he told us, because it was the only employment possibility open to him after he had failed to complete his schooling in rural Limpopo; at training college, a superior had seen him sketching and referred him for the Identikit programme. Sketching was his passion, but after nearly twenty years he was getting tired of just doing faces of bad people. He loved to draw everything – bodies, animals, the folds in fabrics – and he wished he had the energy to do so after his exhausting workdays were over. Bringing the faces of Shorty and Poppy-Eyes and The Colonel to life beneath the tap of his fingers on the computer keyboard, Captain Phaahla seemed to give us some control over them and the memory of what they did to us, although we experienced distress, at times, at what we could remember, and even more at what we could not. From time to time the outside world would intervene on our colloquy and interrupt Captain Phaahla's concentration, but this was nothing that a little breathing could not set right.

After two hours, we were all exhausted, and Phaahla had another appointment. 'Do you mind working after hours?' he asked. Of course we did not, and so we suggested that he visit us at Katie and Bea's flat, at his convenience, to continue the job in a more salubrious environment. When he came to Wildsview the following afternoon, he told us how sorry he was for our experience; how sorry he was, too, that all the work he had done for us would come to nought, because the police services did not have funds to publish and distribute Identikits except in the most high-profile cases.

Later we would discover that despite his humanity, Captain Phaahla did not know the law. Because our Identikits had been drawn collectively, they would be inadmissible as evidence in a court.

*

The police investigation did not start off with much promise either. Through a friend in the cellphone industry, we had managed to put tails on our stolen Blackberrys, which were tracked through the course of the twenty-four hours following the attack and eventually seemed to have settled down in a low-income housing complex just across The Wilds. We conveyed this information to Nkomo and Dlamini (interestingly, perhaps influenced by too much detective fiction, we never called them by their first names), but nothing seemed to come of it. Eventually we got their boss 'Apples', on the line, who explained to us that they had gone to the complex but did not enter it, as it was 'too big'. He offered to take us there himself, to show us how big it was. Enraged, I contacted an ex-crime intelligence boss who is the neighbour of friends: he offered to make some calls. A week later, Nkomo and Dlamini had not yet visited Gugu to question her son and search her house and Apples had failed to respond to a list of questions Bea had sent him. I called the head of detective services at Hillbrow and gave him a lecture on Batho Pele, liberally sprinkled with references to my career as a journalist.

Bea and Katie found a private investigator whom we arranged to meet one evening. I will call him Theuns: he was a short man with oversized, rough features and the ruddy face of one who has spent much of his life outdoors and drinking. His enormous hands continually massaged the huge belly straining against his short-sleeved striped polyester shirt. He appeared to have a case of acid indigestion so extreme that he would often, in mid sentence, have to stop talking to suppress a belch with a deathmask-like grimace, and get up to walk around. He was an ex-cop, he told us, and had been in 'the business' for decades. It was not a pretty story: he had spent time in a Central African jail, and had not been lucky in love. Even now, he had a huge teddy-bear in the back of his car: it was Valentine's Day and he hoped to see his girlfriend when he was finished with us to make up with her.

When we began telling him our story he interrupted us aggressively, cutting to the chase: 'You're not going to get your stuff back. So what do you want?'

We looked at each other, somewhat confused, before Bea said, 'Justice. We want justice. We want to see these men caught, and punished, and behind bars.'

'It's not going to happen,' he shot back. 'Forget it. Trust me. I know these guys, and I know the courts. Even if your guys do get caught, they'll be given bail, and they'll easily be able to pay it because they're obviously part of an organised crime ring and earn well from their jobs, and before you know it they'll be across the border. So they'll never come to trial.'

Theuns paused a moment to let this sink in, then asked again: 'So what do you want?'

'I'm not sure what you mean?' Bea asked, slowly.

'Well,' he said, cocking his head at me with a look I have come to know well – something between a smile and a sneer that people use when they're talking to journalists and want to make themselves feel more important than they are – 'I would tell you what I mean, but I don't think I can, because of the presence of *journalists* in the room ...'

'Please,' I snapped back. 'I'm not a journalist today. I'm the victim of a crime. And that's why you are here. It's really not worth continuing this conversation if you are unable to be frank.'

His sneering smile widened, downwards, into a performance of distaste that inadequately masked the actual pleasure he took in saying what came next. 'Well, let's just say there are many people in this town who would take a lot of pleasure' – here he gave a dry little laugh, 'heh heh' – 'in making sure these guys never bothered anyone again.'

I looked up and saw how the horror in Bea's eyes – she was sitting directly opposite me – mirrored my own. He must have seen it, too, for he was quick to offer a clarification: 'I'm not necessarily saying anyone will be killed ...'

'No,' I interrupted, 'that's out of the question ...'

'We want to see them caught and sent to jail, that's the only thing we're interested in,' Bea added, but in the silence that followed, we heard Katie's burble: 'Well, I don't know. I'm not sure if I would mind if they fell off a building ...'

Afterwards, the three of us rolled about laughing at this moment; at how Katie had thrown this curveball and how Bea and I looked at each other in something of a panic and tried to smooth things over. But our laughter was edgy, for in her comment Katie vocalized the fears of all three of us: that any quest for justice might lead to retribution. If being attacked in this way makes you feel vulnerable as you never have before, how much more so if you cannot trust the system put there supposedly to protect you?

When, during our meeting with Theuns, we all regained our composure, Katie pursued her line of thought, and asked about the possibility of retribution. He responded that it was very low: these men were busy 'professionals'; it was not in their interest to waste their time and risk their lives by going back to teach someone a lesson when they could be 'earning' more through another attack.

In this respect, at least, our time with Theuns was very useful: he was a 'professional' too, and he knew his field. He was so convinced that Gugu was not a suspect that he said we did not even need to ask her to take a polygraph. Why, he asked, would she concoct an elaborate story about losing a key rather than just making a copy? Similarly, if the culprit were the son, why would he render his mother – and thus himself – a suspect by removing the key and not copying and replacing it? Besides, he explained to us after he looked at the kitchen door, a key was not necessary: the lock was so basic that you could open it with a blank. No: our assailants were jobbers rather than insiders. If polygraphs are to be trusted, he was right: Katie and Bea asked Gugu to take the test anyway, and she was cleared.

We cross-questioned Theuns, but he countered our hypotheses of an inside job, one by one. All the information our assailants seemed to have – such as the hour that Jonah went off-duty – could have been gleaned by casual intelligence-gathering or observation. And as for the safe, well, in the township they believe that every white household has one, and weren't they proven correct anyway? He believed that Katie and Bea might have been targeted, over others in the building, because women are less likely to carry firearms. And the gangsters' compassionate behaviour might have been because of internal dynamics: there is always a 'nice guy' in a gang of three.

Still, he held strongly to some analysis that we just knew to be wrong, perhaps because of the way he typecast his adversaries in a battle between good and evil that clearly had ideological roots: he told us he had been in the police Special Branch in the 1980s ('you don't want to know the kind of things we did') but had quit in disgust when F.W. de Klerk had released Nelson Mandela. He told us, for example, that Bea's assailants had been driven by 'sadism' when they sexually assaulted her, when her actual experience was very different.

In explaining how I had come to my own theory of an inside job, I mentioned that my feet had been left unbound, perhaps – I reasoned – as a mark of compassion: 'I thought, maybe they wanted to make it possible for me to get help once they left.'

He scoffed at this: 'No, they wanted you to get up and challenge them or run for help so they could shoot you dead.'

It took me a few moments to find my words, through the shock. 'Why would they want that? Surely that would only make their job more difficult?'

'No. You know, when they go back to the taverns in the townships they want to be able to boast, "I killed a white man. I didn't want to do it, but I had to, because he resisted."'

Much as I do not like to, I concede the presence, beneath Theuns's crudeness, of some logic to this analysis. If, indeed, you were once a 'good boy' – if you have a mother who tried to raise you well and maybe you even accompany her to church on Sundays – you will construct a moral framework that permits what you are doing. I rob because we are poor and we are oppressed and these white people still have everything, even now. I am angry with them, so angry I could kill them. But I am a pro; I am a soldier. I don't take a life unless it's in self-defence. He's getting up to run, he's threatening us. Bang: he's dead. I can score another notch on my rifle. I've seen war. I'm not a useless fuck who can't get a job or even a wife because I have no money to get married. I'm a man.

Still, I argued with Theuns. Surely, if one person in the group (let's assume it's Poppy-Eyes) feels this way, the other two would prevail? Shorty saw my legs were untied. Why wouldn't he have tied me up? Theuns had an answer for this: perhaps Shorty – he was short, after all – was insecure about his position in the gang, and did not want to contradict the others.

Who is to know? I do not accept Theuns's take on my unbound legs, but maybe this is because the narrative I have constructed about my attackers does not allow it. Theuns's reading, compromised though it is by the hatred boiling in his own gut, must be allowed. I like to believe that we all lived through the ordeal because, in the end, we were six reasonable people, Poppy-Eyes included. And indeed, even accepting Theuns's reading, I lived because I was reasonable: I did not get up and run. But as time and distance draw me away from the attack, I am developing a perspective both sharper and more troubled. You can act reasonably. You can exercise your agency by working in a team both with your fellow victims and your assailants; by humanising them through communication and cooperation so that they humanise you and feel the need to look after you rather than hurt you. But still, in the end, when three armed and desperate men under the influence of drugs and alcohol break into your home, you have no control over what will happen to you. It is random and it is chaotic, and even if your reasonable behaviour lessens the odds of your being hurt or killed, it guarantees you nothing. You have no control over when, and how, you will die. Once you understand this, you accept that life is a gift.

*

Our pressure on the police seemed to be having some effect. Team Apples kicked into gear. We came to understand our men, and their challenges, and also their modus operandi. So overworked were they – Dlamini told me he had dozens of dockets open on his desk at any one time – that they simply did not have the time to put in the footwork we might have come to expect after many evenings watching *Prime Suspect* or *Wallander*. Rather, they relied on circles of informers who serviced several cases at once. Knowing how difficult it was to secure a conviction, particularly given the very shoddy state of the court system, they also tended to depend on forensics supplied by the labs before venturing into the streets to chase wild geese. No doubt, the danger the streets presented made this more cautious approach more attractive too, as did the fact that it gave them some breathing space, given the heavy backlog in the forensics labs. If I were entirely cynical, I might say that they, cynically, blamed their inactivity on bureaucratic problems elsewhere. But having watched them work, I felt a bit more sympathetic. It just meant that things had to go slowly, more slowly than three crime victims would have liked, three crime victims who were seeking the healing that an arrest and conviction would bring.

'Slowly, slowly,' Nkomo said at one point. 'More haste, less speed.' And at another: 'Slowly catches the thief.' Such homilies seemed to suit his naturally phlegmatic manner. But in our case, astonishingly, slowly did catch the thief, or at least one of them.

*

In late March, Nkomo called Bea to tell her that the fingerprints analysis had finally come back, and that there were two positive identifications with previous offenders: one for a man who had participated in a housebreaking in the nearby suburb of Parkview, and another for a man who had very recently been convicted of robbery in Hillbrow. The officer who had initially arrested the latter was one of Apples' own staff, and said she would recognise the man immediately. And so Nkomo and Dlamini accompanied their colleague to the address the man had given when he was first arrested, found him and arrested him again.

'Is he an experienced criminal?' I asked Dlamini

He snorted: 'He's a *loser* criminal!' What gangster gives his actual address along with his fingerprints to the police, and then stays there after committing another crime without gloves? Following the detective's reasoning, the *moegoe* – the South African word for hick, or rube – had been caught; the two scary guys were still at large.

We were called to an identity parade in mid March. The experience was, in the beginning, as alienating as our previous visits to police stations, with administrative chaos and unexplained waiting in a dark, windowless anteroom adjoining the cells behind Hillbrow Police Station, the sounds of prisoners' singing and shouting rebounding around us. We chatted, for a while, with each other and with the other crime victim called to the same parade, a jittery commercial driver who had been carjacked. Then we lapsed into silence. 'I feel calm,' I said to Bea and Katie. 'I haven't felt this calm since we were under attack.'

'That's because you're in the moment,' Bea responded. 'You're not churning about what happened yesterday, or what you should or might be doing tomorrow. You're just here, now.'

We were called in, one by one, by the supervising officer, a huge slab of *ancien régime* Boer. Bea went first, and then me. There were seventeen men behind the one-way glass, each holding a number. I looked carefully at them one by one, but did not recognise any of them. And yet I knew one of them must have been my assailant. Was Poppy-Eyes in the room? I looked at all the big-eyed men: no. Shorty? I looked at all the short men: no again. I looked for The Colonel. There were three very dark men in the room, who looked like they could be Zimbabwean. I did not get a good look at The Colonel during the attack, but in the Identikit session Bea and Katie had made so much of his handsome features and his muscular physique that we had giggled we were turning him into a matinee idol: just put a pencil-thin moustache on him and he would be Clark Gable. By process of elimination, then, it could only be the man with the muscles bulging out of the soccer shirt. 'I think it's him,' I said.

'Are you sure?' the police officer asked me.

'No, I cannot be sure,' I responded.

'We need 100 per cent positive identification or it won't stand up in court.'

'This is the best I can give you,' I said.

Team Apples was elated. Not allowed to communicate with us before the parade, they were waiting at the exit. When I told them whom I had identified they high-fived one another, and backslapped me, and called me their 'star witness'. Bea and Katie had failed to identify their assailant; the fact that I had called him out, the policemen said, would at the very least give them some leverage in trying to secure his cooperation.

The pleasure that Team Apples took, in having purportedly gotten their man, was very gratifying. We had kept our faith in the police rather than thrown in the towel, or gone private with Theuns, and although they might have resented our cajoling and threatening, they had risen to the occasion and appeared to have done their job.

Certainly, we were lucky: a *moegoe* had left his fingerprints, had given his correct address on a previous offence and had been stupid enough to stay there while committing more crime. Still, we had insisted that the system work for us, and for now, at least, it seemed to have done so. This gave me a sense of the way the trauma of crime victims in a country like South Africa, is exacerbated by the lack of results, by the inability of the system to restore a sense not only of security, but one of justice too.

The ID parade was a turning point for me. When I pointed the man out he was instructed to walk forward, toward the one-way glass. I saw a muscle flinch in the temple of his taut, military face, and I felt his discomfort through the glass as he stood only a few centimetres away from me. In trying to confirm my deduction that he was my man, I tried to reconstruct the feeling of having him close to me, of feeling his breath on my face, but I failed. When I thought of The Colonel, all I could see, or think about, was his gun. Still, he did not know that; nor did he know that I was not able to give the kind of definitive positive identification that would hold weight in court. It seemed to me that he thought I was recognising him and that he was thus done for. He broke into a sweat.

This felt like a triumph even if, later, it made me feel sick: had I become like him? And what had transformed him, this man who took great care of himself even in the holding cells of the Hillbrow Police Station, into an armed assailant and maybe a killer? If he had made me play the dirty game of power, who had made him play it? Robert Mugabe? Xenophobic South Africans? An absent or abusive father? The ANC government's ineffective economic policies and border controls? The trade union movement with its job reservation for members and its insistence on an inflexible labour market? The banks and capitalists who caused the global crash? The Chinese who killed Africa's manufacturing industry by flooding the continent with cheap goods? The rich who got richer while the poor got poorer?

Me?

*

In early November 2012, eight months after the attack, I came back to Johannesburg to give evidence in the trial. Two men had been charged with aggravated robbery, it turned out, a charge which carried a minimum sentence of fifteen years. The first was the man whose fingerprints had been found and whom I had apparently pointed out at Hillbrow Police Station: his name was Thabani Sibanda, and he was a Zimbabwean immigrant. After his arrest, Sibanda had pointed out the second man, named Thabo George, a South African. At their first appearance a few months previously, both had signalled that they would plead not guilty: George had been granted bail, but not Sibanda.

This was my first time in court as anything other than a journalist or a disinterested observer. As we waited on a wooden bench outside Court Seventeen, I was struck by the way that busy courts, like busy hospitals, were places both of banal bureaucracy and intense personal drama; places where the bounds of familial intimacy were brutally ruptured as the workings of medicine or of justice exposed people's private vulnerabilities to the world. All around us, men and women bustled by in black robes carrying thick folders, while small groups of people gathered in anxious little pools along the corridor, or around the embers of cigarettes against the low brick walls of the building's handsome courtyards. The journalist in me wanted to know the stories: why was that woman crying silently to herself, ignored by her companions? And that short man with the snakeskin tie: was the indignation with which he poked his lawyer's chest a sign of his guilt, or his innocence? But the victim in me wanted to cry with the woman – I was scared to see my assailant again, and very anxious I would mess up my testimony – and the aggrieved party in me wanted to poke someone's robed chest too, and deliver a tirade on the failures of the South African criminal justice system: I had flown all the way from Paris just to testify and it looked like our case might not be heard, due to the magistrate's absence.

A Johannesburg magistrate's courtroom, on a Monday morning, seems more like a clanking shunting yard of justice than a cool chamber of reason. Cases postponed, cases remanded, cases discharged: were any cases ever heard? Finally, the following day, the magistrate, a middle-aged man named Vincent Ratshibvumo, reappeared and Thabani Sibanda was brought into the dock from the holding cells below. My heartbeat quickened as I watched him climb the steps, and I found myself annoyed by his military bearing, by the way he carried himself like a prisoner of war rather than the thug I presumed him to be. I watched him scan the gallery for his people: he did not seem to recognise anyone and he looked down in a scowl somewhere between contempt and disappointment. I felt something between *schadenfreude* and relief at his aloneness: there would be nobody to confront – no recriminating woman with a baby on her back, no threatening older brother – at tea-break.

Sibanda's codefendant, Thabo George, stepped into the dock to join him. Like Bea and Katie, I was absolutely certain that I had never seen this man before, and that he had not been one of our assailants. Katie and Bea were equally certain that Sibanda was our man, the attacker we called 'The Colonel'. But was I? Pacing a courtyard just before I was to give evidence, I suffered a crisis of confidence. I felt the unbearable pressure of a man's freedom in my hands and I asked myself if this pressure alone might be the cause of my self-doubt. Still, I had identified Sibanda in the identity parade, albeit not definitively, and the police had confirmed after the parade that the man I had pointed out was the man they had arrested, and that his fingerprints had been on my mother's car. I was also certain that the man I had pointed out in the line-up was the man now in the dock.

I took the witness stand still unsure of what I would say. As I recounted the story of our attack for the court, it was translated laboriously for the defendants into their two native languages. I watched, as if from above, as the anger rose in my gorge. This was not only because of the way one of the translators was turning my testimony into a township burlesque with his plosive sound effects and expansive gestures. It was also in outrage at the expenditure allocated – my tax money, money that could be building schools or training police to do their jobs properly – to give this man a fair trial. Katie and Bea were not allowed in the courtroom, as they were still to give their own testimonies, but I held silent communion with them: 'Maybe we were wrong. Maybe we should have taken the street-justice route and gotten this man's kneecaps broken.'

I noticed how Thabo George followed me, nodding and shaking his head as I spoke in English, and then doing so again as the translator spoke my words. We looked each other in the eye: I felt his distress, and he clearly felt mine. I did not know whether to read this as guilt or innocence, but I appreciated the contact. The man standing next to him could not have reacted more differently: Thabani Sibanda refused to meet my gaze and kept his head down. I watched his face darken and the blood pump through his temples as I told the court about how our assailant had threatened and mocked Katie and me when we had started weeping after hearing Bea's screams from the next room. Suddenly, and for the first time, I connected with my anger and almost felt overwhelmed by it. I felt the blood pumping through my own temples, a sheet of red rage descending over my eyes at last. *Look me in the eye, you fucker!*, I shouted silently while waiting for my words to be translated two times over, *Admit to what you have done, you fucking coward! Behave like a soldier, if you are one, and not a useless* moegoe*!*

I was so angry I needed to sit down. But this was unsatisfying, and so I leaped up again, holding onto the rail of the witness stand and causing the chair to fall. Startled by the minor commotion, Sibanda looked up, but so fleetingly that I missed his glance. I found myself reciting the words 'mutual release', in some kind of mantra, to calm myself down. The words are Hannah Arendt's: my brother Peter, a psychotherapist, had offered them to me from Arendt's book, *The Human Condition*, to help me prepare for the trial, because of her philosophy of forgiveness. 'Only through [the] constant mutual release from what they do can men remain free agents,' Arendt writes, 'only by the constant willingness to change their minds and start again can they be trusted with so great a power as that to begin something new.'

I sluiced the hate out of my head with these words as I focused on the prosecutor's next question. I imagined my brain as a bed of live coral, exposed to the elements again after the red tide has ebbed away, glistening and vulnerable, still stained with rage. I loosened my grip on the witness box, and came back to myself, elevated above the court, looking across the paraphernalia of justice before me – the clerks, the stenographers, the translators, the lawyers with their grubby folders clustered untidily around old wooden schooldesks – to Sibanda's downturned face, to his throbbing temples. Release me, I instructed him, I pleaded with him. Look me in the eye and say sorry. Change your mind. Start again. I will tell the court how you held the mug so Bea could drink the tea, how you buttoned her shirt for her. Look me in the eye and say you're sorry, and I will forgive you, and we can both start something new.

Of course, the only thing awaiting Thabani Sibanda, should he confess, would be a fifteen-year jail sentence. His downturned face remained eloquently silent.

*

I told the court that I had never seen Thabo George before. But I was certain that Thabani Sibanda was the man who had attacked me, and whom I had identified in the parade at Hillbrow Police Station.

It was a difficult moment, and one I do not recall – in the absence of mutual release – with any of the satisfactions of vengeance, not least because of what followed. There were, it transpired in my cross-examination, two Thabani Sibandas in the line-up at the identity parade that day at Hillbrow Police Station, and according to the parade master's report, I had identified the wrong one. The shiny-faced state-appointed defence attorney hectored me with all the theatrics of a B-grade courtroom drama, and although I stood my ground, the magistrate accepted this evidence: it was there in black and white in a police report before him that I had identified the Thabani Sibanda carrying the number 15, and not the Thabani Sibanda carrying the number 14, the Thabani Sibanda in the dock before me today.

I left the witness box shaken. This was, in part, because the prosecutor had been so ill-prepared that he had actually led me in my evidence about my identification of Sibanda in the parade, thereby not only exposing me but opening a hole in his own case. But I was also distressed because of the doubt the whole episode cast on the workings of my own memory.

I needed to know the truth. What had happened in that identity parade? Our lawyers told me to drop it. Given that I had been unable to make a conclusive positive identification in the parade it would have no material bearing on the case anyway, and if I dug up a problem in the police investigation there would be a mistrial anyway. Still, I found myself unable to let the matter go, and after what seemed like a ridiculously convoluted process, our lawyers managed to find the case docket, which had been languishing in some bureaucratic no-man's-land between the Hillbrow Police Station and the Johannesburg Magistrate's Court. There would be photos inside the docket, I was assured, that would lay the matter to rest.

There were, of course, no photos in the docket. They had gone missing. Eventually, they were found somewhere. When the case was next heard, a few months later – a further postponement because the fingerprints expert was on leave – I would receive, on my laptop in Paris, some blurry scans of the line-up photos, shot in court for me by Bea on her iPad. There they were, standing next to each other, the two Thabani Sibandas: Number 14, short, dark and well-built in a white soccer-shirt with a V-neck, and Number 15 next to him, a little lighter, a little taller, much more slender, and wearing a buttoned-up yellow polo neck.

The parade master's report, a copy of which I have, is very clear that I identified Number 15, although it marks my uncertainty: 'Result of parade: No pointing out – Point out no 15. Not sure.' It seems impossible that I would have pointed out this man when the very process of elimination I went through in my mind to identify my assailant was to look for a very dark man with a very muscular physique.

How did it come to be that two people with exactly the same name – not a particularly common one – were standing next to each other in the parade in the first place? Had the parade master written down the wrong number, either in error or with nefarious intent? Had

Team Apples been mistaken when they slapped me on the back in congratulation when I spoke to them after the parade? Or was the mistake mine? Had I in fact identified the wrong man – albeit, through bizarre coincidence, carrying the right name?

Was my memory in the courtroom conforming itself to the presence of Thabani Sibanda before me the way water assumes the shape of the vessel containing it? Is that what memory does?

*

The case was finally concluded seven months later, in July 2013. By coincidence, I was returning to Johannesburg on the day that Thabani Sibanda was to take the witness stand, and I went straight from the airport to the Magistrate's Court. Thabo George had been discharged, due to lack of evidence, but I arrived in time to see Sibanda defend himself. He was wearing factory-faded jeans and a white button-down shirt with an extravagant blue floral motif, and the eighteen months in jail showed: he clearly had been keeping his body in shape – his chest was more pumped up than before – but his facial features were drawn and haggard.

This time, Court Seventeen seemed as intimate as a living room, and its denizens felt like old acquaintances: Vincent Ratshibvumo, the magistrate who leavened his self-conscious gravitas with charm and a slightly wicked sense of humour; Penwell Mhaga, the amiable and solicitous prosecutor; Meshack Maluleke, the assiduous state defence attorney always with a well-thumbed self-help book by his side; Rosemary Meyer, the ample and proficient isiZulu translator, hanging onto the witness stand as if about to deliver an aria. We had our gripes with them, certainly, and we were enraged that Sibanda had been awaiting trial for seventeen months by this point, but as we watched the day's proceedings, we remarked to one another that the wheels of justice seemed to turn quite well in Court Seventeen.

When Sibanda had to walk from the dock to the witness stand, he was forced to make a choice: to brush physically past us, sitting in the pew behind the prosecutor, or to shift some furniture so to avoid us.

He took the first option, walking with a limp that seemed, to me, to be exaggerated to underscore the allegation he would make, several times in his testimony, that he had been 'severely assaulted' by the police.

Sibanda accepted that the palm-print on my mother's green BMW was his own, but denied that he had anything to do with the car having been stolen, or with the attack on us. He washed cars outside nightclubs in Rockey Street, he explained in isiZulu: in this line of work he touched many cars and the BMW must have been one of them. I scrawled a note, which I passed over to Mhaga, the prosecutor: 'The car would have had to be cleaned between midnight, when it was stolen, and seven in the morning when it was retrieved! Also, it was certainly not clean when I collected it from the police pound!'

Mhaga decided to put me back on the stand, and the case now seemed to revolve around whether the car might ever have been in Yeoville, either before or after it had been stolen. I had never taken it there, I said, but the defence attorney, Malukeke, did his best to cast reasonable doubt on my testimony: since the car belonged to my mother, was it not possible that she had driven it to Yeoville, perhaps in the days preceding the trial? I explained that my mother had been out of town at the time. And anyway, I said, she was an elderly white woman from Sandton: there is no way she would have taken a drive down Rockey Street. So sharp do the geographical distinctions remain in Johannesburg that everyone knew exactly what I meant.

Ratshibvumo adjourned the court and told us that he would deliver judgement the following day. But when we arrived, he said he was not ready to do so: he needed to hear from my mother herself that the car had not been in Yeoville. My mother was abroad, however, and so the case was postponed once again – for another month – until her return.

Sibanda shook in the dock, with fury or with fear, at this further delay, this further injustice. I have never been more conscious, as I was in that moment, of my privilege in relationship to his abjection: the privilege represented by having a mother abroad, a mother with a spare car; by my status in the courtroom as a well-known author jetting in from France; by my education and my access to lawyers and the power I had to ensure that the justice system worked for me.

All this entitlement was lined up against a man who made pennies as a car washer; an economic migrant from devastated Zimbabwe who had been retrenched over three years previously and had not managed to find work since. But there was nothing I could do for Sibanda; nothing, either, that I would want to do for him. Even as I felt guilt about my privilege, I felt an immense relief at it too.

I felt rage rise against Sibanda once more, this time for making me so aware of my place in the world. I hated him for having made me hateful, and I hated myself for hating him. I struggled to balance this against the sadness I felt at the sight of this lost man, shuffling down into the cells below the Johannesburg Magistrate's Court.

*

On the 2 September 2013, my mother testified that she had not been to Rockey Street in Yeoville in fifty years, and that she had certainly not driven her green BMW there in the days preceding its theft.

The following day, magistrate Ratshibvumo delivered his judgement. He said that despite the fact that we were only able to make what is known as 'dock identifications' – in other words, that we were unable to identify Thabani Sibanda in the identity parade – he found us to be credible witnesses. Sibanda, on the other hand, had not managed to provide a credible explanation for why his palm-print was on the stolen car: he was found guilty on all three charges of housebreaking and robbery with aggravating circumstances.

Ratshibvumo upbraided the prosecution for not charging Sibanda with rape, too. He referred to the doctrine of 'common purpose' – a controversial apartheid-era formulation that makes all participants in a crime liable for the activity that ensues – and said he would have found Sibanda guilty had he been so charged, even though he was not a direct participant in Bea's sexual assault.

When Maluleke, the defence attorney, presented evidence in mitigation of the sentence, we found out more about our assailant: he was twenty-eight years old, he was single, he had two children aged six and one, and his work as a car-washer brought him about R4,500 (£300) a month, his Zimbabwean family's sole income. The magistrate did not find these reasons to be 'compelling and substantive' enough to reduce the mandatory minimum sentence, and so Sibanda was handed down fifteen years in jail. Maluleke also argued that, because his client had been held in custody awaiting trial for seventeen months, this time should be taken off his sentence; Ratshibvumo responded that seventeen months was a pretty average amount of time to await trial at the Johannesburg Magistrates' Court, and so he could not make an exception on this account. At the time of writing these words, in October 2013, Thabani Sibanda has applied for leave to appeal both the sentence and the conviction.

During the sentencing, Ratshibvumo explained to Sibanda why the law compelled him to favour the principles of punishment and retribution over that of mercy: 'Members of the society are moving out of certain areas such as the townships to very expensive areas such as the suburbs for the simple reason that they need security and peace of mind,' he said. 'Recently, there was even a trend to move into a golf estate, and the only difference between the golf estate and such suburbs I mentioned above is twenty-four-hour security. Most of the population cannot afford to move into those expensive premises. But each one of us, rich and poor, have a right to live in our homes in peace without fear that while we are watching TV and enjoying our family, a certain Sibanda might pounce, coming to reap what he did not sow. In essence, the interest of our society requires that criminals such as you be moved out of society for a reasonably longer period ...'

As the magistrate was delivering this judgement, my eye wandered over to a 2013 Department of Justice calendar below him, stuck onto the wood panelling of his bench: 'All people in South Africa are and feel safe,' it read.

PART THREE

DISPATCHER

HOMEWARD BOUND

Hope in Alexandra

The vision of Hope Molefe as she billowed through the haze of Alfred Nzo Street towards the Engen Garage, where I was awaiting her, felt like something out of a dream, or a film. There was something of the timeless ingénue in Hope's demeanour as she looked up and recognised me from the middle of the intersection; in the way she threw her head back in laughter and raised her arm up in generous greeting. I had seen her only once or twice in the last twenty years, but we embraced as old friends: she is the oldest daughter of Bettinah, my childhood nanny; she is three years younger than me and we have known each other since we were children.

It was February 2012, about a month after the attack, and a good few months before the trial was to begin. I was in Johannesburg to finish writing this book –and I had planned to stay for at least another three months. Of course, the temptation to leave the city immediately after the attack was great: I had a home in Paris, after all, a life and a husband there. But it had not seemed the right time to go, and not just because of the work still on my plate: Johannesburg was my home town, my soul town, and I did not want to run away from it. 'If you close the door too quickly, you'll never be able to come back,' someone had said, perhaps a tad melodramatically, but still, it rang true. I needed to make my peace with Johannesburg before I could leave, so that I could return with ease. I also needed to be around friends, and carers, who could connect with what I was going through, because it was their lived reality too. Most of all, I still needed to be with Katie and Bea, and they needed to be with me.

But I found myself unable to write. So I set myself a task: rather than stewing over my computer, I would throw myself into my final round of research which would require me to be on the street, among people, in the city centre and in townships. I would begin, I decided, on page 75 of the *Holmden's*, in Alexandra, the township that first alerted my consciousness to the presence of borders and boundaries in my city. I was at ease in Soweto, in Thokoza, in Evaton, in Mamelodi; I could travel the streets of these and many others, but I still barely knew the township closest to my own childhood, unreachable across the Sandspruit at the edge of page 77. I do not know if there was some reason, beyond random circumstance, for my lack of familiarity with the township: perhaps an atavistic fear percolated through from my childhood, or a lingering discomfort in its dark, crime-ridden streets, swollen with too many people, or a need to keep some corner of Johannesburg's street guide a place for the secret fantasies of a Dispatcher game rather than the real-life missions of a journalist and explorer. Whichever: here I was now, walking with Hopey – as she was universally known, in her family and mine – back across Alfred Nzo to her home in Alexandra.

*

Alexandra functions as the picaresque in the South African imagination: its mean streets kill you or teach you; embrace or extinguish you. Its characters are resourceful and ebullient and streetwise but they can also be rogues; it is a place of music and gunfire, where Nelson Mandela found his politics and Hugh Masekela his beat. Alexandrans seem to take a perverse kind of pride in their mean streets. For the 1950s activist Michael Dingake, his home-township was 'the stepchild of step-parenthood', a dumping ground, a place of 'social cannibalism'; for Mongane Serote, whose poems about Alexandra I had been holding close since my own adolescence, it was a 'troubled stomach', a 'terrible stew', a place that absorbed all of apartheid's evils 'like a sponge'.

And yet, in the true spirit of the picaresque, there was the promise of something redemptive in this hostile environment. 'Out there in the streets, something with a loud bang, called soul, screamed and popped and dragged our children along,' writes Serote in his novel of the Eighties, *To Every Birth Its Blood*. In one of the finest passages in South African literature Serote seemed deliberately to omit the word 'music' after 'soul', as if to suggest that he might be talking about something more than just a beat: 'It overspilled out of house windows and doors; it leaped over stadium walls; peeped through bars at shops, got off out of fast-moving taxis and buses – soul, it followed us everywhere.' Finally, he gets specific: 'The children, responding to this soul music, discovered their cocks and cunts and buttocks and thighs and stomachs and navels as they spiralled and twisted and jerked and pointed to the sky and looked at the earth, and cried and laughed – bewildering the old; the old had nothing to do, they could do nothing; soul did it, the old remained silent. The children, with unkempt hair, and the girls in hotpants which forever want to expose but never do – these our children crowded the streets, walking aimlessly.' And then, the punchline, the crash: 'These same streets, which now took our children – and souled them, so to say – still claimed corpses.'

Alexandra provided the African National Congress with an inordinate number of its political leaders; many of them doubled as gangsters. Even after the fall of apartheid it has maintained its notoriety, despite a massive infusion of state funding through an Alexandra Renewal Project (ARP). This, the ARP director Job Sithole told me when I spent my time in the township in February 2012, had everything to do with demographics: 'The only way to renew Alexandra is to move half the people out of it. Instead, more and more people are moving in, every day. It's the cheapest and most convenient place to begin your life in Gauteng province.'

Alexandra was proclaimed in 1912 a freehold township for people of all races, and it would be particularly targeted at those prosperous black people forced out of the countryside by the Land Act of the following year. Wealthy black sharecroppers came to town and bought handsome homes on Alexandra's large plots, often taking on extortionate mortgages that they were unable to service due to their rapid impoverishment as wage-labourers. To keep their properties they became slumlords, in effect, erecting dormitories in their yards that they rented by the room to the new arrivals streaming into town. Thus did the township develop around communal yards.

'Everything was shared in Alexandra,' Paul Mashatile told me. 'The tap, the toilet once it came [Alexandra got sanitation only in the 1980s]. So we were forced into accepting to live together as human beings.' Mashatile is the township's most powerful politician, the arts and culture minister in Jacob Zuma's cabinet when I met him in 2012. His politics were formed in the yards: 'In other townships, you go into your own yard and close the gate. In Alex, you go home, and there are five other families there, each one from a different ethnic group: here Zulu, here Shangaan, here Xhosa. It *teaches* you.'

In the Forties, Alexandra led the protest movement against incipient apartheid with its famous bus boycotts, and in the Eighties, with its youth uprisings. It was unique, among urban black freehold communities, in resisting the fate of places like District Six in Cape Town or Sophiatown in Johannesburg: through effective protest against clearance, it survived. But there was a price. The plan was to clear Alexandra and turn it into a massive migrant-labour hostel: the title deeds of landowners were cancelled and everyone – whether a landlord in the main house or a denizen of the yard – was transformed into a tenant of the state. The state's next step was to take control of the yards: migrant labourers, fresh from the countryside, were allocated backrooms, regardless of the wishes of other tenants around the yard. Thus did a tension arise in Alexandra, which persists to this day: between the so-called 'Bona Fides', who claim to be the township's original residents, and the parvenus, who are disparagingly called *amagoduka*, the isiZulu word for migrant labourers. This simmering conflict twice erupted into murderous violence: in the early Nineties, in conflicts between the ANC-supporting comrades and Inkatha-supporting hostel-dwellers; then in 2008, in the bloody massacre of people presumed to be new migrants from other parts of Africa.

Maps never bleed, of course, and none of this is visible on page 77 of the *Holmden's*, or any other map of the township, which appears in plan form as a rigid and regular grid, somewhat at odds with the curves and acute angles of the white suburbs that surround it.

And yet, whenever I have spoken to people like Paul Mashatile, I am struck by Alexandra's alternative topography: the warren of uncharted lanes connecting the yards that run alongside the regimented streets, and through which comrades and gangsters alike could pass.

Mashatile – a couple of years younger than me – laughed when I asked him if he ever used *Holmden's* or the *Street Guide to Witwatersrand*. 'We had our own maps,' he said. 'They were in our heads. There were no straight lines on them. How do you think we organised so effectively? If I wanted to get a message out, my comrades would move' – here he made a motion with his hand, swivelling it from side to side as if a fish in the ocean – 'from yard to yard, between the streets. The cops would never see us.' The reality of life in Alexandra – roiling and transitory, unstable and unlit (it remained without electricity until the 1980s) – defies its Cartesian geometry, its tyranny of line.

In all the indicators of social malaise, from infant mortality to AIDS to homicide rates to xenophobia, Alexandra remains near the bottom of South Africa's charts, and is dramatically worse, of course, than the now racially mixed middle-class suburbs that directly surround it. Its decrepitude is all the more striking when compared with the boom-town that is now Soweto; more striking yet with the gaudy towers of Sandton leering over it. And yet it did feel exhilarating to be enveloped by so intense an urbanity, I thought, as I waited for Hope Molefe and looked down over the jumble of roofs and yards from my vantage-point at the Engen Garage. Its sheer density brought Mumbai, or Lagos, or Cairo to mind. I would spend the better part of the next two weeks coming here: I would follow a film crew; I would meet activists and politicians, businessmen and artists and old-timers too, but most of all, I would reacquaint myself with Hopey, who has lived in Alex most of her life and has raised her children here.

Hopey and I are contemporaries. We eyed each other across the frontier of the backyard. I wanted to understand how she might actually have shuttled across the boundaries of the *Holmden's* while I only fantasised about doing so from the back seat of my father's Mercedes.

*

Everyone seemed to know and love Hopey on her street. '*Ma Thabang! Ma Thabang!*' they called, in the African custom of naming a parent after her child, obviously intrigued by the *umlungu* at her side.

'I hope they don't think I'm your new boyfriend,' I teased.

'No,' she laughed with her easy smile. 'They know I am a good girl.' *Goood giiirl*: she strung the vowels out into diphthongs, affecting that gymslippy girlish voice that one often hears from grown women in South Africa and that must have its roots in the kind of township burlesque performative style now the norm on TV soaps. Hopey, I would come to realise after my few days in her company, could deploy the wit and the ferocity of a street-smart township woman if need be, but she put much stock in being, as she frequently put it, 'decent'. She came from a devout churchgoing family and was 'a quiet somebody', she told me, 'too shy for Alex'. There was something charming in the only slightly selfconscious way she wore her considerable beauty.

As the early evening hubbub of a township homecoming percolated all around us, we sat sipping tea in her immaculate flat, while her eldest son Thuso obsessively scrubbed every surface of the kitchen and the bathroom and her younger children – fifteen-year-old Thabang and seven-year-old Thuthu – perfected dance routines to tinny hip-hop off a cellphone in the bedroom. Hopey and I were not really childhood friends, but we did that thing childhood friends do when reunited after many years: we exchanged stories about our mothers and asked after each other's siblings; we updated each other on our respective lives, our families and careers.

The flat had some markers of prosperity – a big television and a desktop computer, stucco on the ceilings and shiny new countertops in the kitchen – but Hopey's toehold on the middle class was clearly tenuous. One of the few things I remembered about her, from my childhood, was her mother's pride in Hopey's academic achievements, and her aspirations of becoming a doctor. 'No, Mark,' Hopey corrected me, when I mentioned this, 'Betty was exaggerating to you. I only wanted to be a nurse.'

She told me, now, that she had not been able to finish her schooling because of illness. She had worked her way up from a cleaner to a clerical post at a furniture company but had lost her job five years previously when the company went bankrupt, and she had not been able to find another one since. She survived off irregular maintenance payments from her children's' father, from whom she was separated, and domestic work, her mother's work, which she justifiably loathed. We discussed her entrepreneurial plans: she is a great cook, and she was thinking of starting a catering business with her sisters; her current boyfriend came from a well-known Free State family, and they were thinking of setting up a company to 'get some tenders' there. When I asked what kind of tenders, she couldn't say: in desperately underemployed South Africa, being well-connected enough to get paid in exchange for some service rendered to the state has become job description enough. There is even a word for it: 'tenderpreneur'.

Hopey's son, Thuso, had just turned twenty-one – there were celebratory cards adorning the mantelpiece – but he too was unemployed. He was devoted to his grandmother's Zion Christian Church, where he had been revealed as a prophet and where he spent most of his time. Most of Hopey's meagre income went towards the education of her younger children, whom she had enrolled in formerly white state schools in the suburbs around Alexandra. These 'Model C schools', as they are still called (after the legislation that permitted some white schools to take in a small number of black students in the early 1990s), cost more than the township schools and, of course, she had to pay for daily transport too.

'When you were a kid in Alexandra', I said, 'you would have needed a pass to cross London Road from Alex into Lombardy. Now you and your kids do it a few times a day.' We laughed, and I used this to segue into an explanation of what I was doing in Alexandra, by way of my

Dispatcher story and the *Holmden's*. 'When I was growing up I played this game imagining what life was like in Alexandra, by giving someone directions about how to get there,' I said, 'but the maps were made in such a way that there was no means of finding the route from Sandton to Alex. Of course, *you* knew the route. You must have crossed that boundary between pages 75 and 77 many times, when you came to visit your mom.'

'I crossed it every day,' she said.

That is how I found out that Hope Molefe had come to live across our backyard in 1983 at the age of fourteen and had stayed for nearly five years. I had no idea. I had already left home, for the University of Cape Town. Still, I came back frequently, and I remained close to Bettinah, in that familiar yet distant way adults have with the servants who raised them. At UCT I had joined the National Union of South African Students and become radicalised; I had spent two months at home after leaving UCT and preparing to go to Yale, where I would write about the plight of black schoolchildren in a South Africa increasingly at war. How could I have missed that one of these children had sought refuge in my family home, across our backyard, sleeping almost directly beneath my bedroom window?

*

Hopey was raised by her grandparents in a village outside Rustenburg, two hours' drive north-west of Johannesburg, a slice of poverty wedged between the wealth of the platinum mines and the obscenity of Sol Kerzner's Sun City casino development.

There were, at times, as many as twenty children in the Molefe family home; all Bettinah's sisters were also domestic workers in the city. The Molefes were pillars of the community: Bettinah's father was an educated man and the local head of the Zion Christian Church. He and his wife had met through the church; they had sought refuge in it, individually, as youngsters, as many did, because they were believed to be possessed by the ancestors and were fleeing their destinies as *sangomas*. Possession is something that runs in families, Hopey told me: this was why her son, Thuso, was a prophet in the ZCC – 'I fear terribly for him' – and why she herself had been forced to leave her village as a little girl.

She had been a very sickly child, often unable to rise from her bed, and neither Western medicine and doctors nor the cleansings of the church had been able to heal her. She was too ill to go to school, and rumours spread through the village that she might be bewitched. In desperation, her mother sent her to a relative in Ga-Rankuwa, one of Pretoria's townships, a woman who was both a *sangoma* and a Christian preacher. 'I was called by the ancestors,' Hopey told me, 'but I didn't follow the calling. It was my choice. I didn't want to. My aunty told me, "You're still young, we'll try to calm them down." And she succeeded.'

Why, I asked Hopey, did *she* think she was so sick as a little girl? 'Even to this day I do not understand it,' she responded. 'But I am thinking that it's maybe because I missed my mother too much. Every time she came home, I cried and cried when she left. I was only three when she left to work. My brother was six, already, he understood that Betty had to go to work.' And why, then, did she think she got better? She cannot explain it, beyond the supernatural interventions of her aunt. But she is certain of one thing: the closer she was, physically, to her mother, the better she was.

Hopey endured a rigorous treatment with her aunt in Ga-Rankuwa: she would be awakened three times a night to pray, and after six months she seemed better. The family decided that she should not return to the village, and she was sent to lodge with an uncle in Soweto. But this did not work out, and so this thirteen-year-old was shunted about yet again and sent to stay with another uncle, in Alexandra.

But despite placing her closer than ever to her mother – just a page away in the *Holmden's* – Alexandra did not work out. First, her illness seemed to be triggered again, this time by the vile stench of the township. 'They had the bucket system,' she explains, 'where you had to leave your shit outside in a bucket each night, to be collected by the *amaBhaca*' – members of the Bhaca tribe, who had cornered the trade, and who would, notoriously, overturn all the buckets in a yard or street if anyone insulted them. 'It was terrible. I was sick all the time.'

Second, and more decisively, she shot into adolescence early, way ahead of her peers. A country girl of uncommon beauty, she attracted a lot of attention, some of it aggressive and abusive. 'I was not safe, Mark,' she told me. 'Once, at lunchtime, a boy abducted me, and pulled me to his place. I started to scream, and the old people heard me and he let me go. *Malumi* [Uncle] was very strict. I got home late, and he screamed at me, "Where have you been?" I was too afraid to tell him what happened. I just cried and cried, and nobody understood why.' The following week she was beaten by a boy when she tried to resist him. She resolved to tell her uncle, but when she did he flew into a rage and beat her himself. 'You must learn to fight for yourself,' he said.

'It was not good for me,' Hopey told me, 'as if the problem were with her rather than with society. 'I am a quiet somebody. Even here, in Alex, today, I like to stay inside and mind my own business.' She had heard of a boarding school in Hammanskraal, north of Pretoria, and when her mother next came to Alexandra, she told her she wished to enrol there. Bettinah did not have enough leave to accompany Hopey there herself to register, but her daughter said that two older girls who were also interested in going to the school would look after her. And so Bettinah gave her the money for the travel.

Thus began the ordeal which would finally shatter Hopey's already dislocated childhood. The bus to Hammanskraal broke down somewhere along the road; after three hours of waiting for a replacement bus, some men drove by and offered the girls a lift. 'We didn't think it was a bad thing at first, but after they were driving us around for hours we started crying and asking them to let us go. Eventually we came to a house, with high walls, and barking dogs. That is when I knew something bad was going to happen. They kept us for maybe two hours more, then an older lady and two men came in, and called us in one by one. The granny touched the other girls' breasts and told them to go, and one of the people with masks took them away. They called me in and asked me my age and whether I was menstruating yet.' Hopey is certain that she was neither raped nor assaulted sexually. 'The granny said to undress me, but when she saw the rope around my waist, she got furious with the two men who had brought me, shouting, "Why do you take this evil to my house? Get her out of here!"'

Like all initiates into the Zion Christian Church, Hopey wore a coloured string around her waist. She had already made a deduction: the old woman, who was draped in beads, was some kind of witch, or evil *sangoma*. This was a time when there was a lot of publicity, particularly in the black press, about '*muti* murders', children abducted, murdered and dismembered for body parts to be used as *muti*, or medicine, in the practice of the dark arts. Perhaps, Hopey told me, 'they feared that if they killed someone from the ZCC, the *muti* would not work'.

Who can know what a fourteen-year-old who has undergone such trauma actually experiences and what she remembers; what phantasms insert themselves into memory and what depredations recede into the brain's deep folds of repression? Whatever the detail, Hopey was taken somewhere against her will and held for several hours, and this is the defining trauma of her life. 'When I get sick, or if there is a problem, let's say, with men, I think: Maybe it's because of this. Maybe this is what's killing me. I think about, What if they would have killed me that night? My mother would struggle to get back the body. She would never know where I am. And of course I worry all the time about my own children.' I noted how strict she was with them, particularly with respect to matters of safety: if my party trick had been reciting world capitals, seven-year-old Thuthu's appeared to be reciting the rules of the road.

When the witch rejected Hopey that night, she was tied up and gagged, and left outside in the yard for several hours. It was mid winter, and all Hopey remembers is the bitter cold; she might have passed out from it. The following morning she was wrapped in a cloth and dumped at Pretoria Station. A security guard found the phone number of a relative on Hopey – given to her by her mother in case of emergency – and called it: 'I was shivering, and in shock, and the cousin came to fetch me, and took me to hospital. I was very sick. The cousin called Betty, who said to put me on a bus back to Alex. Betty decided I must come and stay with her, and asked your mother. She said, "yes", and that's how I came to stay at Betty's Place.'

*

The refuge at 'Betty's Place' helped heal Hopey, she told me: it gave her quiet, and it gave her space, and she had her mother's warm body next to her every evening. In the beginning she harboured an irrational fear of Welshman, the Zimbabwean man who replaced the beloved James in our household, because he closely resembled one of her abductors, but she came to trust him. And Maggie, the cook, looked after her as her own daughter, particularly when Bettinah was unavailable. My mother was particularly nice: 'She and Betty have always been the two role models to me. Betty would come and say to me, "Get dressed nicely," and then your mother would take me in the car to buy snacks and would ask me, "How is school? How are you coping?" And I thought, "Yes, I am happy, here, at Betty's Place."'

I was moved by the way Hopey referred to our home as Betty's Place, even if I was a little uncomfortable with the way she spoke of her own mother as Betty, as we Gevisser children did, rather than by her Setswana name, or simply as 'Mom' or 'Mama'. She might have said 'your house', or she might have said 'my Mom's place', but by calling it Betty's Place it occurred to me that she was striking a subtle balance. She was claiming possession of it for her mother, who would after all live there for over forty years. But she was also acknowledging that her mother was someone else while there, someone with responsibilities to other children; someone, even, with another name.

This led me to consider what it would mean if the only 'home' you could go back to, after such a violation, was in the backyard behind the place where your mother worked as a nanny and whom you only saw when she climbed into bed next to you, dog-tired, after spending the day looking after white children, white children who didn't even know you were there. A place where you were not even allowed to be:

the apartheid regulations were very clear that domestic workers were not permitted to have their families on the property, even if my parents had chosen to turn a blind eye.

I tried to imagine, listening to Hopey's story, how a fourteen-year-old would recover from such a trauma, with none of the access to the kind of professional services I had just received after my own attack. Here I was, trying to find a way to be safe again in my home town; how on earth, I wondered, does a fourteen-year-old ever feel safe again in the world, in her skin, after such an experience at the cusp of her adolescence?

*

It would be another few years before black children could begin attending white schools. In 1983, when Hopey came to live at Betty's place, there were not yet any schools in Sandton that would have taken her, and so once she was well again – it took her many weeks to recover – she was re-enrolled at Alexandra High, and had to find a way to commute.

It was surprisingly easy. In the mornings, she would do the half-hour walk to Jan Smuts Avenue, where a bus bringing farmworkers' children to Alex would stop to pick her up. In the afternoons, she would either get this bus home or – after she became involved in an after-school programme – would get a lift from the white woman who ran the programme and lived nearby. Two other kids commuted from our suburb to Alex, a boy and a girl who stayed in servants' quarters with their parents, like Hopey, and they became her constant companions. She still feared the attentions of older boys, but her friends waited for her after class, and protected her.

This was the mid Eighties, the most turbulent time in South Africa's history, and Alexandra had responded vigorously and passionately to the ANC's cry to 'make the country ungovernable'. After the shooting of a young man by a security guard at one of the Indian stores on London Road in early 1986, the township ignited in what became known as the 'Six-Day War', in which gangs of comrades – many of them students from Alexandra High – formed militias to attack anyone assumed to be collaborators, such as policemen, councillors and state officials. The security forces responded with brutality and mass detentions, and at least thirty children were killed. Huge crowds gathered in protest in the Alexandra Stadium, marching through the township and attending fiercely angry mass funerals.

When Hopey was at school in Alexandra, commuting daily from the leafy suburban laager in which I had been reared to Alex High, the township was perhaps the most radical place in the country. It was a place of rumour and conspiracy and the perpetual flashfire of rebellion, a place that spawned both the students' movements and the civics movements of the era, and which resisted pacification to such an extent that it was almost obliterated in the 'Six-Day War'. What was it like, I asked her, living in the suburbs and commuting to this war zone daily.

She shrugged. 'What can I say?'

'What did the other kids think of you?'

'We were teased a lot,' she allowed.

'Were you called coconuts?' Black outside and white inside: a slur which became more common as more kids commuted from the townships to the suburbs to attend schools and started talking like whites.

'Of course we were. There was a lot of that. They would look at my lunchbox, at the food made by Betty, maybe the leftovers of what you had eaten for supper, and they would say, "*Ooh Hopey, you think you are better because you are living with the whites.*"' Hopey assumed an uncharacteristic posture of mild defiance: 'But I didn't bother, because it was true. I *did* have better food in my lunchbox. I *was* living a better life than them. It *was* better in the suburbs than the townships, where the girls were running around, and the boys chasing them.' For the first time in our conversation, she did not refer to her mother as Betty: 'And I was next to my mom. I had no problem where I was staying.'

At the outset of the 'Six-Day War', she told me, she was commandeered with the other students to a march on the Indian shop on London Road where the protesting boy had been killed by the guard: 'We were *toyi-toying*, but I was crying. One of the comrades came up to me and said, "Hopey, what is wrong?", and I said I was not feeling well. So they let me go home but they said, "Tomorrow we want you here." She did not go back to school for several days: while she was at Betty's Place, the Indian shopkeeper had his shop torched, many of her schoolmates were injured and detained, and two of her friends were killed. I was in my junior year at Yale.

Later that year, her mother sent her to Alexandra on a Saturday with a cousin to get their hair done, for they were going to be brides-maids at an aunt's wedding in Rustenburg. 'We were walking in the street, and the police stopped us and put us in a mellow-yellow (police van). It was terrible. They took us to Bramley Police Station. Betty was at home, waiting for us, waiting to go to Rustenburg, and the worst was that she would be worried about where we were. At the police station, they showed us a picture of Mandela, with Sellotape over his eyes. They asked us, "Who is this man?" I knew it was Mandela, but I knew the whites didn't like him, so I said, "I don't know, I'm not one of the comrades. I'm from Sandton."'

Hopey had wet herself with fear, 'Lucky you,' the policeman, a black man, had said. 'You stay in Sandton, not in Dark City.' He threw her a bucket and mop: 'Wipe up your mess, and I'll drive you home.'

Hopey and her cousin made the wedding. But that year, 1986, the year Alexandra caught fire, she became very ill again. She collapsed in class one day, and was taken to Hillbrow Hospital, where she spent many weeks. She did not go back to school.

*

In 2004 I met the celebrated South African writer K. Sello Duiker at a writers' retreat at Monkey Valley, outside Cape Town. 'I recognise your family name,' he said. 'Did you go to Redhill?'

Duiker was one of South Africa's most vibrant and iconoclastic young talents – both his novels had won major awards – and I was intrigued to hear that we shared an alma mater. He told me that he had started at Redhill when my youngest brother, Peter, was in his final year, in 1989; Duiker had been the school's first black scholarship student, through a programme initiated by my father, then the chair-man of the school's board of trustees. Duiker's parents were university-educated and ambitious for their children, and he came from a comfortable Soweto home. But his Redhill experience was nonetheless deeply dislocating.

I will never forget his words: 'It's hard to describe what it was like travelling that distance every day, from Orlando to Morningside, and being virtually the only one doing it. No one in Soweto knew or understood the place I was going to, and no one at Redhill knew or understood the place I was coming from.' It was a cost, he told me, that he was ultimately very grateful to have paid: 'It made me into an artist. I had a teacher who said, "follow your dreams". There wouldn't have been those horizons in a Soweto high school.' The daily crossing, from Soweto to the Northern Suburbs, put him on a trajectory which got him to Rhodes University and to his first novel, *Thirteen Cents*, published at the age of twenty-six, which won him the Commonwealth Writers' First Book Award for Africa. Still, he told me, being the only township child at Redhill came very close to destroying him, something he could admit to no one at the time, given the pride his scholarship brought his family and the sense of benevolence it brought the Redhill community.

We stayed up talking for hours on the Monkey Valley terrace, the Atlantic Ocean crashing against the shore directly beneath us. It was very painful to listen to this young man describing such anguish at a place that had been so empowering and nurturing for me. I had never previously heard anyone describe the 'coconut' condition so acutely, but when I urged him to consider writing about it, his response was startling. *Thirteen Cents* drew on his experiences of becoming homeless in his early twenties; his second novel, *The Quiet Violence of Dreams*, was a sexually explicit *roman-à-clef* with a gay rentboy protagonist. His fiction shattered so many stereotypes about what was acceptable for a young, upwardly-mobile, educated black man in postapartheid South Africa and yet, he told me, he would never write about his experiences at Redhill: it was territory he could not own publicly. It was still too shameful.

We never met again, although we corresponded several times by email. And then, a few months later, I heard that he had killed himself. He was not yet thirty. He had been open to me in our conversation at Monkey Valley about his struggles with mental health, and clearly he was possessed of one of those fragile psyches that create brilliant art but make living so difficult. I could not help but be haunted by our conversation, and by thoughts about how his adolescence at Redhill might have destabilised him further, even as it revealed to him his calling and offered him the alienation that is the writer's greatest gift.

Certainly, there is an entire generation of 'Model C graduates' (I use quotation marks because Redhill was a private school, not a government Model C one) from Sello Duiker's time who are successful, or happy, or both. Duiker's experiences strike me nonetheless as representative of one of the great taboos, still to be shattered, about the South African transition. The story of the first generation of border-crossers in South African schools, those kids who first went into white schools as apartheid crumbled, and who have come out with the educations and networks and 'model C accents' that prime them for success, but who also carry the baggage of a profound alienation, the depths and costs of which have not yet been socially understood.

A large number of the kids in the 'Model C' demographic are, like Hopey Molefe, children of domestic workers who have come to the suburbs to live with their mothers – in no small part so as to be able to access the superior educations of suburban schools. Hopey was just a few years too old to be one of these children herself; had she arrived at 'Betty's Place' four or five years later, she would have been enrolled in Hyde Park High, or Sandown High, and her life might have been very different. So, too, might have been that of Nora Kubeka, Bram Fischer's informally adopted daughter, had she been able to attend school with her 'sisters', Ilse and Ruth, in the late Fifties.

Spending time with Hopey, I thought about the stories I knew, from my own social world, of such children. The apartheid-era spatial divisions remain in Johannesburg houses. There is a main house, where the owners live, although they are not necessarily white any more, and there is, across the yard, the servants' quarters. In some instances, the feudal constructs of this space have crumbled: the servants' quarters have been converted into a 'garden cottage', and the household is no longer run by live-in servants. In other instances, the feudal relationship has morphed, somewhat, and new borderlands have opened up along the frontier that once segmented space so rigidly across the threshold of the yard.

South African literature is replete with stories from the *platteland* [countryside], where the boundaries have always been blurred between the farmer's white children and the farmworkers' black ones. Now, in the post-apartheid years, with the collapse of the Group Areas Act, which allocated each racial group its own residential zone, such border-crossing narratives have found new expression in the suburbs. These new suburban borderlands are, in the way of all liminal zones, both creative and troubled. Black and white children have grown up together and have often gone off to the same schools together in the morning; they have eaten meals together, before the white child goes to bed in the main house and the black child in his mother's room at the back. Deep friendships and kinships have developed, but so too have a whole new difficult set of relationships. A white child has become so attached to her surrogate backyard siblings that she has to be urged by her parents to speak in English rather than Zulu. The adorable child of the domestic worker, with full run of the house, has turned into a troublesome adolescent; this has seen him ejected from paradise along a path that has led to banishment and drug abuse. A sibling-like relationship among children is shattered – as is the black child's education prospects – when a domestic worker quits after a conflict with the madam. A couple has fallen in love with their maid's baby and is in the process of adopting him; he has moved into the house while she remains across the yard.

*

'Did Betty's Place become home for you?' I asked Hopey.

'More than those words,' she responded. 'Of course I met different kids staying in the suburbs, and some had to sneak in and out. They weren't allowed to be there. But for me, I felt it was my home. I was free. Even when Betty was busy in the kitchen I can go through, I can go upstairs and ask for whatever . . .'

During school holidays, Hopey's three siblings came to stay, and sometimes on weekends her friend Olga would spend the night. The two of them would sleep in a spare room in the servants' quarters, and take towels to lie out on the grassy verge of the pavement during the day just as her mother and the other maids did. Sometimes she helped her mother with the ironing – maybe this is why she loathes that particular task now – and when she was sixteen, she got a packing job at Checkers in Sandton City; this is where she would spend most weekends. Occasionally, my younger brothers would come and ask her to play, but this interaction would never last long: 'You boys were very busy, you had your exams, you had your sports, all that.'

Hopey quickly intuited that a part of me needed to pity her, perhaps so that I could express some remorse and even ask some forgiveness: for my callous insouciance about her presence in my family home, for the fact that Bettinah's obligations to me and my brothers had denied her a mother, for nothing less than her thwarted dreams. She was having none of it: 'Now when I'm thinking about my life, I think, even if I'm not successful, like having a job or education, still I'm decent. Girls my age who grew up in the township, I look at them today, and they've got hard faces. They lived tough lives – boyfriends, drink, all that. Living in the suburbs led you to be *decent*. I am so happy for that.'

It took me a while to ask the question, but I had to, of course: 'How did you feel about us?'

She did not, at first, seem to understand, so I rephrased it. 'Did you ever resent us? I mean, there we were, inside the house, with all that *stuff*. There was a garden, with a pool, and you had to sit on the pavement! And Betty was looking after us rather than you, her own children.'

She took some time to answer. 'We understood,' she said. And she paused again, weighing her words. 'We understood that Betty had to look after you so that she could earn the money to look after us. That's how it was.'

'It must be a sign of what a good mother you had,' I responded. 'Maybe you felt loved enough by Betty, taken care enough by her, that you didn't need to resent these other children for taking her away from you?'

Hopey agreed wholeheartedly.

I chose to believe her.

*

Hopey and I spent a few days tooling around Alexandra. I told her I was writing about the township, and I employed her as a fixer and translator, a job she acquitted ably. On one of our excursions, I wanted to provide for our hosts, and so Hopey accompanied me down Seventeenth Street to buy some drinks and biscuits. We passed a couple of *spaza* shops – tuck shops, in effect, run out of homes – but Hopey said we should continue to the 'container' on the corner. The shop, a general store of sorts, was a rail container which had been set on an open piece of land, and the tradesman, a Somali, seemed literally caged in: we stood outside, and gave him our orders through bars. This was the only time I witnessed Hopey being anything other than sweet and polite: she spoke to the man in isiZulu, and when he struggled to respond, she scowled at him and cursed under her breath. As we walked away, I asked her what had prompted her ill humour, and she unleashed a tirade against foreigners from other parts of Africa: 'They take our jobs and they take our women. They leave their own woman back home, and then they come here and marry a local woman, and with this they get papers, they get an RDP [government] house, and then they bring their family and dump her and leave her!'

'Why did we shop from him, then?' I asked.

'We have to, Mark,' she responded, somewhat exasperated. 'He's the cheapest. Unless we want to go all the way up to Pan-Africa Mall to buy from Pick 'n Pay.' The common perception in the township is that Somali and Ethiopian traders are undercutting local businesses because they use their networks to buy in bulk, but this of course makes them no different from the big commercial retailers such as Pick 'n Pay.

The 2008 xenophobic violence had began in Alexandra, and I heard the scowling bass-note of resentment toward foreigners everywhere

I went, now, over four years later: they take our homes, they take our women, they take our work. The township administrators and politicians might make the fervent point, as the Alexandra Renewal Project's Job Sithole put it to me, that 'There are no ancestors in the ground here, there are no "bona fides" in Alexandra, or, rather, we are all "bona fides". We all come from somewhere else originally.' But the popular opinion that held sway was articulated more accurately, to me, by one of Hopey's neighbours, a bumptious gangster-turned-preacher who is also a community activist.

Hopey brought 'Bra Gib', as I will call him, to meet me one Sunday morning. Like many others I spoke to, he expressed rage that new Zimbabwean and Mozambican migrants were 'jumping the queue over the *bona fides*' and getting state housing just because they had erected their shanties on the floodplains of the Jukskei. In truth, this has been happening: by 2012 the authorities had twice cleared Setswetla, the squatter camp in the floodplain, moving its residents into formal housing; each time, a new generation of shanty-dwellers just replaced them. But Bra Gib reserved his particular ire for the Somali traders. 'Are they *really* refugees?', he asked, rising to the fullest heights of pulpit outrage. 'Why must they be treated as such? If Somalis are killing one another, why should they run here? We have been fighting here [as South Africans], we have had our war, did *we* run anywhere else?'

Before I could engage Bra Gib in a discussion about the tens of thousands of South Africans who had gone into exile during the apartheid years, he had leaped forward into dark prophesy: 'We are sitting on a time bomb here,' he warned. 'Alex is really unpredictable. Young people are saying, "Somalis are taking jobs, you are forcing us to crime."' Just the other day, he told me, he was called in to defuse a situation at the very 'container' Hopey and I had visited, on Seventeenth Street. 'The Somali had been warned, "We are not going to fight you, but you cannot carry on doing business here."'

'How was he warned?' I asked.

'Violently. *Violently*. "You go or you die."'

*

In 2011, two of South Africa's most creative proponents of public art, Stephen Hobbs and Marcus Neustetter, began working in Alexandra in direct response to the xenophobic violence, in collaboration with a group of local artists. They instituted several projects, including the construction of an ephemeral one-day museum on the banks of the Jukskei River, washed away just like the shanties of Setswetla were during floods. But the one that caught my eye was called 'Borderless Intervention', and it entailed driving a herd of goats from Alex all of three kilometres across the Sandspruit and the M1 highway, to water them in the faux-Tuscan fountains of the Michelangelo Hotel at Sandton Square. Why goats in Sandton Square, when dealing with xenophobic violence?

'We wanted to respond to the fact that these new borders within Alex,' Hobbs told me, 'between the "bona fides" and the *makwerekwere* [foreigners] were reflected in the old, uncrossable borders between Alex and Sandton too.' Goats made 'instinctive sense' for a project exploring boundaries and borders, because 'in Alex the goat is a symbol of porousness and fluidity. It goes anywhere, and you just let it pass, because it belongs to someone else. This became an embodiment of the economic and geographic reality of people from Alex: you could be free to roam within your bounds, but in the next neighbourhood over, you were a foreign object, unwelcome and unhealthy.'

As Hobbs said this, I remembered the words of some of my contemporaries whom I had interviewed in Alexandra – men like the ARP's Job Sithole or the Arts Minister Paul Mashatile – who spoke about their experiences as kids visiting the gleaming new Sandton City for the first time. The huge shopping mall was a wonderland for them just as it was for us suburban white kids, but whereas it represented a whole new world of leisure possibility for us – shops, moviehouses, games arcades, girls – it represented, primarily, for them, the game of dodging the law. 'If you were there, you were obviously up to no good,' recalled Sithole. 'So the security would chase you. You're seen as dirty black kids, you don't wash, you're bringing trouble and crime.'

The way Sithole had it, Sandton was nothing less than his *Treasure Island* as a boy: 'The police would stand at the bridge [over the Old Pretoria Road] and if they saw you, they'd sjambok you back to the location. Outwitting the police *became* the adventure. That's why we'd go. You'd laugh if they caught you, if you couldn't manoeuvre [*sic*] them – what's the worst that could happen? They just sjambok you home! And then you'd try again the following weekend.'

Sizakele Nkosi, she of the '*shhhit* from Sandton' remark, had a similar experience of the possibilities for adventure on the other side of the Sandpruit. 'You'd begin', she told me, 'by going to the white farms to steal fruit. But then you'd be more daring, particularly during the December holidays, when the white people were away on holiday. We didn't understand why we should go to Jukskei and drown forever there in the dangerous currents when there are all these beautiful swimming pools with nobody in them. We'd jump over the walls – fortunately they were lower then – into the white man's house, and take everything off and swim. And I mean *everything*. We didn't even wear our panties, because you are scared to arrive at home with a wet panty; you'd have to explain. There were days when, whilst you are swimming, the owner will arrive and he'll find these small black little faces in his swimming pool, and you'll jump out and run away and whoever is caught, well, it's his business!'

In a 2012 retrospective of their work, Hobbs and Neustetter exhibited a large-format photograph from 'Borderless Intervention'. A Michelangelo doorman, replete with yellow-and-black top hat and tails and looking like a ludicrous bumblebee minstrel, is holding a recalcitrant goat by its horns and patting it tenderly on the backside. 'We loved this moment', Neustetter said during a guided walk through the exhibition, 'because here was this guy representing Sandton in all its outlandish finery, surrounded by all this ostentatious fake-Tuscan nonsense, and yet he obviously had his own experiences, back in the townships or the rural areas, and he could see that none of us knew what we were doing, so he stepped out of his role and bounded across the forecourt to show us how to get a goat to move!'

I had been thinking about how to bring 'Borderless Intervention' and goats into my disturbing conversation with Bra Gib when we got drowned out by a tremendous racket. Thuthu, Hopey's little boy, came bounding into the living room to pull me outside to look: a huge procession from one of the township's charismatic churches was passing through the yard below as part of its Sunday morning devotional activity. There must have been a hundred people: women dancing, men drumming, robes flowing and bodies swaying, massed prayer on the move. Bra Gib and I decided to call it quits, and I lingered on the landing outside Hopey's flat, watching the spectacle. The devotees seemed to sweep the other sounds of a Sunday morning township into their liturgy: the honking taxis down Alfred Nzo Street, the women bellowing to each other across the washing-line, the kids screaming as they scampered up and down the stairwells, the youths pumping mindless bass out of open cars, the more matronly church music wafting up from Alex's many places of worship, Thabang and Thuthu doing their interminable dance routines.

A swell of sound rose up the stairwell, a gasp or a cheer, and I watched, rapt, as two young men made their entrance on the landing carrying baskets of laundry. They were wearing denim hotpants, tight black singlets, heads shaven into dyed faux-hawks and loads of clunky jewellery, and they were performing a campy satire of the hymn being sung by the faithful below, swinging their hips and pouting their lips but performing with much affection and emotion too. One of them spotted the *mlungu*, put down his laundry, and swung over to greet me, with a sweetness and a politeness that shone through the ravages of the previous night's excesses. 'Hello,' he said, extending a hand with painted nails. 'I am Dumisane.'

'Hello Dumisane. I am Mark, Hopey's friend. Pleased to meet you.'

'You have such *soft* hands,' he said, holding onto them.

*

'Dumisane's very naughty,' Hopey told me later, smiling indulgently. She clearly adored him, as did Thabang and Thuthu, and she did her bit helping look after his family, a single mother and three young men – all out of school and unemployed – crammed into the one room next door.

'Is it a problem that Dumisane is different?' I asked Hopey, choosing my words carefully. She knew, of course, about me: Betty and C were fast friends.

'The mother accepts,' she responded. 'With the brothers, some problems at first, but now it's okay.' She did not wish to elaborate: it was other people's business. Once, Hopey told me, there were some boys in the yard who were harassing Dumisane, and a rage rose in her as never before. She stormed downstairs and bawled them out: 'Leave him alone! Why are you bothering him? He's not your child. If his own family has a problem with him, leave it to them. It's none of your business!' Her neighbours had never previously heard her voice raised in anything but laughter; when I suggested that her anger might have come from her own childhood experience of being harassed, her response made it clear that something more immediate was at stake: 'No, Mark, people must *accept*. We are all human beings.'

Later in the day, I accompanied Hopey and her family to listen to Thabang sing with her church choir in a fundraiser choral competition at a hall on the Far East Bank. Each group would take to the stage in a set of home-made uniforms and sing a series of mildly choreographed popular hymns. I was struck by how intergenerational the groups were: each one had kids as young as Thabang, all the way up to old men and women who swung about on sticks. It was a scorching afternoon, and the audience participation was languid: every now and then someone would be moved by the spirit into standing up and singing along, and might shuffle her way gently forward – there were very few men in the hall – to offer some coins to the group on stage. I did a double-take when I realised that one of the more ardent participants in this ritual was transgendered, a biological man dressed almost identically to her companion in township streetwear: tight jeans, strappy sandals, frilly tops, hoops in the ears. What differentiated her was a big wig, a little too much make-up, and oversized sunglasses that were not entirely necessary indoors. But I noticed that despite the occasional titter, the others in the hall seemed entirely unfazed by her presence: I seemed to be the only one looking at her.

*

It was only a few months later, once I had given my evidence and the trial was over, that I realised how deeply affected I had been by my time in Alexandra. Johannesburg had resettled inside me, as the 'central privileged space' of my imagination, the village from my childhood from which outward journeys could once more be undertaken. I can put my finger on when this happened: when I was leaning against the railings of the landing outside Hopey's flat with Thuthu standing next to me, looking out over the township, listening to the song coming from the church procession beneath me, and watching Dumisane and his friend ascend the stairwell.

This was not just because of the comfort I felt among strangers again, and the dispelling of any racial profiling that might still have been lurking within me, waiting to be reactivated by the experience of coming face to face with Sibanda in court. It was not, either, just about the sensory delight of that moment on the stairwell, even though this alone carries immense capacity for regeneration. It was also something spatial, something that re-imprinted onto my consciousness the way I like to be in the world. Hopey's easy hospitality, and the way she had made her flat available to me to conduct interviews with people, had established it as a provisional Alexandra 'home' for me. By standing on the landing with my back to the open door of this 'home', I was looking out at the affairs of the world from the familiar portal of my own experience and taking pleasure in trying to make sense of them, again. *Terra incognita* was still there – it is always there, it lurks in the events of that mysterious identity parade and the two Thabani Sibandas – but it no longer existed as a fantasy space between pages 75 and 77 of the *Holmden's*. I had crossed the Sandspruit; I had made one page of the map. I was home.

Open City

Let's play Dispatcher, one more time.

It is about 6.30 on Sunday evening, 30 March 2012. It is two weeks after you have identified your man at the line-up at the holding cells of Hillbrow Police Station; it will still be three months before you give testimony in the trial. It is your last day in Johannesburg before you return to Paris, to your married life, and you have spent it in Alexandra with Hope and her family. You take your leave of them as dusk is falling, after the choral meeting: you are expected at your mother's for a farewell dinner.

According to the *Holmden's*, here is your route. You are to travel west up Roosevelt, (as Alfred Nzo was previously called), crossing into the industrial area of Wynberg and continuing along 2nd, over the Old Pretoria Road bridge. And here, as you hit Andries Street at the top edge of page 75, you will find yourself in trouble. For here you are, up against that uncrossable divide between pages 75 and 77, the frontier of the Sandspruit but now viewed from the other side, from the perspective of Hopey, who took the bus across here to get to school every day; of Job Sithole, who dodged the sjamboks of policemen with probably not as much bravado as he musters today; of Paul Mashatile, who was carried across here in the back of a mellow-yellow to be detained at John Vorster Square and held in custody without trial for four years; of those goats in the back of a truck.

As an adult you made a discovery that there was, in fact, no direct route across the Sandspruit between Alexandra and Sandton during the *Holmden's* years of your early childhood. Until the M1 highway to Pretoria was laid along the Sandspruit valley in the mid 1970s and the

326

Grayston Interchange built connecting Wynberg/Alexandra and Sandton, one had either to pick one's way through the veld along the river or do a lengthy loop back around Corlett Drive. Both routes were invisible to an inexperienced dispatcher sitting in the back of his parents' Mercedes. And so the edge of Wynberg at the top of page 75 in your *Holmden's* remains, for ever, the symbol of your childhood's uncrossable frontiers.

But it's okay, you're an adult now. You know the way. You know there is now a Grayston Interchange and that you can slip across it onto page 77, along Katherine Street and past Sandton City, which is also not yet built. I don't even need to tell you what to do from here, you could do it with your eyes closed, you could drive it if you were blind, homing to that triangle of streets as cloyingly familiar as the sickly sweet smell of jasmine from your childhood, through the open gate and up the brick driveway where you park and see Bettinah in the kitchen window basting the leg of lamb that your mother has ordered in your honour.

You embrace Bettinah, at work all this Sunday to make your meal while you have been hanging out with her children, and you hand her the gift Hopey has sent her. She blushes with pride as you tell her about Thabang's performance at the choir meeting, even though you know she can barely stand the pain of having three of her four adult children unemployed. 'You've got a wonderful family, Betty, you've done well!', you say, before you climb the stairs to your mother and a whiskey. You sink down into the plush frayed couch of your childhood, your father's varnished pine logs a soaring chapel to his memory above you, *Psychopathia Sexualis* somewhere in the upper reaches of your grandfather's library, also above you, the cupboards to your left stashed with the photo-albums of your childhood, the wall of ancestors straight ahead: hello Zalman, hello Minnie.

You sit opposite your mother at dinner, at the table you have shared with your parents and your brothers since you were a little boy. It is a hot evening, and she gets up to open the doors into the garden, but this time you let it be: her company is enfolding, warm and light and rich, and it is unexpectedly pleasant to have the fresh air brushing against you, fragrant with the possibility of a night shower as it rustles through the big old blue gums in the garden, carrying the subtlest suggestion of Alexandra coalsmoke, too, across the Sandspruit. You don't even mind the infernal fucking shrieking of the hadeda ibises this evening. Are they same ones you heard in Alexandra earlier, rising above the hooting of the taxis along Alfred Nzo, oblivious to the *Holmden's* boundaries?

*

Your dinner is over. You are to travel southward, along the William Nicol Highway that runs through the centre of page 79 and across descending numbers that take you closer to town – 37 to 25 to 23 – past Rosebank, where you used to have your Saturday afternoon trysts with Adam in the basement of the Children's Bookshop, and through Forest Town, where you shiver, as always, at the thought of those two queer parties, both outlawed yet inaccessible to each other. Cross over Oxford Road into page 19 and Killarney and wind your way up the ridge along the palisade fence to Wildsview. Park the car against Michael's exuberant bank of hydrangeas, say hello to Jonah the door-man, and bound through the grand lavender lobby into the lift and up to the fourth floor, to say goodbye to Katie and Bea.

Your time with them is tender, but taut. They know you must go, but they are not ready for it. You are leaving Johannesburg for a place where you do not need to dash across the dark and deserted garage, heart thumping, from your car to the lift; where you do not need to triple-bolt your doors and walk around your flat with a panic button attached to a lanyard round your neck; where you do not need to barricade yourself into your bedroom every night after dinner. This is the place where the three of you were attacked, but it is also Katie and Bea's home. As time passes, things will get easier for them: they will paint the walls vibrant colours and rearrange the furniture to shake out the terror still lurking in the corners of their home; they will throw uproarious dinner parties and reclaim their comfort. But tonight, as you are pulled into the kind of three-way embrace you do, an Almodovarish sort of neck-smooch, you feel the wetness of Katie's eyes. It makes you want to leave and to stay at the same time.

*

It's been a long day and it's time to go home, to your bed, but you are not to take the most direct route, back along the gauntlet of Westcliff Drive and over page 23 into page 45 and Melville, a route you have sped along in terror coming home from Wildsview or your friends in Parkview in the nights after the attack. No: you are to take a detour, through The Wilds on page 19, along the drive where you first discovered geography as you sat in the back of your parents' car in the Sunday afternoon traffic on its way to page 3, plotting Granny Gertie's home to her Hillbrow hotel.

It is 9.30 p.m., the very hour that your assailants entered Katie and Bea's flat, having walked down from Hillbrow in the opposite direction to which you are driving. Are there men slipping up The Wilds' stone pathways right now, brushing against the milkwoods and tramping over the clivia toward the palisade fence as you speed along Houghton Drive beneath them in your tube of tar and metal and halogen light? This uncomfortable thought carries you past the housing development to which your cellphone was traced but which the police would not enter, and under Louis Botha Avenue into Yeoville, the formerly Jewish working-class suburb with its pokey Victorian bungalows and art-deco apartment blocks, once the bohemian mixed-race heart of the city, the centre of the world in the early 1990s when you came back to South Africa and the heart today – tonight – of Afropolitan Johannesburg.

This free zone, with people from all over the continent, is perhaps where the Somali shopkeeper from Alexandra scuttles home to each night. You will turn off Raleigh Street, Yeoville's main drag, heavy with Congolese *kwasa* beat and the smell of *nyama choma*, and make your way up Grafton Street to Saunders Street to stop outside number 31, a striking three-story block that has had the name 'BELLAIRS' painted roughly in blue over its overhanging concrete portico to replace the letterplates which have long been filched. It must have been built in the Fifties, and it is loyal to the principles of Le Corbusier, even if cheaper in detail than he would have liked; a series of cubes seemingly suspended on stilts with alternating recessed balconies and *brise-soleil* concrete shutters, now a dilapidated slum where immigrants seem to rent space by the square metre, where the balconies are caged in with rusting burglar bars and where the parking bays between the concrete stilts swirl with litter and dead leaves, one dark recess illuminated by a gas-lamp revealing the vibrant neon colours of the wrappings of a hundred sweets and lollipops laid out by a late-night vendor.

Why have you stopped here? Because this is where Thabani Sibanda was arrested. The police picked him up from the room he shared with his girlfriend; she was very pregnant, they told you, not happy at all. Is that her, now, sitting on the steps of the building, hugely swollen with child, with the dead look of hunger in her eye?

*

Your route home is through Hillbrow, along Abel Street, near to where your mother's car was found, past the Hillbrow Police Station where you identified Sibanda, and westwards into Empire Road. But you cannot resist a little detour, and so you find yourself on Claim Hill, looking up at Hillbrow from the vantage point of the Lloyd, Granny Gertie's hotel on the corner of Paul Nel Street, your very first perspective on the city. There are people everywhere, weaving precariously into the traffic from drunkenness or exhaustion or just because they are overloaded with sleeping children and chequered hessian bags full of the weekend's necessities, trudging toward Monday with resignation or staving it off at that tavern directly beneath Granny Gertie's room. And because it is so frantic, because the crush of humanity brings fear to your gorge, because you have just looked into The Colonel's window, you are to stop, right here, on the corner of Paul Nel and Claim. Yes, it is indeed busy, but no busier than Alfred Nzo and you were fine there, weren't you? Do not mind the jousting men spilling out of the tavern or the roiling

Nigerian crowd outside the kidnapped building to your left: just because they are loud does not mean they are gangsters.

Listen: even now, late on Sunday night, there is church song. Put your hazard lights on and look around you, at the life that fills this street, your first city street, the place you took your granny home to every Sunday evening. Look up Claim Hill and feel, in your groin, the thrill of Estoril and Exclusives, of the Skyline and Gotham City; none of that is there any more, but something else is, some other kid is finding his way, her feet, his city, her path, his future, her *umtshotsho*. Look up, at the Lloyd. Yes, it is dilapidated, why wouldn't it be? Whole families now live in the single rooms once occupied by Jewish dowagers called Muriel and Gittel. Look up there, on the balcony right next to your granny's Room 608: is that Poppy-Eyes and Shorty leaning over the rails having a fag, plotting their next heist, figuring out how to spring The Colonel from jail? But there, on the next balcony, two children are looking out over the street. They are pulled inside by their mother. It's bedtime: there's school tomorrow.

Look directly to your right, at that ugly and rather ominous stone edifice, built in an almost-fascist Thirties style, directly opposite the Lloyd. This is Temple Israel, the synagogue where you used to go to holiday classes when you were a kid. Since the white flight from Hillbrow it has been derelict, until a dynamic new management took control under a former cosmetics-queen who grew up in the congregation; they put two openly gay lay-rabbis on the *bimah* and have begun to attract a small but keen small congregation determined to remain part of the inner city and come to grips with it.

You were here just six months ago, remember, for Yom Kippur, and your spirit soared as you sat listening to the Kol Nidrei sung in the old way – just four beautiful acapella voices doing the *ashkenaz* liturgy your grandfather would have sung in Želva – to a congregation that included more black people than you have ever seen in a *shul* before, including the two adopted children of your friend Lael, one of the lay-rabbis. Just next to you was a couple, a middle-aged black woman and a much older white man, both modestly dressed; what was their story? She was singing the Kol Nidrei like a regular, drawing out those mad

Aramaic diphthongs with the intensely performed abjection the prayer requires, no less immersed in her liturgy and faith than those women in the church procession beneath Hopey's flat last weekend.

Think about that, as you idle here for a few moments, on the corner of Claim and Paul Nel: think about what makes you feel at home, at home among strangers, leaning against the rails of the landing outside Hopey's flat, or sitting among congregants in a reclaimed city *shul*, or walking on a city street or driving along it, looking left, looking right, as you move forward. For it is the Dispatcher's route that threads it all together, sending you out and bringing you home, sending you out and bringing you home, sending you out and bringing you home, stitching you together tighter and tighter until the stitches lose their individual definition and become a seam, a road, a river, the Sandspruit itself, holding page 75 and page 77 together across its banks rather than keeping them apart; stitching Poppy-Eyes on one balcony of the Lloyd to the schoolkids on the next; joining the Lloyd and Temple Israel across Paul Nel Street; creating one life of the past and the present, the rough and the smooth, black and white, Alexandra and Sandton, Bachelors and Maidens, your bound terror at the end of a gun in Killarney and your unbound release on the landing outside Hopey's flat, the horror of death threats made against a Somali shopkeeper and the exuberance of the church procession passing beneath you, the unexpected pleasure taken by two gay boys bringing the laundry up from the line and the victimisation and even violence that you know they must endure.

Welcome home.

BIBLIOGRAPHY

This bibliography does not include maps, photographs, atlases and street guides.

Arendt, Hannah, *The Human Condition*, New York: Doubleday Anchor, 1959.

Barrie, J.M., *Peter Pan: Peter and Wendy and Peter Pan in Kensington Gardens*, London: Penguin Classics, 2004.

Barthes, Roland, *Camera Lucida: Reflections on Photography*, New York: Hill & Wang, 1980.

Beall, Jo, Crankshaw, Owen and Parnell, Susan, *Uniting a Divided City*, London: Earthscan, 2002.

Beavon, Keith, *Johannesburg: The Making and Shaping of the City*, Pretoria: University of South Africa Press, 2004.

Beningfield, Jennifer, *The Frightened Land: Land, Landscape and Politics in South Africa in the Twentieth Century*, London: Routledge, 2006.

Benjamin, Walter, *Berlin Childhood around 1900*, Cambridge Mass: Belknap, 2006.

Bernstein, Hilda, *The Rift: The Exile Experience of South Africans*, London: Jonathan Cape, 1994.

Beukes, Lauren, *Zoo City*, Johannesburg: Jacana, 2010 .

Beylis, Shloyme, *Portretten und Problemen*, Warsaw: Yiddish Books, 1964.

Biko, Steve, *I Write What I Like*, Oxford: Heinemann, 1978.

Bizos, George, *Odyssey to Freedom*, Johannesburg: Random House, 2007.

Bonner, Philip and Segal, Lauren, *Soweto: A History*, Cape Town: Maskew Miller Longman, 2001.

Bonner, Philip and Nieftagodien, Noor, *Alexandra: A History*, Johannesburg: Wits University Press, 2008.

Cammy, Justin, '"Yung-Vilne", A Cultural History of a Yiddish Literary Movement in Inter-War Poland', Ph.D thesis, Harvard University, 2003.

Chipkin, Clive, *Johannesburg Transition: Architecture & Society from 1950*, Johannesburg: STA, 2008.

Clingman, Stephen, *Bram Fischer: Afrikaner Revolutionary*, Cape Town: David Philip, 1998.

Coeman, C., *Tabulae geographicae quibus Colonia Bonae Spei antiqua depingitur: eighteenth-century cartography of Cape Colony.* Amsterdam: Hollandsch-Afrikaansche Uitg. Mij, 1952.

Cole, Ernest, *House of Bondage*, New York: Random House, 1967.

Cole, Teju, *Open City*, London: Faber and Faber, 2011.

Coplan, David, *In Township Tonight!: Three Centuries of South African Black City Music and Theatre*, Johannesburg: Jacana, 2007.

De Certeau, Michel, *The Practise of Everyday Life*, Berkeley: University of California Press, 1998.

Dennie, Garrey, 'The Cultural Geography of Burial in Johannesburg, 1886–1941', n.d., Wits Historical Papers, University of the Witwatersrand.

Dennie, Garry, 'The Standard of Dying: Race, Indigence, and the Disposal of the Dead Body in Johannesburg, 1886–1960', *African Studies*, 68, 3, December 2009.

Dhlomo, H.I.E., *Valley of a Thousand Hills: A Poem*, Durban: Knox, 1941.

Dikobe, Modikwe, *The Marabi Dance*, London: Heinemann, 1973.

Duiker, K. Sello, *Thirteen Cents*, Cape Town: David Philip, 2000.

Duiker, K. Sello, *The Quiet Violence of Dreams*, Cape Town: Kwela Books, 2001.

Duminy, Andrew, *Mapping South Africa: A Historical Survey of South African Maps and Charts*, Johannesburg: Jacana, 2011.

Durrheim, Kevin and Dixon, John, 'The Role of Place and Metaphor in Racial Exclusion: South Africa's Beaches as Sites of Shifting Racialisation', *Ethnic and Racial Studies*, 24, 3, May 2001.

Dyer, Geoff, *The Ongoing Moment*, London: Abacus, 2001.

Ellman, Richard, *James Joyce*, Oxford: Oxford University Press, 1982.

Foster, Jeremy, 'From Socio-nature to Spectral Presence: Re-imagining the Once and Future Landscape of Johannesburg', *Safundi: The Journal of South African and American Studies*, 10, 2, April 2009.

Foster, Jeremy, 'The Wilds and the Township: Articulating Modernity, Capital, and Socio-Nature in the Cityscape of Pre-Apartheid Johannesburg', *Journal of the Society of Architectural Historians*, 71, 1, March 2012.

Frescura, Franco, 'Johannesburg, Egoli, Rawutini: A Brief Historical Survey of an Apartheid City, 1886-1976', Dept of Archaeology, University of Witwatersrand, 1994.

Gevisser, David, *The Unlikely Forester*, Johannesburg: Jacana, 2006.

Gevisser, Israel, 'The Village Orphan', unpublished memoir in Yiddish, 1956.

Gevisser, Mark, 'A Different Fight for Freedom: A History of South African Lesbian and Gay Organisation from the 1950s to the 1990s' in *Defiant Desire*, ed. M. Gevisser and E. Cameron, London: Routledge, 1995.

Gevisser, Mark, 'Between a Rock and a Hard Place', *New York Times Magazine*, March 2000.

Gevisser, Mark, 'Mandela's Stepchildren', in *Different Rainbows*, ed. P. Drucker, London: Gay Men's Press, 2000.

Gevisser, Mark, 'Inheritance', in *Beautiful Ugly: African Diaspora Aesthetics*, ed. Sarah Nuttall, Durham: Duke, 2006.

Gevisser, Mark, 'Why I Won't Give ANC My Vote', *The Star*, 21 April, 2009.

Gevisser, Mark, 'South African Rites', *New York Times Magazine*, 16 July 2009

Gevisser, Mark, 'Under Covers, Out in the Open: Nicholas Hlobo and Umtshotsho', in *Umtshotsho*, Nicholas Hlobo, Cape Town: Stevenson, 2009.

Gevisser, Mark, 'Edenvale', in *Granta 112: Aliens*, ed. John Freeman, London: Granta, 2011.

Gevisser, Mark, 'To be Black and Gay in Soweto', *Mail & Guardian*, 4 March 2011.

Gevisser, Mark, 'Going Back to my Routes: Finding a Way to Call Joburg Home', *Mail & Guardian*, 23 September 2011.

Goldblatt, David, *TJ: Johannesburg Photographs 1948–2010*, Johannesburg: Umuzi, 2010.

Gordimer, Nadine, *Burger's Daughter*, London: Penguin, 1979.

Gordimer, Nadine, 'The New Black Poets', in *Telling Times: Writing and Living, 1954–2008*, New York: W.W. Norton & Co., 2010.

Greenbaum, Masha, *The Jews of Lithuania: A History of a Remarkable Community 1316–1945*, Jerusalem: Gefen, 1995.

Haasbroek, Hannes, *'n Seun soos Bram: 'n Portret can Bram Fischer en sy ma Ella*, Cape Town: Umuzi, 2011.

Hayes, Patricia, 'Poisoned Landscapes', in Mofokeng, Santu, *Chasing Shadows: Thirty Years of Photographic Essays* (ed. Corinne Diserens), Munich: Prestel, 2012.

Hellman, Ellen, 'Native Life in a Johannesburg Slum Yard', in *Africa, Journal of the International African Institute*, 8, 1, January 1935.

Hoad, Neville, Martin, Karen and Reid, Graeme (eds), *Sex and Politics in South Africa*, Cape Town: Double Story, 2005.

Hudson, W., et al., *Anatomy of South Africa: A Scientific Study of Present Day Attitudes*, Cape Town, Purnell and Sons, 1966.

Hyman, Louis, *The Jews of Ireland: From Earliest Times to the Year 1910*, Shannon: Irish University Press, 1972.

Hyslop, Jonathan, 'Gandhi, Mandela and the African Modern', in *Johannesburg: The Elusive Metropolis*, ed. Achille Mbembe and Sarah Nuttall, Johannesburg: Wits University Press, 2008.

Ignatieff, M., 'Berlin in Autumn: The Philosopher in Old Age', UC Berkeley: Townsend Center for the Humanities.

Joyce, James, *Ulysses*, London, Penguin 2000.

Judin, Hilton and Vladislavic, Ivan (eds), *Blank: Architecture, Aparthied and After*, Rotterdam: NAI, 1999.

Kane-Berman, John, *South Africa's Silent Revolution*, Johannesburg: South African Institute of Race Relations, 1990.

Kardas-Nelson, M., 'Rising Water, Rising Fear: SA's Mining Legacy', *Mail & Guardian*, 12 November 2010.

Kentridge, William, 'Meeting the World Halfway: A Johannesburg Biography', The 2010 Kyoto Prize Commemorative Lectures, Kyoto, 2010 (unpublished).

Keogh, Dermot, *Jews in Twentieth-Century Ireland: Refugees, Anti-Semitism and the Holocaust*, Cork: Cork University Press, 1998.

Krafft-Ebing, Richard V., *Psychopathia Sexualis*, London: Rebman, 1901.

Landau, Loren B. (ed.), *Exorcising the Demons Within: Xenophobia, Violence and Statecraft in Contemporary South Africa*, Johannesburg: Wits University Press, 2011.

Le Corbusier, *Aircraft*, London: The Studio Ltd, 1935.

Le Vaillant, François, *Travels into the Interior of Africa via the Cape of Good Hope*, vol. 1, (trans. and ed. I. Glenn et al.), Cape Town: Van Riebeeck Society, 2007.

Levi, Primo, *If This is a Man / The Truce*, London: Abacus, 1987.

Lewin, Hugh, *Stones Against the Mirror: Friendship in the Time of the South African Struggle*, Cape Town: Umuzi, 2011.

Liefferink, Mariette, 'Assessing the past and present role of the National Nuclear Regulator as public protector against potential health injuries: The West and Far West Rand as case study', *New Contree*, 62, October 2011.

Louw, Joe 'My Flight To Love', *Drum*, June 1962.

Mandela, Nelson, *Long Walk to Freedom*, London: Little Brown, 1996.

Markham, Beryl, *West with the Night*, London: Houghton Mifflin, 1942.

Mbembe, Achille and Nuttall, Sarah, 'Afropolis', in *Johannesburg: The Elusive Metropolis*, ed. Achille Mbembe and Sarah Nuttall, Johannesburg: Wits University Press, 2008.

Miłosz, Czesław, *Native Realm: A Search for Self-Definition*, tr. Catherine S. Leach, New York: Farrar, Straus & Giroux, 2002.

—— 'Notes on Exile', *Books Abroad*, 50, 2, Spring 1976.

Modisane, Bloke, *Blame Me on History*, London: Thames and Hudson, 1963.

Mofokeng, Santu, *Chasing Shadows: Thirty Years of Photographic Essays*, ed. Corinne Desirens, Munich: Prestel, 2012.

Mtshali, Mbuyiseni Oswald, *Sounds of a Cowhide Drum / Imisindo Yesighubu Sesikhumba Senkomo*, bilingual edition, Johannesburg: Jacana Media, 2012.

Nabhan, Gary P. and Trimble, Stephen, *The Geography of Childhood: Why Children Need Wild Places*, Boston: Beacon, 1994.

Naidoo, G.R., 'All the Fun of the (Crazy) Sardine Fish Madness', *Drum*, September 1963.

Nakasa, Nat, 'Fringe Country: Where There is No Colour-Bar', *Drum*, March 1961.

Nakasa, Nat, 'Johannesburg , Johannesburg' in *The World of Nat Nakasa*, ed. Ebrahim Patel, Johannesburg: Ravan Press/Bateleur Press, 1975.

Nkabinde, Nkunzi Z., *Black Bull, Ancestors and Me: My Life as a Lesbian Sangoma*, Johannesburg: Fanele, 2008.

Ó Gráda, Cormac, 'Lost in Little Jerusalem: Leopold Bloom and Irish Jewry', *Journal of Modern Literature*, 27, 4, Summer 2004.

Ó Gráda, Cormac, *Jewish Ireland in the Age of Joyce: A Socio-Economic History*, Princeton: Princeton University Press, 2006.

Pamuk, Orhan, *Istanbul: Memories and the City*, tr. M. Freely, London: Faber, 2005.

Parnell, Susan, 'Johannesburg Slums and Racial Segregation in Cities, 1910–1937', Ph.D thesis, Wits University, 1993.

Passop (People Against Suffering Oppression and Poverty), 'A Dream Deferred: Is the Equality Clause in the South African Constitution's Bill of Rights (1996) Just a Far-off Hope for LGBTI Asylum Seekers and Refugees?', www.passop.org.za

Paton, Alan, *Cry, the Beloved Country*, London: Vintage, 2002.

Rankin, Nicholas, Dead Man's Chest: Travels After Robert Louis Stevenson, London: Faber, 1897.

Reid, Graeme, *Above the Skyline: Reverend Tsietsi Thandekiso and the Founding of an African Gay Church*, Pretoria: UNISA, 2011.

Retief, Glen, 'Keeping Sodom out of the Laager', in *Defiant Desire: Gay and Lesbian Lives in South Africa*, ed Mark Gevisser and Edwin Cameron, London: Routledge, 1995.

Robinson, Jennifer, 'Johannesburg's 1936 Empire Exhibition: Interaction, Segregation and Modernity of a South African City', *Journal of South African Studies*, 2003.

Saint-Exupéry, Antoine de, *Southern Mail*, London: Heinemann, 1971.

'Sandspruit Self-Guided Trail', Johannesburg Municipality Coordinaring Committee for Community Open Space, 1988.

Serote, Mongane Wally, *To Every Birth Its Blood*, Johannesburg: Ravan Press, 1981

Serote, Mongane Wally, *Yakhal'inkomo*, Johannesburg: A.D. Donker, 1972.

Shain, Milton and Mendelsohn, Richard, *The Jews in South Africa: An Illustrated History*, Johannesburg: Jonathan Ball, 2008.

Smith, Anna, *Johannesburg Street Names: A Dictionary of Street, Suburb and Other Place-names*, Cape Town: Juta, 1971.

Solnit, Rebecca, *A Field Guide to Getting Lost*, London: Canongate, 2006.

Sontag, Susan, *On Photography*, London: Penguin, 2008.

South African Police, *Annual Report of the Commissioner of the South African Police*, Pretoria: Government Printers, 1963 and 1964.

South African Police Services, *Crime Report 2010/11*, www.saps.gov.za

Stevenson, Robert Louis, *Treasure Island*, London: Heinemann, 1964.

Swift, John, *Alexandra I Love You: A Record of Seventy Years*, Braamfontein: Alexandra Liaison Committee, 1983.

Turton, Anthony, et al., 'Gold, Scorched Earth and Water: The Hydropolitics of Johannesburg', *Water Resources Development*, 22, 2, June 2006.

Van Onselen, Charles, *New Babylon, New Nineveh: everyday life on the Witwatersrand 1886-1914*, Johannesburg: Jonathan Ball 2001.

'Venus de Milo Suspect', *Rand Daily Mail*, 11 November 1964.

Vermaak, Chris, *Bram Fischer: The Man With Two Faces*, Johannesburg: ABP Publishers, 1966.

Vladislavic, Ivan, *Portrait with Keys: Joburg and What-What*, Cape Town: Umuzi, 2006.

Wexler, Laura, 'Seeing Sentiment: Photography, Race and the Innocent Eye', in *Female Subjects in Black and White: Race, Psychoanalysis, Feminism*, ed. Elizabeth Abel et al., Berkeley: UC Press, 1997.

Wylie, Diana, *Art+Revolution: The Life and Death of Thami Mnyele, South African Artist*, Johannesburg: Jacana, 2008.

ILLUSTRATION CREDITS

The author would like to thank the copyright holders and archives listed
below for permission to reproduce the images in the pages of this book.

p. 7   Cover of *Holmden's Register of Johannesburg: Randburg and*
        Sandton Townships, 9th edition. Together with the pub-
        lishers, the author has made every effort to contact all
        possible copyright holders for this volume.

p. 8   Map from *Holmden's Register of Johannesburg: Randburg*
        and Sandton Townships, 9th edition. Together with the
        publishers, the author has made every effort to contact
        all possible copyright holders for this volume.

p. 9   Photograph of (back to front) Mark, Antony, John, and
        Peter Gevisser. Courtesy of the Gevisser Family Archive.

p. 10   Map from *Holmden's Register of Johannesburg: Randburg*
        and Sandton Townships, 9th edition. Together with the
        publishers, the author has made every effort to contact
        all possible copyright holders for this volume.

p. 11   Map from *Holmden's Register of Johannesburg: Randburg*
        and Sandton Townships, 9th edition. Together with the
        publishers, the author has made every effort to contact
        all possible copyright holders for this volume.

p. 42   Photograph of a handmade map on view at the Želva Secondary School History Museum. Copyright © by Akvile Grigoriavicute. Reproduced by permission of Akvile Grigoriavicute.

p. 49   Detail from an early map of Johannesburg showing the town cemetery. Courtesy of the Johannesburg Public Library.

p. 51   Photographs of Zalman and Minnie Blum. Courtesy of the Gevisser Family Archive.

p. 52   Photograph of Beila Gitl Gevisser with her sons Israel and Bere-Leib and her daughter-in-law Fanny. Courtesy of the Gevisser Family Archive.

pp. 58–59   Detail from Gevisser family tree, compiled by Julius Gevisser. Courtesy of the Gevisser Family Archive.

p. 62   Photograph of Shloyme Beylis and Dvorah Ginzberg with their daughter 'Bebele'. Courtesy of Wiktoria Czernobielska and Judita Hecner.

p. 64   Photograph of (from left to right) Israel, Bere-Leib, and Morris Gevisser. Courtesy of the Gevisser Family Archive.

p. 66   Photograph of the wedding of Morris Gevisser and Janie Moshal, 1912. Courtesy of the Gevisser Family Archive.

p. 67   Photograph of David Gevisser. Courtesy of the Gevisser Family Archive.

p. 72   Front page of the *Rand Daily Mail*, November 11, 1964. Courtesy of the Johannesburg Public Library.

p. 78   Map of Africa from *Hamlyn's New World Relief Atlas*: Published by Geographical Projects (London: Aldus Books, 1966), p. 94.

343

p. 83   Photograph of David (left) and Mark Gevisser. Courtesy of the Gevisser Family Archive.

p. 84   Photograph of James. Courtesy of the Gevisser Family Archive.

p. 90   'The King's Map': *Partie Méridionale de l'Afrique depuis le Tropique du Capricorne jusqu'au Cap de Bonne Espérance contenant les Pays des Hottentots, des Cafres et de quelques autres Nations / Dressée pour le Roi sur les observations de M. le Vaillant par M. de Laborde, ancien premier Valet de chambre du Roi, Gouverneur du Louvre, l'un des Fermiers généraux de Sa Majesté / 1790.* Copyright © by Bibliothèque Nationale de France. Reproduced by permission of the Bibliothèque Nationale de France.

p. 90   *Narina Fille Gonaquoise* by François le Vaillant. Copyright © by South African Parliamentary Library. Reproduced by permission of the South African Parliamentary Library.

p. 96   Aerial view of Soweto: Photograph copyright © by Patrick Robert Brian Lewis. Courtesy of Wits Historical Papers.

p. 97   *Women's Hostel, Alexandra Township, 26 June 2009.* Copyright © 2009 by David Goldblatt. Reproduced by permission of David Goldblatt.

p. 100   Photograph of David Cohen. Courtesy of the Gevisser Family Archive.

pp. 102–3   Pages from *Drum*, March 1961: '"Fringe Country": Where There Is No Colour-Bar' by Nat Nakasa. Copyright © by Baileys' African History Archives (BAHA). Reproduced by permission of BAHA.

p. 109   Photograph of David and Hedda Gevisser on their wedding day. Courtesy of the Gevisser Family Archive.

p. 110   Photograph of David and Hedda Gevisser. Courtesy of the Gevisser Family Archive.

p. 111   Photograph from '"Fringe Country": Where There Is No Colour-Bar', *Drum*, March 1961: Unidentified *Drum* photographer. Copyright © by Baileys' African History Archives (BAHA). Reproduced by permission of BAHA.

p. 113   Photograph from '"Fringe Country": Where There Is No Colour-Bar', *Drum*, March 1961: Unidentified *Drum* photographer. Copyright © Baileys' African History Archives (BAHA). Reproduced by permission of BAHA.

p. 116   Pamela Beira and Joe Louw illustrated in 'My Flight to Love' by Joe Louw, *Drum*, June 1962. Copyright © Baileys' African History Archives (BAHA). Reproduced by permission of BAHA.

p. 120   Photograph of the Fischer swimming pool. Courtesy of Ilse Wilson.

pp. 126–127 Photographs of the practice of '*tausa*' in the Johannesburg Central Prison. Copyright © 1956 Baileys' African History Archives (BAHA) / Bob Gosani. Reproduced by permission of BAHA.

p. 128   Photograph of Gertie Cohen. Courtesy of the Gevisser Family Archive.

p. 138   *Arriving Family, King George Street, (circa 1955)*. Copyright © 1955 David Goldblatt. Reproduced by permission of David Goldblatt.

p. 142   Photograph of Janie Gevisser and Zelda Moshal on West Street, Durban. Courtesy of the Gevisser Family Archive.

p. 143   Photograph of Michele Bruno and his friend Louis (in the background) on Eloff Street, Johannesburg. Courtesy of Michele Bruno.

p. 147   Vertical projection on the main reef leader of the Crown Reef mine. Courtesy of the Johannesburg Public Library.

p. 148   Vertical projection of a mine, 1897. Courtesy of the Johannesburg Public Library.

p. 158   Photographs of the Gevisser family on Clifton 4th Beach, Cape Town. Courtesy of the Gevisser Family Archive.

p. 160   Photograph of Joe Garmeson and friends at Bachelors Cove, Cape Town, 1950s. Courtesy of Joe Garmeson and Gay and Lesbian Memory in Action (GALA). Copyright © GALA. Reproduced by permission of GALA.

p. 161   Photograph of Joe Garmeson and friends at Blue Lagoon, Durban, 1951. Courtesy of Joe Garmeson and Gay and Lesbian Memory in Action (GALA). Copyright © GALA. Reproduced by permission of GALA.

p. 162   Photograph of Michele Bruno. Courtesy of Michele Bruno.

p. 163   Detail from the Afrikaans *Beeld* newspaper. Courtesy of Gay and Lesbian Memory in Action (GALA).

p. 179   *Izithunzi* by Nicholas Hlobo, from his *Umtshotsho* installation: Rubber inner tube, ribbon, organza, lace, found objects, steel, couch, and 8 sculptures. Copyright © 2009 by Nicholas Hlobo and Stevenson Gallery, Cape Town and Johannesburg. Reproduced by permission of Nicholas Hlobo and the Stevenson Gallery.

p. 181   *UkuSoma* by Nicholas Hlobo. Copyright © 2009 by Nicholas Hlobo and Stevenson Gallery, Cape Town and Johannesburg. Reproduced by permission of Nicholas Hlobo and the Stevenson Gallery.

p. 183   Advertisement for the Butterfly Bar in *Exit* magazine. Courtesy of Gay and Lesbian Memory in Action (GALA).

p. 205   Photograph of Edgar's wedding ring. Copyright © by Zethu Mathebeni and Gay and Lesbian Memory in Action (GALA). Reproduced by permission of Zethu Mathebeni and GALA.

p. 219   Drawings for *Other Faces*. Copyright © 2011 by William Kentridge. Reproduced by permission of William Kentridge.

p. 226   *Sangoma Cleansing Ritual at Klip River, Soweto*: Pigment print by Santu Mofokeng. Copyright © 2011 by Santu Mofokeng and Maker Studios. Reproduced by permission of Santu Mofokeng and Maker Studios.

p. 230   *Baptism* by Ernest Cole, early 1960s. Copyright © by The Ernest Cole Family Trust. Reproduced by permission of The Ernest Cole Family Trust.

p. 231   Photographs of a swimming pool baptism, 1996. Copyright © by Graeme Reid.

p. 234   *Sardine Fishing* by Ranjith Kally. Copyright © by Bailey's African History Archives (BAHA) and Ranjith Kally. Reproduced by permission of BAHA.

p. 235   Sardine run photograph: From William Hudson, Gideon François Jacobs, and Simon Biesheuwel, *Anatomy of South Africa: A Scientific Study of Present Day Attitudes* (Cape Town: Purnell, 1966). Photographer unidentified.

TEXT CREDITS

ACKNOWLEDGEMENTS

The research for this book was made possible by a grant from the Faculty of the Humanities, University of Pretoria, where I was Writing Fellow for three years. I am particularly grateful to Sandra Klopper, to the office of the Dean of Humanities, and to Pippa Green and my colleagues in the journalism department. Some of this work was developed while I was a Carnegie Equity Fellow at Wits University, and I am grateful to Norman Duncan and the Apartheid Archive Project.

For invaluable archival assistance and permission to reproduce their images I thank Gay and Lesbian Memory in Action (GALA) at Wits University, Bailey's African History Archives, Wits Historical Papers, MuseumAfrica, the Johannesburg Public Library, the Ernest Cole Family Trust, the South African National Archives in Bloemfontein, the library at the Jewish Board of Deputies in Johannesburg, the Hebrew University Archives, the Warsaw Jewish Institute, the Lithuanian National Archives in Kaunas, the *Bibliothèque Nationale de France*, the Cullen Collection and Wits Historical Papers at Wits University, and the Times Media Photographic Archives. Particular thanks are due to Bongi Maswangani at BAHA, Linda Chernis at MuseumAfrica, Alastair Marshall at Johannesburg Public Library, Michelle Pickover at Wits Historical Papers, and to Anthony Manion and his team at GALA. Some of the initial research for this book was done for GALA's exhibition, 'Jo'burg Tracks', and I would like thank my collaborators on that project, Zethu Mathebeni, S'bu Kheswa, Paul Mokgethi, Oliver Barstow and Theresa Collins.

I would like to acknowledge Patricia Hayes as the source of the citation from H.I.E. Dhlomo's *Valley of a Thousand Hills*, and to thank Mongane Wally Serote for permission to cite 'Black Bells', and Mbuyiseni Oswald Mtshali and Jacana Media for permission to reproduce 'The Swing'. Together with my publishers, I have made every effort to track down all copyright holders to the lyrics of 'Golden City Blues', sung by Dolly Rathebe, from *Jim Comes to Johannesburg*. I thank David Goldblatt, Nicholas Hlobo, Stephen Hobbs, William Kentridge, Marcus Neustatter, Santu Mofokeng, Graeme Reid and the estate of Eli Weinberg for permission to reproduce their artworks and photographs. I also thank Michele Bruno, Ilse Wilson, Nora Kubeka, Wiktoria Czernobielska and Judita Hecner, and, most of all, Hedda and the late David Gevisser, for making their family photographic archives available to me.

For help with family genealogies and archives I would like to thank Hedda Gevisser, Jonny Gevisser, the other Mark Gevisser, Aaron and Liebe Klug, John Moshal, Ines Mureinik and especially Zena Zulman, who made Issy Gevisser's personal archive available to me. I am particularly grateful to Adrian Freedman, to the late Julius Gevisser and to the late Sarah Zway, without whose respective research the Freedman, Gevisser and Cohen family histories would have been lost.

Several sections of this book have been published, in different form, in other publications: 'Inheritance' in *Beautiful Ugly: African Diaspora Aesthetics* (Duke, 2006); 'Edenvale' in *Granta 114: Aliens* (Granta, 2011); 'Under Covers, Out in the Open: Nicholas Hlobo and Umtshotsho' in *Izithunzi* (Stevenson, 2009); 'Between a Rock and a Hard Place' and 'South African Rights' in *The New York Times Magazine*; and 'Going Back to My Routes: Looking For a Way to Make Johannesburg Home', 'Affairs of the Heart' and 'To be Black and Gay in South Africa' in the *Mail & Guardian*. I have also cited work published previously in my essays 'A Different Fight For Freedom: Gay and Lesbian Organisation in South Africa from the 1950s to the 1990s' in *Defiant Desire* (Routledge, 1995) and 'Mandela's Stepchildren', in *Different Rainbows* (ed. P. Drucker, GMP, 2000), and in my book, *A Legacy of Liberation: Thabo Mbeki and the Future of the*

South African Dream (Palgrave Macmillan, 2009). I am particularly grateful to Sarah Nuttall, the editor of *Beautiful Ugly*, and Ellah Allfrey of *Granta* for their help in developing the ideas that would become this book.

For research assistance and picture research I would like to thank Felicity Nyikadzino Berold, Ryan Brown, Michele Hay, Micah Reddy, and especially Theresa Collins, Deena Dinat and Margot Rubin; for archival photography, the late John Hodgkiss; for administrative assistance, Jackie Downs; for Yiddish translation and research, Akvile Grigoriaviciute; for Polish translation, Olga Zienkiewicz and Agnieszka Zolkiewska; for Lithuanian translation and guiding, Simon Davidovitch; for Hebrew/Aramaic translation, Sheree Zohar and Louise Bethlehem; for sharing their collections of Johannesburg street maps, William Kentridge, Keith Beavon and Ismail Farouk; for sharing their research on Alexandra, Philip Bonner and Noor Nieftagadien, and Rehad Desai and Uhuru Productions; for writing space, Jud Cornell, Miriam Wheeldon, and Jonny Broomberg and Lauren Segal.

For help with research and ideas I would like to thank: Tesfalem Araia, Keith Beavon, Alan Buff, Justin Cammy, Milan Chersonskij, T.J. de Klerk, Hugh Denman, Jane Eagle, Rehana Ebr.-Vally, Jeremy Foster, Michael Godby, Vitalija Gircyte, Sandra Klopper, Gideon Koppel, Hanna Le Roux, Mariette Liefferink, Alan Mabin, Terrence McCarthy, Santu Mofokeng, Noor Nieftegadien, Cormac O'Grada, Ilona Murauskaite, Sue Parnell, Gordon Pirie, Frédérique Pressmann, Graeme Reid, Stuart Rosenblatt, Ilse Wilson, Tanya Zack, and especially Jessica Dubow, my navigator in the world of cultural geography. I owe huge debts, too, to William Kentridge, for the way he has imagined Johannesburg, to David Goldblatt, for the way he has documented it, and to Ivan Vladislavic, for the paths he has cut through the city before me. I am also grateful to Laura Wexler's Photographic Memory Workshop at Yale, the English Academy of South Africa, the Apartheid Archive, the Wits Arts Faculty and the Wits Institute for Social and Economic Research, for giving me the opportunities to test the ideas of this book.

For reading all or part of the manuscript, I would like to thank: Hedda, Antony, John and Peter Gevisser, and also Maggie Davey, Jacob Dlamini, Jessica Dubow, Damon Galgut, Michiel Heyns, Bridget Impey, Claire Messud, Phillip Miller, Carol Steinberg and, more than ever, Jonny Steinberg.

This book would not have seen the light of day without the publishing nous and deep intellect of my agent David Godwin; I thank him and all at DGA Literary Agency. I have been blessed with two extraordinary editors, in Ellah Allfrey at Granta Books, and Ileene Smith at Farrar, Straus & Giroux. I would like to thank all at both publishers, especially Max Porter and Christine Lo at Granta and John Knight at FSG, as well as Jeremy Boraine and his team at Jonathan Ball. Particular thanks is due, too, to Paul Elie, who first commissioned this book for FSG and helped it take its first steps.

Finally, as always, my deepest gratitude and love to Dhianaraj Chetty.

Keep in touch with
Granta Books:

Visit grantabooks.com to discover more.

GRANTA